WALKING AND TREKKING
IN ICELAND

About the author

Paddy Dillon is a prolific walker and guidebook writer, with over 50 books to his name and contributions to 25 other books. He has also written extensively for several outdoor magazines and other publications, and has appeared on TV and radio. He uses a palmtop computer to write his route descriptions while walking. His descriptions are therefore precise, having been written at the very point at which the reader uses them.

Paddy has walked all of Britain's National Trails and several major European trails. He has led guided walking holidays and has walked throughout Europe, as well as in Nepal, Tibet, and the Rocky Mountains of Canada and the US. He is a member of the Outdoor Writers and Photographers Guild.

Other Cicerone guides by the author

WALKING AND TREKKING IN ICELAND

by Paddy Dillon

2 POLICE SQUARE, MILNTHORPE, CUMBRIA LA7 7PY
www.cicerone.co.uk

© Paddy Dillon 2012
First edition 2012
ISBN: 978 1 85284 647 3

Printed in China on behalf of Latitude Press Ltd.
A catalogue record for this book is available from the British Library.
All photographs are by the author unless otherwise stated.

lovelljohns.com

Mapping produced by Lovell Johns Ltd www.lovelljohns.com.

Advice to readers

While every effort is made by our authors to ensure the accuracy of guidebooks as they go to print, changes can occur during the lifetime of an edition. If we know of any, there will be an Updates tab on this book's page on the Cicerone website (www.cicerone.co.uk), so please check before planning your trip. We also advise that you check information about such things as transport, accommodation and shops locally. Even rights of way can be altered over time. We are always grateful for information about any discrepancies between a guidebook and the facts on the ground, sent by email to info@cicerone.co.uk or by post to Cicerone, 2 Police Square, Milnthorpe LA7 7PY, United Kingdom.

Warning

Walking across remote Arctic tundra, volcanic terrain and glaciers can be a dangerous activity, carrying a risk of personal injury or death. It should be undertaken only by those with a full understanding of the risks, and with the training and experience to evaluate them. While every care and effort has been taken in the preparation of this guide, the user should be aware that weather conditions and the level of water in rivers can be highly variable and can change quickly, materially affecting the seriousness of these treks. Therefore, except for any liability which cannot be excluded by law, neither Cicerone nor the author accept liability for damage of any nature (including damage to property, personal injury or death) arising directly or indirectly from the information in this book. For mountain/wilderness rescue in Iceland, contact ICE-SAR, tel 112 www.landsbjorg.is.

Front cover: Öræfajökull, as seen from the Glacier Lagoon of Jökulsárlón (Walk 25)

CONTENTS

Descending a steep, stony slope with shapely fells seen either side of Álftavatn (Trek 2 Stage 5)

Map key

▬▬▬▬	primary road	→	route direction
═══	secondary road	→	continuation
───	track	◌₁₀₀	contour (100m interval)
▬▬▬	route		glacier
••••••••••••	alternative route		lake
••••••••••••	adjacent route	───	river
─ ─ ─ ─ ─	other path/track	▲	peak
─ ─ ─ ─ ─	ferry	■	building
⊢ ═ ═ ═ ═ ⊣	tunnel	⋀	campsite
(人)	start point	⸸	church
(人)	finish point	●	hot spot
(人)	start/finish point	⊕	airport
		•	other features

9

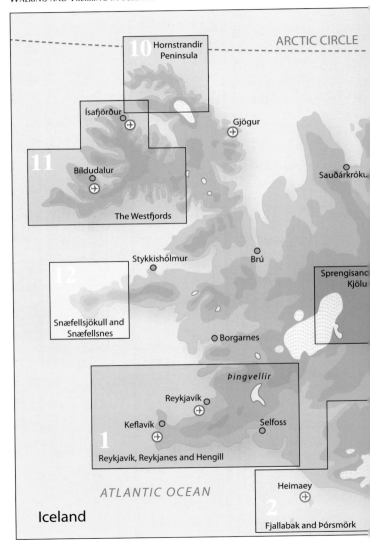

ARCTIC CIRCLE

10 Hornstrandir Peninsula

Ísafjörður

Gjögur

11

Bíldudalur

Sauðárkróku.

The Westfjords

Stykkishólmur

Brú

Sprengisanc Kjölu

12

Snæfellsjökull and Snæfellsnes

Borgarnes

Þingvellir

Reykjavík

Keflavík

Selfoss

1 Reykjavík, Reykjanes and Hengill

Heimaey

2 Fjallabak and Þórsmörk

ATLANTIC OCEAN

Iceland

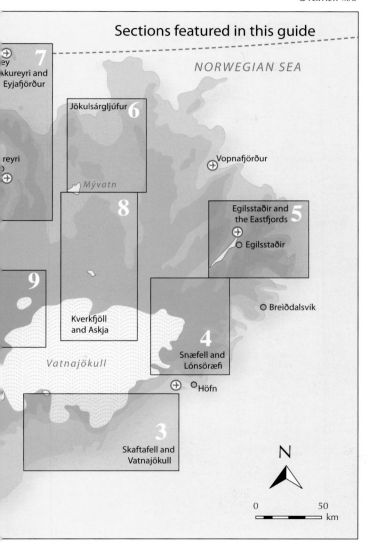

Sections featured in this guide

Splendid views are available from the edge of the Morinsheiði plateau on the Skógar Trail (Trek 2 Stage 8)

INTRODUCTION

Iceland is often referred to as 'The Land of Ice and Fire', and it doesn't take visitors long to discover why. The country boasts ice-caps and glaciers, volcanoes and hot springs. The bleak and barren landscape is sparsely populated, yet visitors can travel day after day visiting amazing waterfalls, admiring huge bird colonies on coastal cliffs, going trekking from hut to hut, or camping along scenic trails. Iceland is an intensely 'outdoor' country, with changeable weather, so it needs to be approached with forethought and careful planning in order to enjoy it safely and to the fullest extent.

The population of Iceland is barely 320,000, and two-thirds of the population live in or near the capital – Reykjavík. Bearing in mind that well over 500,000 tourists visit Iceland each year, the chances are that visitors are more likely to meet other visitors than Icelanders! A few small towns and villages, with scattered farms in between, are dotted around the coastal fringes, while the interior is uninhabited, and even regarded as uninhabitable.

Many visitors motor around the Ring Road, which encircles Iceland in 1340km (835 miles), but this doesn't reach the best walking areas, as it avoids the whole interior and the fascinating Westfjords. The bulk of Iceland's roads are dirt roads, requiring special care to explore, although there are bus services along some of them.

Over 10 per cent of Iceland is permanently glaciated. The largest ice-cap is Vatnajökull, followed in size by Langajökull, Hofsjökull, Mýrdalsjökull, Drangajökull, Eyjafjallajökull and dozens of smaller ice-bound peaks. There are three national parks – Þingvellir, Snæfellsjökull and the mighty Vatnajökull, the largest national park in Europe.

The country offers an incredible variety of landscapes, from the desert-like interior to the green coastal margins, from cliff coastlines and occasional sandy beaches to towering mountains capped with ice. Canyons carved by furious torrents suddenly give way to broad floodplains. Powerful waterfalls abound, as do unique geothermal areas.

There are 100 days of walking in this guidebook, stretching over 1722km (1070 miles), split almost evenly between day walks and long-distance trails. The walks are loosely grouped into a dozen areas, with enough variety to satisfy all kinds of walkers. They range from easy nature trails to challenging treks, spread all around Iceland, from sea level to the highest peaks. Facilities are sparse around the country, and more so on the longer trails, where trekkers need to be completely self-sufficient. The descriptions in this guidebook help with choosing appropriate routes and highlight walking opportunities throughout the country, so that walkers will want to return time and time again.

LOCATION

Iceland lies just south of the Arctic Circle, west of Norway, east of Greenland, and north-west of the British Isles. From some parts of the south coast, a line drawn directly south encounters no land whatsoever until Antarctica! Although renowned for its ice-caps and glaciers, Iceland is less chilly than might be expected, benefitting from the warm Gulf Stream. The island was settled by the Norse, along with British and Irish Celts, spawning a hardy race of people able to survive on largely unproductive land while harvesting the oceans.

Iceland covers almost 103,500km² (40,000 square miles) – a little less than the area of England. It is over twice the size of its former colonial master, Denmark, and about the same size as the US state of Kentucky. Bear this in mind if you are tempted to 'do' Iceland in a week. It is better, and cheaper, to explore one or two areas in detail, returning to explore other areas later. Iceland is far too interesting and awe-inspiring to be rushed!

GEOLOGY AND LANDSCAPE

Iceland is a new addition to the face of the Earth. Neighbouring countries boast rocks whose ages are measured in billions of years, but Iceland is no more than 18 million years old. As the European and North American plates parted, a rift opened along the floor of the North Atlantic above a mantle

Some geothermal hot-spots have been exploited to produce hot water and power

Looking back along the Laugavegur to the steam rising from hot springs at Stórihver (Trek 2 Stage 4)

plume, and massive outpourings of lava rose above the sea to create the island. As the continents continue to drift, Iceland increases in size. The oldest parts are the western and eastern extremities, while the youngest parts lie on a widening rift roughly through the centre of the island, bending towards the south-east. This region contains a great number of faults, is dotted with active volcanoes, and exudes copious amounts of hot water, steam and sulphurous gases.

Iceland is estimated to have produced one-third of the lava in the world since 1500. There is on average a volcanic eruption every five years, and this has increased in recent years. Few will forget the chaos caused to flights around Europe in May 2010, when Eyafjallajökull erupted. This was followed in 2011 by the eruption of Grímsvötn, beneath Vatnajökull, then Katla beneath Mýrdalsjökull. All three eruptions caused a glacier flood, or 'jökulhlaup', but none reached the proportions of a flood in 1996, which for a few hours formed a torrent second only to the flow of the Amazon! Every so often big destructive events – quite literally dark periods in the history of the country – cause devastation and enormous loss of life.

The bulk of the bedrock is basaltic, varying from fine ash and honeycombed pumice to unyielding lava and vitreous black obsidian. Basalt sometimes fractures into distinctive polygonal columns as it cools. Lava flows often cool so that their crusts fracture, leaving slabs tilting at all angles. Sometimes the lava has concentric ripples on its surface and is referred to as 'ropy', as it looks remarkably like

The cascade of Dynjandi is one of the highlights of travel through the Westfjords

twisted ropes. Occasionally there are areas of more 'acidic' rhyolite, forming light, pastel-shaded, crumbling slopes. Areas of high geothermal activity often feature mineral-stained water and bubbling mud-pots, and some areas have been exploited for power and heat.

In recent geological time Iceland was completely covered by ice, of which only remnants remain, including the enormous ice-cap of Vatnajökull – the largest in Europe. The most recent deposits in Iceland occur as the glaciers melt, leaving vast areas of ill-sorted moraine. This is washed by powerful glacial rivers, spreading huge amounts of mud, sand, grit and gravel across the land.

The reason most walkers visit Iceland is to experience the landscape. The rugged basalt bedrock, sometimes smooth, sometimes broken into massive blocks, forms extensive lava flows, or breaks into cliffs in the fells and around the coast. Some areas are covered in volcanic ash or fine grey windblown sand. Other areas have been ground to rubble by long-vanished glaciers, leaving heaps of moraine and vast, empty, stony deserts.

Although Iceland boasted extensive birch forests at the time of Settlement in the late ninth and early tenth centuries, these were brutally hacked for timber and fuel. Some areas were cleared and improved for grazing, while others were overgrazed and became barren. Despite centuries of man-management, vast areas of Iceland remain uninhabited, and the overall aspect is one of bleak, empty landscapes, often starkly beautiful in good weather, but capable of being truly frightening in bad weather.

The bulk of Iceland's bedrock is basaltic lava, seen here in its 'ropy' form

HISTORY TIMELINE

- **860s** Naddoddr was blown off course, landed briefly, and called the place 'Snæland' (Snowland). Garðar Svavarsson circumnavigated the island and called it 'Garðarshólmur' (Garðar's Island). Hrafna-Flóki had a good summer, a harsh winter and a late spring. He coined the name 'Ísland' (Iceland), then abandoned his settlement and never returned.
- **874** Ingólfur Arnarson settled at Reykjavík. Start of the 'Age of Settlement'. Norse and Celts claimed territory and established farms.
- **930** The end of the 'Age of Settlement', with most of the land claimed. The 'Commonwealth' was established and the parliament, or 'Alþing', was founded at the remarkable geological site of Þingvellir. Oral 'sagas' were composed, keeping alive memories of people and events.
- **982** Discovery of Greenland by Eiríkr Rauði Þorvaldsson (Eric the Red).
- **985** Southern Greenland was partially settled from Iceland.
- **1000** Under pressure from Norway, Iceland adopted Christianity.
- **1056** Iceland's first bishop was appointed – Ísleifur Gissurason.
- **1097** Church authorities began to claim tithes.
- **1104** Hekla erupted and destroyed a settlement at Þjórsárdalur.
- **1106** Iceland's second bishop was appointed – Jón Ögmundsson.
- **1117** Iceland's laws were written down instead of being recited orally.
- **1122** The 'Íslendingabók' was written, detailing the Settlement of Iceland.
- **1197** The death of Iceland's most powerful chieftain – Jón Loftsson. There followed a time of increasing strife and civil unrest around the country, known as the 'Sturlung Age'.
- **1262** Icelanders were forced to become subjects of the king of Norway.
- **1280** The 'Jónsbók' was written, detailing the laws of Iceland.
- **1362** Öræfajökull erupted and covered one-third of Iceland in ash.
- **1402** The Black Death killed half the population in two years.
- **1412** English fishing fleets began operating in Icelandic waters, at the start of what was known as the 'English Century'. The English established a base in the Vestmannaeyjar, from where they launched pirate raids.
- **1494** A second plague ravaged Iceland.
- **1539–1550** Reformation swept through Iceland with violent incidents, culminating in the beheading of Jón Arason, the last Catholic bishop.
- **1558** The English were expelled from the Vestmannaeyjar.
- **1584** The Bible became the first book to be printed in Icelandic.
- **1602** A trade monopoly allowed only Danish traders to control trade between Iceland and the rest of the world.

- **1627** Algerian pirates raided the Vestmannaeyjar, killing some islanders and kidnapping others for slave markets.
- **1661** Icelanders were forced to accept the absolute monarchy of the king of Denmark.
- **1707** The bubonic plague killed one-third of the population of Iceland.
- **1760** Salted fish were exported to Spain.
- **1783** The huge Laki eruptions caused the death of a quarter of the population and half the livestock, as well as crop failures around Europe, drought in India and famine as far away as Japan.
- **1787** End of the trade monopoly.
- **1800** The Danes abolished the 'Alþing', which had long ceased to wield any power.
- **1809** Jørgen Jørgensen, nicknamed 'Jörundur Hundadagakonungur', proclaimed himself king for the summer until deposed by the Danes.
- **1843** The king of Denmark agreed to the resumption of the 'Alþing' parliament, which was re-established in Reykjavík.
- **1874** 1000 years of the Settlement celebrated. The king of Denmark granted Iceland a constitution.
- **1875** Eruption of the Askja volcano.
- **1875–1939** Icelanders mounted a series of demands for independence and formed a number of political parties.
- **1940** British forces invaded and occupied Iceland to prevent Nazi forces doing the same.
- **1941** British forces withdrew and left American forces in occupation.
- **1944** Iceland became a republic, free of Danish control.
- **1946** The Keflavík Agreement – under which American forces were permitted to maintain a base in Iceland.
- **1949** Iceland became a founder member of NATO, despite having no army. Riots took place in Reykjavík.
- **1963** The volcanic island of Surtsey emerged from the sea.
- **1973** Eldfell erupted on Heimaey, forcing complete evacuation.
- **1976** Agreement reached between Britain and Iceland after years of disputes over fishing limits, known as the 'Cod Wars'.
- **2006** American forces withdrew from Keflavík.
- **2008** The start of Iceland's financial crisis and collapse of its major banks.
- **2010** The Eyafjallajökull eruption led to the grounding of air traffic throughout northern Europe.

WILDLIFE

Trees and flowers

Q – What do you do when you get lost in an Icelandic forest? **A** – Stand up!

It's an old joke, and no longer as valid as it was years ago, now that more trees are being planted. The dominant tree species are dwarf birch and creeping willow – the latter boasting bewildering varieties. Creeping juniper is also common, and rowan is sometimes noticed. Birch and willow sometimes grow tall, but Icelandic 'forests' usually look like moorland and are trampled underfoot. In recent years some areas have been planted with native trees, and other species have been imported, notably conifers. Dense natural woodland is found around Þórsmörk, while plantations are found near urban areas, such as Reykjavík and Akureyri. Close to Eglisstaðir, Hallormsstaðaskógur features plenty of imported species, which can be seen on Walk 30.

Much of Iceland is barren, but tiny plants grow in some inhospitable places. One of the primary colonisers is lambagrass, which looks like moss but sprouts tiny pink or purple flowers. Thrift and campion are also common in stony areas, while windblown sand is colonised by lyme grass. Some areas, including rugged lava flows, are covered with thick, soft masses of fragile moss. In some sensitive areas, such as Laki, it is forbidden to walk on it. In some barren areas, moss accompanies little streams, bringing vivid streaks of green into otherwise grey landscapes. Many rivers are flanked by angelica, while riverside gravel may sprout arctic riverbeauty.

There are vast expanses of sub-Arctic tundra, featuring low-lying birch and willow, abundant crowberry and bilberry, sometimes with heather, horsetails and bearberry, scented with wild thyme. Wetter areas feature cotton grass and insectivorous butterwort. Some mountainous areas support saxifrages and gentians, while lowland meadows sprout buttercups and dandelions. Many places are threatened by invasive lupin, whose flowers look attractive, but whose leaves crowd out native species. In some places, particularly in the national park at Skaftafell, measures are taken to control its spread.

Creeping willow and birch are common and make up the bulk of Iceland's flat 'forests'

Arctic riverbeauty, related to rosebay willowherb, often thrives on riverside gravel

A handy reference book is *A Guide to the Flowering Plants and Ferns of Iceland*, by Hörður Kristinsson, published by Mál og Menning.

Birds and animals
Iceland is renowned for its bird life, which includes everything from non-migratory ptarmigan to migratory Arctic terns, flying between the Arctic and Antarctic. The summer months witness an invasion of species, all intent on nesting and feeding. Coastal cliffs such as Látrabjarg, on Walk 47, support gulls, guillemots and razorbills, while cliff-top burrows

are popular with puffins. Rocky stacks are important, and the remote Eldey, seen from Trek 1 Stage 7, supports a huge colony of gannets. Some coastal heaths are used by eiders, and some of their down is harvested. Beaches attract oystercatchers and turnstones, while fulmars nest on coastal cliffs, as well as cliffs far inland. Beware of the great skua, which kills small birds or animals approaching its nest, and will injure everything else, including humans!

Broad moorland and tundra is often alive with the sight and sound of curlew and plover, with 'drumming'

Diminutive Icelandic horses come in 30 colourings – each with its own name

21

Beware the great skua – a bad-tempered bird that can cause injury if approached

snipe common in the long summer evenings. Lonely pools attract wildfowl, including ducks, geese and swans. Rugged fells are the haunt of ravens, while birds of prey include gyrfalcon and merlins, often hunting for pipits. Many small birds control insect numbers around Iceland, but flies reach plague proportions around Mývatn (Trek 7) each summer.

Bird-watching guides abound, but it is worth noting that most maps published by Mál og Menning feature several species on the reverse side.

Large animals have been introduced to Iceland since the Settlement, including cattle and sheep. Horses have not been imported for a long time, so the Icelandic horse is distinctive. There are 30 varieties of colouring, each with its own name. Horse-trekking is popular, and these small,

strong horses can negotiate rugged terrain, coming into their own during autumn sheep round-ups when they carry shepherds to remote locations to collect strays (see www.feif.org).

The largest native land mammal is the Arctic fox. It can be observed on rare occasions almost anywhere, but its stronghold is the remote northwestern peninsula of Hornstrandir, explored on Trek 9. Reindeer were introduced to eastern Iceland and have slowly expanded their range. Polar bears turn up very, very rarely on the north coast, and are generally shot on sight.

Whale-watching trips are popular, and while they are offered from Reykjavík, the most popular are from Húsavík on the north coast. Sightings can never be guaranteed, but when whales do appear they are spectacular. Dolphins, porpoises and seals are also likely to be spotted. To discover what fish are in the sea, watch what the fishing boats off-load or look in a supermarket!

NATIONAL PARKS

Iceland's first national park was established in 1928 at Þingvellir, east of Reykjavík. Geologically fascinating, and of immense historical and cultural significance, this is essentially a rift valley formed at a point where the European and North American plates are torn apart. It was chosen as a meeting place for the Icelandic parliament, or 'Alþing'. It has an interesting arrangement of cliffs and outcrops, with peculiar acoustics. As Iceland's laws were recited orally and committed to memory, it was useful to be able to speak them out loud in a place where the greatest number of people could hear them.

Further national parks weren't established until 1967, when Skaftafell was designated on the southern part of Vatnajökull. Jökulsárgljúfur, far to the north of Vatnajökull, was designated in 1978 beside the glacial river of Jökulsá á Fjöllum and its powerful waterfalls. Snæfellsjökull, at the western end of Snæfellsnes, was designated in 2001. In 2008 the enormous Vatnajökull national park was created, covering the huge ice-cap and surrounding land, including Laki, Nýidalur, Askja and Snæfell. The former Skaftafell and Jökulsárgljúfur national parks were absorbed into this new creation, which now covers 13

Wild camping is perfectly acceptable around large parts of Iceland

per cent of Iceland and is the largest national park in Europe.

Over one quarter of the walks in this book are in national parks, and another quarter lie in specially designated reserves, such as Reykjanes, Fjallabaki, Lónsöræfi and Hornstrandir. Even areas that haven't been given special protection can be wild, remote, scenic and interesting.

GETTING TO ICELAND

By air

There are no 'budget' deals, but it is worth checking prices thoroughly. Flights operate daily and, given the position of Iceland in the North Atlantic, there are options to fly from Europe and North America. There are flights to Keflavík from all Scandinavian countries, especially Norway. Flights also operate from the German cities of Berlin, Frankfurt and Munich. Other major European cities with direct flights include Amsterdam, Brussels, Paris, Milan, Madrid and Barcelona. Icelandair (www.icelandair.com) flies from London, Manchester and Glasgow, as well as other European and North American airports. Iceland Express (www.icelandexpress.com) offers further options, including flights from London, a few European airports, and New York.

People travelling between Europe and North America, with a change of flights at Keflavík, are encouraged to take a stop-over and explore at least the south-west of Iceland. There are walking opportunities within easy reach of the airport at Keflavík (see Walks 3–6).

By ferry

The Norröna sails something of a mini-cruise – from Hirtshals in Denmark, via the Faroe Islands, to Seyðisfjörður in Iceland (www.smyrilline.com). Sailings from Denmark are on Saturday and Tuesday, arriving in Iceland on Tuesday and Thursday. Sailings from Iceland are on Wednesday and Thursday, arriving in Denmark on Saturday. The ferry is essential if you are taking a vehicle to Iceland. It is possible to step off the ferry at Seyðisfjörður and immediately start walking a long-distance trail through the Eastfjords (see Trek 4).

GETTING AROUND ICELAND

Fleets of buses leave Reykjavík every morning for most parts of Iceland, with the exception of the north-west and east, which require a change of buses and possibly another day's travelling. Avoiding a second day's travel is usually possible by taking a flight instead.

Driving in Iceland often involves long journeys, and it is inadvisable to attempt to explore the whole country in a single visit. Time spent on long drives means less time spent walking.

Car hire

One of the biggest mistakes visitors make is to assume that they have to hire a car, and then to look for a cheap deal. Cheap cars have stickers on the dashboard saying that they can't be driven on 'F' roads, or dirt roads, which is one way of saying you won't get much further than the Ring Road encircling Iceland. Hiring a 4WD allows the use of 'F' roads. More walks can be reached, but at a hefty price, and fuel is expensive. Hiring a car to access a long-distance trail is pointless, as it sits unused for a week and is awkward and costly to retrieve. If you want to access short day-walks and keep moving, and cost is no object, then hire a car. If you have no previous experience of driving dirt roads or fording rivers, note that damage is not covered by insurance and has to be paid for. Driving off dirt roads, across open country, is illegal.

Buses

Most of the routes in this guidebook can be accessed by bus services. Buses are expensive, but if you just want to reach a long-distance trek, then you only have to pay to get there and back, with no further costs. Some buses run only once a day, or less frequently, so check timetables. Buses are good for getting from place to place, but it isn't always possible to commute to and from a walking route in a day. So if you are planning to commute from a base, be sure to study timetables very carefully. The main bus transport hubs are the BSÍ terminal in Reykjavík, tourist information offices in Akureyri, Mývatn and Egilsstaðir, and Skaftafell visitor centre. In other towns and villages, ask where the buses stop and always be on time.

Check bus timetables carefully to be able to reach remote walking areas

Orange Stræto city buses run regularly around Reykjavík's urban sprawl. Get free city plans, bus maps and timetables, and either use a day pass or buy a strip of ten journey tickets from the bus station at Hlemmur (www.straeto.is).

Scheduled buses are operated by Sterna (tel 5511166, www.sterna.is). Reykjavík Excursions mainly operate tours, but also run scheduled buses (tel 5805400, www.re.is). SBA Norðurleið operate from Akureyri, providing tours and scheduled buses (tel 5500720, www.sba.is). These three companies cover most of Iceland, and operators in the Westfjords work with them. Timetables are available from bus or tourist information offices, so obtain and keep hold of them. Bus 'passports' (www.icelandonyourown.is) offer better value than paying several single fares.

There are other bus services, particularly in eastern Iceland, that aren't widely known, but offer access to interesting places. These one-off services are mentioned, where they occur, along with a telephone contact in the information box at the start of each walk or trek.

By air
Getting from one part of Iceland to another can take one or two days by bus. It is much quicker and possibly cheaper to fly. Air Iceland (www. airiceland.is) flies from Reykjavík to Akureyri, Ísafjörður, Grímsey, Egilsstaðir and Vopnafjörður. Eagle Air

(www.eagleair.is) flies from Reykjavík to Vestmannaeyjar, Höfn, Húsavík, Sauðárkrókur, Gjögur and Bildudalur.

By ferry
Ferries are used to reach four islands in this book – Heimaey (Walk 19), Hrísey (Walk 36), Grímsey (Walk 37) and Flatey (Walk 49). A ferry is also required to reach the remote northwest peninsula of Hornstrandir (Trek 9). Ferry contact details are given in the information box before each route description.

WHEN TO GO

This guidebook is written for walkers visiting Iceland in the long days of summer, although it is still important to make the best use of good weather forecasts and to be absolutely certain of your walking abilities and experience. Easy urban walks, such as Walk 1 from Reykjavík, could be covered any day of the year, but the bulk of walks are not recommended in the winter months. Spring varies, and 2011 saw the latest spring since 1947. May can be a good month to walk in low-lying places, as the days lengthen and snow melts, but rivers run high and may be impassable. Highland roads are closed and few bus services operate.

The roads authority aims to open highland roads by mid-June, but there can be delays. From mid-June to mid-August most popular walking areas are busy, and buses run all over the country. The Laugavegur and Skógar Trail (Trek 2 Stages 4–9) get very busy, and many walkers get frustrated because they are unable to book huts or, if they have secured bookings, find the huts too crowded. Be assured that there are plenty of quieter trails around Iceland.

The main concern for many walkers is not so much where to go, but what the weather will be. It is always changeable, and is unpredictable for more than a couple of days ahead. Even with 24hr daylight in the middle of summer and clear blue sky, the temperature barely touches 15°C, struggles to get near 20°C, and is truly record-breaking if it reaches 30°C. However, 15°C is quite refreshing if you are walking long and hard routes with a big pack. Dry, windy days result in unpleasant dust storms in some areas. When it rains, and the wind approaches gale force and the cloud is low, even the most scenic places seem dull and uninteresting. If shelter is unavailable the prospects for survival cause genuine worry. The weather may worsen around the end of August, which is when bus services cease and accommodation shuts down.

Avoid making hard-and-fast plans in advance. Do what most Icelanders do – get a weather forecast for the next few days and go where the sun is shining. This guidebook will surely contain appropriate routes somewhere in the country. Tourist information offices will either look up the weather for you or have it printed and posted on a board. Five-day forecasts are fairly accurate for two days, then increasingly inaccurate, so keep checking (www.vedur.is) or tel 9020600 to hear a recorded message. Seismic and volcanic activity can also be checked on the website.

Highland roads should be open by mid-June, but be sure to check before using them

ACCOMMODATION

Iceland is mostly remote and unin-habited, so most areas don't have any accommodation at all. This is no problem for those who are prepared to camp and have all the equipment. However, if you are relying exclusively on huts, hostels or other indoor accom-modation, remember that some places become fully booked in the summer.

The absolute budget approach is to camp in the wilds, free of charge, and this is acceptable in many places, but restricted in national parks. If you prefer campsites, these cost around kr1000 (see Money for the current exchange rate) per person per night, but hot showers are extra. Many huts allow camping alongside, and use of their facilities, for a similar fee.

Hut accommodation is very popular in some places, but you can be the sole occupier of a hut even in high summer. Ferðafélag Íslands

(FÍ, or Iceland Touring Association, www.fi.is) has nearly 40 huts around Iceland, and prices range from kr2000–3000 per night for mem-bers to kr3500–5000 per night for non-members. Either book and pay in advance, or turn up and hope for the best. Some huts have wardens, while others don't, providing an 'hon-esty box' for payment. Útivist (www. utivist.is) operates half a dozen huts in the south of Iceland, with prices lower than FÍ. Huts do not provide meals or sell food, but usually have cooking facilities. There may be flush toilets or 'dry' toilets. If showers are available they cost extra, but some huts don't even have a water supply. There are private huts, too, and details are given in the route/trek description.

There are 36 youth hostels, gener-ally near the coast and the Ring Road, often in towns and villages. Prices range from around kr3000 to kr4000,

The hut at Hvítárnes stands beside a channel of the grey, glacial Fúlakvísl (Trek 8 Stage 7)

depending on whether or not you are a member and whether you book through the central office (www.hostel. is) or directly with hostels. Possibly the most 'authentic' hostel is Fljótsdalur (see Walk 18), with its grass roof and amazing library, owned by Dick Phillips (www.icelandic-travel.com).

Bed and breakfast, guest houses and hotels are available at a variety of prices, with varying facilities. Consider anything less than kr10,000 per night to be a bargain, and steel yourself for quotes exceeding kr25,000. Some guest houses allow the use of their kitchens and washing machines. Breakfasts are generally all-you-can-eat buffets. Watch out for places listing 'sleeping-bag accommodation', which include some guesthouses and hotels, where prices are drastically reduced if you use your sleeping bag instead of their bedding.

FOOD AND DRINK

The most popular eatery in the whole of Iceland is reputed to be a hot-dog stall in Reykjavík. Dining at a quality restaurant is very expensive, so check prices before ordering. Alcohol of any strength has to be bought from state liquor stores, rather than supermarkets. Little cafés and filling stations often allow unlimited amounts of filter coffee to be drunk for a single payment.

If you want to buy and cook your own food, the cheapest supermarket is Bónus. A greater choice is available at Samkaup. Most towns and some villages will have one or both of these supermarkets, although there are others. There are familiar imported products on the shelves, but prices are higher than you pay at home. Iceland has a thriving dairy industry, so buying a carton of milk leads to a multitude of choices. Dairy products feature on the website www.ms.is. The most popular Icelandic meat is smoked lamb, and if you could eat a horse, that is also available! Fish is very popular, but Icelandic cured shark smells dreadfully of ammonia and is an acquired taste. Protein-rich dried fish proves versatile and useful on long treks. If you can't figure out Icelandic food names, ask the shop staff to assist. Food is often left in huts and hostels for anyone to use, and huge amounts are usually available at the city campsite in Reykjavík.

Sometimes there is little option but to buy food from a remote filling station, and prices are very high. Fuel for cooking is also expensive. Meths is known as 'rauðsprit', and most gas canisters are Coleman pierceable and screw-top. Fuel is often left at huts or campsites. If you want specialist lightweight trekking food, take it with you to Iceland. If staying in hotels or guest houses, breakfasts are all-you-can-eat buffets – great value if you are hungry!

MONEY

Even following the banking collapse and currency devaluation, Iceland remains expensive, and it can be

29

difficult to control costs while travelling. Food, drink, accommodation, fuel, car hire and bus travel are all expensive, but it is possible to set limits. 'Budget' options involve flying to Keflavík, bringing food with you, walking trails on Reykjanes, and wild camping. A whole week's walking need cost little more than the flight! The same can be done by arriving by ferry at Seyðisfjörður in East Iceland.

The Icelandic currency is the króna (plural krónur) or 'crown'. Notes come in denominations of 5000, 2000, 1000 and 500. Coins are 100, 50, 10, 5 and 1. US dollars and euros are sometimes accepted around Keflavík and Reykjavík. Currently, the approximate exchange rates are:

- £1   kr200
- €1   kr160
- $1   kr125

The rate is very variable so check before converting (see www.xe.com for the latest rates). Currency can be exchanged in Iceland at better rates than in your home country.

A large percentage of transactions are made with credit or debit cards. It is possible to use a card on many buses, and to be given the door code of some of the remote, locked huts by phoning card details to the owner. However, it is wise to carry some cash because there are a few places that don't accept cards. All towns and some villages have ATMs where cash can be withdrawn.

COMMUNICATIONS

Iceland has a lot of empty spaces, but there are also a lot of mobile phone masts, so coverage is surprisingly good. However, it is easy to lose a signal simply by crossing a gully or turning a corner on a fell, so if coverage is important keep an eye on signal strength, but note that opportunities to recharge may be very limited.

LANGUAGE

Icelandic is spoken by 350,000 Icelanders and very few other people in the world. Almost all Icelanders have a good command of English, as do most visitors to Iceland. If you are interested in picking up some Icelandic ask a native speaker, who will be able to correct you instantly – and in English. Icelandic has a complex grammatical structure, but its pronunciation is easily grasped. Most letters are the same as those in English and are pronounced in the same way, but there are some additional accented letters and 'special' characters that have to be learned.

Accented letters include Áá, Éé, Íí, Óó, Öö, Úú and Ýý. The Icelandic word for 'Iceland' is written as 'Ísland', and is pronounced almost the same as 'Iceland'.

The special characters of Þþ (*thorn*) and Ðð (*eth*) give two variants of the 'th' sound – the same as the difference between the 'th' sound in the words 'tru**th**' and 'tru**th**s'. Sometimes, when English booklets and brochures are produced in Iceland, the characters are substituted with 'th'. Another special character is the compound Ææ, which has vanished from the English language but used to appear in words such as 'encyclopædia'.

The Icelandic pronunciation of 'll', as used in words such as 'fell', is difficult for visitors to grasp. The closest approximation would be to make the sound 'tl', which would make 'fell' sound almost like 'fettle'. However, this is only an approximation, and it is best to listen carefully to an Icelander, then repeat, and be prepared to be corrected!

Very basic Icelandic pleasantries are easily grasped, but conversational Icelandic requires an understanding of its complex grammar. If you try and speak Icelandic and make a hash of it, you will be answered in English to put you out of your misery!

hello/hi	hallo/hæ
good morning/ afternoon	góðan daginn
good night	góða nótt
goodbye/bye	bless/bæ
thank you	takk
thank you very much	takk fyrir
yes	ja
no	nei

Icelanders have no surnames, but are generally named after their fathers. If a man called Jón has a son, Erik, and a daughter, Björk, then they will be known as Erik Jónsson and Björk Jónsdóttir. Basically, they are the 'son' and 'daughter' of 'Jón'. If Erik has a son, Þor, he will be known as Þor Eriksson. If Björk has children, they will take the name of their father, except in very rare circumstances.

It is useful for walkers to know the meaning of at least a few place-name elements, and the most common are given in Appendix B.

TOURIST INFORMATION OFFICES

Never pass a tourist information office without a good browse. You often find free maps, some of them good enough for walks. They offer advice about accommodation, attractions and transport, as well as providing the latest weather forecast. One of the most important and useful publications you can obtain is the free book *Around Iceland*, which lists every conceivable service and facility in Iceland, and includes road maps, street plans and a wealth of interesting information. Consider a copy as an essential accompaniment to this guide (see www.heimur.is/heimur/world and click 'Around Iceland'). There are plenty of tourism websites, but start with www.visiticeland.com.

Bláhnúkur peeps over a rugged lava flow beyond the busy campsite at Landmannalaugar (Walk 15)

WHAT TO TAKE

Iceland's summer weather is a little cooler and wetter than Britain's, and it changes all the time. Wear warm, waterproof clothing on wet, windy days, but don't omit sun protection, as the air is often remarkably clear when the sun shines.

Camping gear is essential on any multi-day routes where huts are unavailable, or where bookings for huts have not been made in advance. Camping gear is also very useful in case your plans don't turn out as expected, and you have to camp somewhere unexpectedly. A tent is good insurance! Take a tent that has been tried and tested on stony ground in severe weather.

If you are carrying food, bring lightweight trekking food, as buying in Iceland is expensive. Water is often abundant and clean, but glacial rivers are filthy. Some stony deserts have little or no water, and supplies may have to be carried some distance.

Use sandals or Crocs for fording rivers, and keep footwear and socks dry. Whether you wear boots or shoes is a personal choice, but the ground is often rocky or stony and may be very abrasive. Boots should be worn, with crampons, on glacier walks, where ropes and ice axes are also required. 'Indoor' shoes must be worn in huts, hostels and some other lodgings.

If in doubt about your abilities or kit choices, put them to the test in harsh conditions before you go to Iceland.

HEALTH AND SAFETY

When walking and trekking in Iceland, dress well against cold and wet weather, always be sure of your position on a route, and never take risks with anything beyond your ability and experience. If camping, tents must be able to withstand severe weather. Many places are rough and rocky, with crumbling slopes and unstable cliffs, where it is easy to twist an ankle, break a bone or take a tumble. In remote places, minor injuries must be dealt with using only the contents of your first aid kit. Trekkers must be completely self-sufficient.

There are specific dangers in some parts of Iceland that have to be given consideration before you start. If in doubt, choose another route, or if you have already started, turn back. It is worth asking Icelanders, particularly national park rangers and hut wardens, some of whom are also members of the Icelandic Association for Search and Rescue (ICE-SAR, www.landsbjorg.is), about the current condition of routes. Some may ask you to leave your details as you start a walk.

Some routes involve fording rivers (see below), and glacial rivers can be dangerous. A few routes cross glaciers, requiring ropes, ice axes, crampons and experience. Hot springs and mud-pots should not be approached closely, and if you are tempted to bathe in hot pools, test the water carefully. Visitors rarely get caught by volcanic eruptions and

A river is followed part of the way through Morudalur to Krossholt (Walk 46)

glacier floods, and the emergency services quickly keep people at safe distances. The chances of contracting pneumonoultramicroscopicsilicovolcanoconiosis by breathing fine volcanic dust are minimal, but it's great to be able to include that word in the book!

If you require medication, take adequate supplies with you. Pharmacies are available in towns and some villages, but it may be some distance to a doctor or dentist, and further still to a hospital. The European Health Insurance Card (EHIC) can be used in Iceland to offset the costs of some treatments or to enable some costs to be recovered, but it is well to carry adequate insurance.

If driving around the country, and especially if driving remote dirt roads, check current road conditions (tel 1777, www.vegaverdin.is).

RIVER CROSSINGS

There are a number of walks and treks in this guidebook that require rivers to be forded. Walkers with experience of fording rivers will know what is required, while others should proceed with caution, bearing in mind that every river and every ford is different.

This guide is written for summer visitors, and at that time of year the two factors that influence the volume of water in rivers are rainfall and meltwater. During and after heavy rain, expect rivers to be swollen and sometimes completely impassable. Glacial rivers generally have the greatest flow as the day wears on, then their levels drop during the night. The best time to ford these rivers is early in the morning, but they always require great care as the water is dirty, obscuring views of the riverbed.

Before stepping into a river, walk up and downstream to select a suitable ford. Narrow stretches are invariably deepest and may feature the strongest currents. Broad stretches are usually shallowest, but beware of broad bends, as the water may be shallow on one side and deep on the other, or feature an undercut riverbank denying exit. If a river is deep and swift, then don't cross, but look elsewhere. If a river is broad and shallow, it may be possible to hop dryshod from boulder to boulder, but only do this is you are sure-footed. Avoid wet and greasy boulders which may result in an awkward fall.

Fording a river barefoot is not recommended. Sharp or uneven stones can injure feet, and progress is likely to be slow, with walkers standing too long in cold water. Remove socks to keep them dry, then either put walking boots or shoes back on, or switch them for something else. 'Crocs', for example, are very light and were designed for river crossings. Ensure that your pack hip-belt and chest strap are unfastened. In the event of falling in deep water, discard your pack. Trekking poles are immensely useful for balance and for probing the riverbed before each step. Proceed cautiously with short steps. With two feet and two poles, ensure that there are always three points of contact with the riverbed. If travelling without poles, two or more people can cross effectively by holding onto each other.

Rivers less than knee-deep are unlikely to pose problems. Rivers running higher, or running swiftly, must

A small ICE-SAR base in the middle of the highlands at Nýidalur (Walks 40 and 41)

be approached with utmost care. There comes a point, which varies from person to person, where the force of water cannot be resisted. Some say you should angle your crossing to walk slightly against the current, while others say you should angle your crossing to walk with the current. In practice, walkers might need to go against and with the current. Cautious walkers will retreat if things aren't going their way, but if you are suddenly swept away, the important thing is to get rid of your pack, then scramble or swim to one of the banks as quickly as possible. Save your life before trying to salvage your gear, and bear in mind that the more things you pack in waterproof liners, the more things will survive total immersion. Despite their apparent weight and bulk, most packs will float!

Deep and fast-flowing rivers have hidden dangers and should be crossed only by those with experience. If you are walking as part of a group and know that there are difficult crossings ahead, then a rope should be carried, and members can assist each other across. If walking solo, then proceed with extreme caution. The most radical river crossing would involve a solo walker, with no safety rope, getting into deep, cold, fast-flowing water, having lashed their pack to an inflatable mattress to form a flotation device. Maintaining a line across a river in these conditions would be extremely difficult, but some people do it!

EMERGENCIES

Emergency services are contacted by phoning 112, and if you are close to towns or villages the police, ambulance or fire service may be able to deal with things. In remote areas, ICE-SAR (www.landsbjorg.is) responds to call-outs with specialist vehicles and equipment. They can stretcher someone off a remote trail or glacier, or tow a bus out of a river. Helicopter pick-ups have to be paid for. Provide rescuers with all the information they require so that they can make an appropriate response, but it is best to avoid such situations in the first place. A mass of information and safety advice is contained in the free multilingual magazine *Safetravel.is* and at www.safetravel.is.

Orange emergency shelters are seen on some remote roads and coasts. They are often sparsely furnished and may contain emergency food rations. Some people use them as 'free' huts, but this is to be discouraged.

FOOTPATHS, WAYMARKING AND ACCESS

There are a number of designated long-distance trails in Iceland, some of which are followed by the routes in this guide. The extremely popular Laugavegur and the Skógar Trail (Trek 2 Stages 4–9) in South Iceland are of course included, but don't neglect other trails around the country, which are much quieter and just as satisfying.

Reykjavegur signpost near Leiti, at the foot of the Bláfjöll massif (Trek 1 Stage 2)

If you have never walked day to day before, start with the easier ones, such as the two-day Jökulsárhlaup (Trek 5) or three-day Mývatn Trail (Trek 7). The Lónsöræfi Trail (Trek 3), however, is one of the toughest trails.

Access in Iceland is often unrestricted, but there are private areas, farmland of no interest to walkers, and places that are downright dangerous whether access is permitted or not. Most walking routes in this guidebook are along clear tracks and paths, or are waymarked. The standard method of marking a route is to stick painted posts or pegs into the ground, which walkers follow, sometimes for days on end. There may or may not be trodden paths on a waymarked route, so keep watching for markers.

There are variations in the standard of waymarking. Routes across Reykjanes (Section 1) are marked with orange plastic posts, bearing codes and numbers for different trails. In nearby Hengill (Section 1), colour-coded posts and signposts make the area better marked than anywhere else in Iceland. Some trails are not marked, including half of the tough Lónsöræfi Trail (Section 3), which requires good map-reading. Some old trails are marked by stout stone cairns. Read the route descriptions carefully to determine if a route is marked or unmarked, and even a well-marked route can be difficult to follow in poor visibility or when snow covers it.

MAPS

A bewildering range of maps cover Iceland, and it may not always be possible to obtain the best one at short notice. Landmælingar Íslands, the National Land Survey of Iceland (www.lmi.is), produces maps at various scales and has a versatile online map of Iceland (http://atlas.lmi.is/kortasja_en). Their maps are published under the brand name Ferðakort (www.ferdakort.is). A 1:250,000 series is useful for general travelling, while 1:100,000 and 1:50,000 maps are best for walking and trekking. Some maps specifically cover popular walking areas.

Many popular areas are mapped by Mál og Menning (www.forlagid.is). The Atlaskort series covers Iceland at 1:100,000. Special Hiking Maps at 1:100,000 have some areas at 1:50,000 printed on the reverse, as well as additional notes and a selection of pictures of interest to bird-watchers.

Good maps cover the national parks, obtainable from national park visitor centres. Walking clubs have mapped some good walking areas, available in specific localities. Tourist information offices give away useful maps, and it is worth browsing their wares. Throughout this guidebook, one, two or three maps are recommended in the information box at the start of each walk, but use them with caution, because some trails are drawn in the wrong places, even if other details are good.

Strokkur, at Geysir, and a host of other roadside attractions, don't require maps and guidebooks

USING THIS GUIDE

There are a variety of walks in this guidebook, so read the descriptions carefully and choose routes to suit your ability and experience. There are suburban routes, coastal routes, and fell and glacier routes. There are stony deserts, broad tundra and woodlands. The routes are spread all around Iceland, grouped into twelve regions, most of which contain a selection of day-walks and a long-distance trail. Each day's walk is in the range 4–40km (2½–25 miles). Trekking routes can last for a week.

Clear tracks and paths are often used, and signposts and waymarks blaze many trails, but markers are sometimes sparse and it is necessary to watch carefully for them. Some of the clearest waymarked routes are around Reykjanes and Hengill.

If you have never walked on glaciers before, or want to climb Iceland's highest mountain – Hvannadalshnúkur, then join a properly guided, roped party, equipped with ice axes and crampons.

In the box at the start of each walk or trek stage, all the information is given to allow you to choose wisely. Usually, two or three maps are recommended, bus access is mentioned, huts are noted, while the distances, ascents, descents and nature of the terrain should indicate whether routes are suitable for your abilities or whether you should choose another route. Timings are 'walking' times only, and do not allow for breaks. Use

them as a rough guide and adjust them in the light of your own performance.

The sketch maps in this guide are at an approximate scale of 1:100,000, but a handful of them cover short walks at a scale of around 1:50,000. They are intended to show the basic relief, with contours at 100m intervals, along with a few rivers and lakes. Man-made features such as bridges, huts and roads are often rare beyond the starting points. Although strong red lines are used to show the routes, it is important to read the route descriptions carefully, especially where paths are scant or absent, and take note of whether the routes are waymarked or not. One of the best maps available in Iceland – Hengill Hiking Trails – can be downloaded for free. Go to www.or.is/English and click on *Hiking trails and pics*.

Some readers may flick through the pages of this guide and wonder what happened to Gullfoss, Geysir, Goðafoss, Dynjandi and a host of other famous features. Quite simply, you look at these places, maybe visiting cafés alongside, but they don't offer more than a half-hour walk. If you use bus services passing these places, the bus will stop, and you'll get to see them anyway. Remote places such as Laki are the subject of bus tours from Skaftafell, and the bus will stop, and the driver explains where you can walk from time to time. You don't need a guidebook for those places, and this guidebook is to help you get off the beaten track and enjoy more of the wonderful trails that Iceland offers.

1 REYKJAVÍK, REYKJANES AND HENGILL

Looking from Hengill towards Reykjanes – two areas that are easily reached from Reykjavík

Thousands of visitors dash from Keflavík airport to the centre of Reykjavík, ignoring the Reykjanes peninsula in the south-west of Iceland. This area abounds in interest, featuring many geothermal hot-spots and offering plenty of well-marked walking routes.

The day-walks include interlinked, low-level walks across lava fields near the airport (Walks 3–5) and in rugged little fells near Seltún (Walks 6–8). An easy coastal walk round the suburbs of Reykjavík (Walk 1) looks towards one of Iceland's most popular mountain climbs on Esja (Walk 2). The interesting little national park of Þingvellir is easily explored nearby (Walk 9). A quick trip from Reykjavík to Hveragerði allows access to a rugged range of fells at Hengill (Walks 10–13), where the signposting and waymarking is possibly the best in Iceland.

The long-distance Reykjavegur (Trek 1) links several of the day-walks in this section, particularly in Hengill, near Seltún, and near Grindavík. Although the trail runs within sight of Reykjavík, it often appears to be very remote and attracts very few walkers.

Many of the walks in this area can be accessed using local bus services from Reykjavík. Walkers intending to use Reykjavík as a base should make a careful study of bus timetables to ensure that outward and return journeys tie in with the time needed to complete walking routes. One of the best ways to see what the Reykjanes peninsula can offer is to enjoy a trip with Salty Tours (tel 8205750, www.saltytours.is).

Reykjavík, Reykjanes and Hengill

Day Walks

Reykjavegur

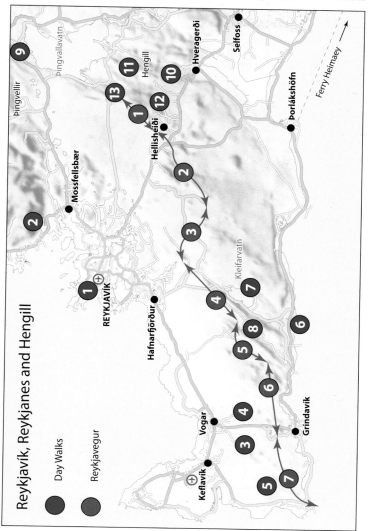

41

WALK 1

Reykjavík and Seltjarnarnes

Start/Finish	Ráðhús (parliament) in Reykjavík
Distance	20km (12½ miles)
Total ascent/descent	100m (330ft)
Time	5hrs
Terrain	Easy, low-level tarmac and gravel coastal paths, with some roads
Map	Free 1:25,000 'Big Map' of Reykjavík from tourist information offices
Transport	Regular Strætó buses run near most of the route

If you are stuck for a day in Reykjavík, the coastal walk around Seltjarnarnes is pleasant. The western parts are grassy, flowery and home to several species of birds. There is also a geothermal beach, an artificial geyser and a fine viewpoint.

The Ráðhús, or parliament building, is in the centre of **Reykjavík**. Follow the road Pósthússtræti towards the harbour, turning left to pass notices and kiosks offering whale-watching and wildlife cruises. Follow a main road and later note the Víkin Maritime Museum down to the right. Go through a roundabout to walk along Ánanaust, past the Olís filling station. Pick up and follow a footpath and cycleway between the road and masses of boulders protecting the coast.

Pass a roundabout and walk beside Eiðsgrandi, enjoying views of distant Snæfellsnes, followed by

the uplands of Akrafjall, Skarðsheiði and Esja. Continue beside Norðurströnd, eventually passing a hut and big anchor. A grassy, flowery area leads towards a prominent lighthouse on a small island at **Grótta**.

The flowery end of the Seltjarnarnes peninsula, looking to the little island of Grótta

> There is no access onto **Grótta** from 1 May to 1 July, while birds breed. After that period, the safe times for crossing a tidal spit are posted. Noticeboards detail the birds that can be seen, from placid eiders to raucous gulls and savage terns.

Follow the path onwards, overlooking the tarn of Bakkatjörn. Before reaching a road, turn right to follow a path around the coastal margin of a golf course at **Suðurnes**. Join and follow a road overlooking Bakkatjörn again, then follow Suðurströnd past a small harbour. Watch for a tarmac path on the right and follow it down Sólbraut. Later, turn left along Skerjabraut and right through a disused car park. Follow the roads Lambastaðabraut and Tjarnarból, then turn right down a main road called Nesvegur.

Turn right along Sörlaskjól to pick up and follow a grassy coastal path parallel to Faxaskjól. Pass a sculpture and follow a tarmac path parallel to Ægisíða, passing a ramshackle fish-drying hut. Pass between a couple of houses and watch for a viewpoint on the right. Views stretch from Vífilsfell and Sveifluháls to Keilir and Keflavik. **Reykjavík airport** is close to hand, and a path runs between the coast and some houses, passing runways.

Pass a geothermal beach at **Nauthólsvík**, where a tarmac footpath and cycleway rise inland. Turn left up another path and left again behind a big building. Turn right up a broken tarmac road and almost immediately left up a forest track. Wind uphill and rejoin the road, but turn left immediately up another track. To the left is an artificial geyser, while the curious building at the top of the hill is Perlan.

The glass dome of **Perlan** ('the pearl'), **www.perlan.is**, sits on a forested hill surrounded by massive drums storing hot water for Reykjavík. It contains the Saga Museum, a conference centre, garden, shops, bar and restaurant.

Go around the back of Perlan and down a tarmac path on a grassy slope, which becomes forested. Turn right along a footpath and cycleway, through an underpass, then turn left up steps and cross a road at a junction. Follow the footpath and cycleway beside Nauthólsvegur and either wait to cross the busy Hringbraut or cross a footbridge. Head towards the BSÍ bus station, which has a café, and keep right of it and the nearby N1 filling station. Cross a footbridge, keep ahead down a tarmac path, and do not cross the Hringbraut. Keep right of a lake in a park called Hljómskalagarður to finish back in the centre of **Reykjavík**.

WALK 2

Þverfellshorn from Esjustofa

Start/Finish	Esjustofa, north of Mossfellsbær
Distance	9km (5½ miles)
Total ascent/descent	800m (2625ft)
Time	3hrs
Terrain	Clear paths on wooded, vegetated and stony slopes. Scrambling is required on the final steep, bouldery, rocky slopes, with chains for assistance.
Map	Free 1:60,000 'Hvalfjarðarhringurinn' from tourist information offices
Transport	Stræto bus 15 from Reykjavík to Háholt, then bus 57 to Esjustofa

The broad mountain of Esja is prominent in views from many places around Reykjavík. It is a favourite fell with local people and boasts several routes. The most popular path is from Esjustofa to a viewpoint at Þverfellshorn.

Bus 57 serves a turning space near **Esjustofa** (café and visitor centre). There is a car park here, and another in a nearby wood. Keep left of the café, cross a footbridge over a river with flowery banks, and turn right. ▶ The path climbs through birch woods, passing a notice at a path junction at Skógarstígur. There are five similar notices on the ascent, allowing progress to be checked.

From the woodland car park, pass a map-board and follow a well-trodden path.

Keep left, up past conifers, and cross a footbridge over a stream. Climb flights of stone steps in a little valley and turn right on a rising traverse across a slope of lupins and cow parsley. Pass a notice at Þvergil and the vegetation thins to low, flowery heath on stony slopes. Reach a notice at a path junction at **Göngubrúin**, and head down to the right. ▶ Cross a stream using a sloping footbridge, then climb stone steps.

Climbing left here offers a steep shortcut.

Another notice is reached at **Vaðið**, where a stream is forded at 393m (1289ft). Marker posts show the way up a bouldery slope, then the path drifts left on a rising

45

Þverfellshorn

780

Steinn

Vaðič

Ford   393

Short Cut

Göngubrú

N

0   1km

Car Park

■ *Esjustofa*

traverse across a steep slope. Reach a boulder called **Steinn**, at 597m (1951ft), where there is a notice and a guestbook. ◀ Climb a steep, stony path to a notice at Klettabeltið, at 676m (2718ft).

The shortcut joins here.

Take care on the last part of the path, climbing and drifting right, passing iron stakes, using short chains on steep, rocky slopes, and climbing to a viewpoint, cairn and guestbook on **Þverfellshorn**, at 780m (2560ft). The higher parts of Esja are broad, bouldery and pathless. Enjoy views of Hengill, Reykjavík and Reykjanes, then retrace steps to **Esjustofa**.

The start of the popular path, known to all the people of Reykjavík, onto the slopes of Esja

WALK 3
Keflavík to Grindavík

Start	Fitjar, near Keflavík
Finish	Grindavík
Distance	18km (11 miles)
Total ascent/descent	150m (490ft)
Time	6hrs
Terrain	Rugged lava crossed by tracks and stony, rocky paths
Map	1:50,000 'Reykjanes Activity Photomap'
Transport	Reykjanes Express serves Fitjar from Keflavík and Reykjavík. Reykjavík Excursions serves Grindavík from Reykjavík.

The coast-to-coast Skipsstígur trail crosses Reykjanes using a traditional cairned route over low-lying, but often rugged lava flows. It is marked by numbered orange plastic posts and sometimes follows hot-water pipelines.

Fitjar is near Keflavík, where a lagoon features several species of birds and a variety of plants, all listed on notice-boards. Behind the Bónus supermarket a main road links Reykjavík and Keflavík. Cross it with care and note a building served by an access road, but head for a hot-water pipeline to find a cairn and Skipsstígur sign. Note orange plastic marker posts bearing the letters SKST and a number. The trail is followed by 'walking by numbers', counting down from 269.

Follow a track parallel to the pipeline over a boulder-strewn moor. To the right are the colourful buildings of a former US military base, followed by bunkers. After post 252 the trail drifts left along a vague path, returning to the track and pipeline at post 236. Go through a fence and cross a narrow road. Post 230 lies on the right, and the path runs onto open stony moorland, winding, rising and falling, marked by cairns.

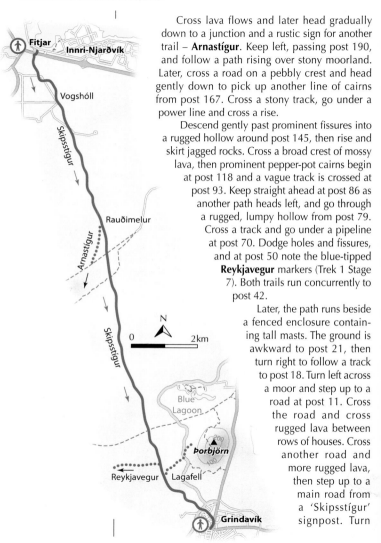

Cross lava flows and later head gradually down to a junction and a rustic sign for another trail – **Arnastígur**. Keep left, passing post 190, and follow a path rising over stony moorland. Later, cross a road on a pebbly crest and head gently down to pick up another line of cairns from post 167. Cross a stony track, go under a power line and cross a rise.

Descend gently past prominent fissures into a rugged hollow around post 145, then rise and skirt jagged rocks. Cross a broad crest of mossy lava, then prominent pepper-pot cairns begin at post 118 and a vague track is crossed at post 93. Keep straight ahead at post 86 as another path heads left, and go through a rugged, lumpy hollow from post 79. Cross a track and go under a pipeline at post 70. Dodge holes and fissures, and at post 50 note the blue-tipped **Reykjavegur** markers (Trek 1 Stage 7). Both trails run concurrently to post 42.

Later, the path runs beside a fenced enclosure containing tall masts. The ground is awkward to post 21, then turn right to follow a track to post 18. Turn left across a moor and step up to a road at post 11. Cross the road and cross rugged lava between rows of houses. Cross another road and more rugged lava, then step up to a main road from a 'Skipsstígur' signpost. Turn

48

The Skipsstígur often looks as though it is heading for the prominent fell of Þorbjörn

right and follow the road past a roundabout into **Grindavík**.

> The fishing village of **Grindavík** has expanded greatly, and its story is told at the Saltfish Museum. Facilities include guesthouses, campsite, bank, post office, shops and restaurants. From here, Reykjavík Excursions head for the Blue Lagoon and Reykjavík.

WALK 4
Grindavík to Vogar

Start	Grindavík
Finish	Vogar
Distance	18km (11 miles)
Total ascent/descent	150m (490ft)
Time	6hrs
Terrain	Gently sloping, stony moorland, rugged lava and loose pumice
Map	1:50,000 'Reykjanes Activity Photomap'
Transport	Reykjavík Excursions serves Grindavík from Reykjavík. Reykjanes Express serves Vogar from Keflavík and Reykjavík.

The coast-to-coast Skógfellavegur trail crosses Reykjanes using a traditional cairned route over low-lying, rugged lava. It is marked by numbered orange plastic posts, counting upwards past the little hills of Stóra-Skógfell and Litla-Skógfell.

Leave **Grindavík** via the Krýsuvík road, almost to the campsite. A 'Skógfellavegur' signpost and cairn stand on the left. Keep left of a football pitch, cross a narrow road and follow orange marker posts bearing numbers. Join and follow a tarmac path and use a pedestrian crossing over a road. Head diagonally right as marked by post 11 and a cairn.

Leave town following posts and cairns across an undulating grass, moss and crowberry moor, which is awkwardly stony. Post 26 is level with the prominent ORF Genetics glasshouse, then the walking is easier. Cross a track at post 37 and rise gently across **Hagafell**, running close to a track.

Cross another track at post 50 and continue gently uphill. An easy stretch crosses bare lava, then the blue-tipped markers of the **Reykjavegur** (Trek 1 Stage 6) are passed at post 56.

Cross a broad track and the trail is rugged underfoot, then from post 65 it is mostly bare lava. From post 70 there are no cairns across an easy slope of crunchy pumice, while jagged lava lies to the right. From post 97 the trail is mostly on moss and lava, with cairns again. By post 107 the trail touches scree on **Stóra-Skógfell**.

Pull away from the fell-foot, keeping left at post 112. Touch the fell-foot again at post 117, where the highest part of the route is reached, at only 75m (245ft), with a glimpse of Vogar far ahead. The ground drops gently, but rugged, then some easy stretches cross the bare lava of **Skógfellahraun**, sometimes bearing a rut worn by horses.

Avoid wheel-marks to reach post 158 at the foot of scree on **Litla-Skógfell**. Vegetation features grass, crowberry, heather, creeping juniper and patches of dwarf birch. Pick a way between stony slopes on the left and rugged lava blocks on the right, reaching a warning notice at post 163. ▶

The area was used as a military range, so don't touch any unusual objects.

The trail is a rugged, stony groove flanked by vegetated rocks and blocks, with occasional clumps of dwarf birch. Drop onto a stony moor and follow a winding path. It is slow going, bouldery later, with easier bare lava between posts 180 and 187. Cross a gentle rise and pass a large cairn at post 190, then cross a broad, rugged dip on the moor. From post 200 to 215 the path rises and falls past lava domes, stony underfoot, struggling towards a main road, and later climbs gently from a broad, vegetated hollow. The path is stony and bouldery again, with few cairns but several posts.

At post 233 there is a clear view to the main road. Cross

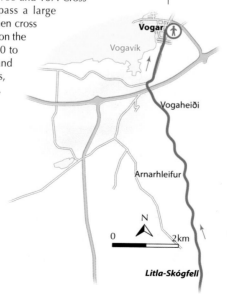

51

One of the numbered waymark posts that help keep track of progress along the Skógfellavegur

a ladder-stile over a fence between posts 238 and 239. Walk under a power line to post 243, where another large notice warns about the former military range. Cross a track and walk to post 246 and a 'Skógafellavegur' signpost.

Go under the busy road and walk past a solitary hut. Turn right along a dirt road, over a crest and along a tarmac road. This is Stapavegur, leading into **Vogar**, past houses and the N1 filling station (also shop, post office and ATM) to the Hótel Vogar. Buses turn at the Gamla Pósthúsið restaurant. With time to spare, visit the harbour, where there is a small park around a hill and a tarn.

WALK 5

Grindavík and Prestastígur

Start	Grindavík
Finish	Hafnir
Distance	21km (13 miles)
Total ascent/descent	150m (490ft)
Time	7hrs
Terrain	Roads at the start and finish, lava and ash in between, crossed by tracks and rugged paths
Map	1:50,000 'Reykjanes Activity Photomap'
Transport	Reykjavík Excursions serves Grindavík from Reykjavík. Pick-up could be arranged with Salty Tours.

The Prestastígur is a traditional route over low-lying, but often rugged lava flows, marked by stout cairns and numbered orange plastic posts. Road-walks at the beginning and end can be omitted if lifts are arranged.

Leave **Grindavík** along Víkurbraut and Vesturbraut, heading for a **golf course** outside town. Rustic wooden signs on the right indicate the Árnastígur and Prestastígur, but this is misleading. Continue along the road, rising and swinging left. A track rises right of the road to a 'Prestastígur' signpost, where orange marker posts bear the letters PRST, with numbers counting upwards. At post 9, a line of stout cairns rises from the golf course. Turn left to follow them, and pick up a path flanked by moss, heather, crowberry and grass.

Map continues on page 54

53

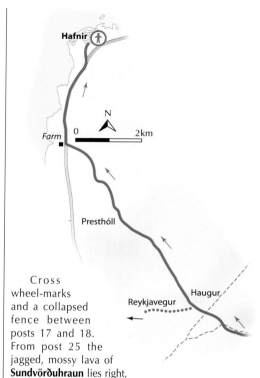

Hafnir

N

Farm

0   2km

Presthóll

Cross wheel-marks and a collapsed fence between posts 17 and 18. From post 25 the jagged, mossy lava of **Sundvörðuhraun** lies right,

Reykjavegur   Haugur

and from 29 to 30 note the groove worn into the bedrock by horses. There is a short, steep, rocky climb, then swing right from post 33 and spot more grooves on the way to post 42. Rise to join the **Reykjavegur** (Trek 1 Stage 7) at post 52, which has blue-tipped markers.

Turn left to follow the combined trails, often grooved to post 63, then crunch on pumice, keeping right of **Rauðhóll**. Between posts 66 and 72 the trails part and rejoin. At post 84 the path runs close to a track, and, if in a hurry, the track can be followed to post 104. Rise gently over a stony moorland crest, go under a power line and cross a track. The Reykjavegur heads left at post

A rustic wooden signpost for the Prestastígur, where it joins a road near a farm

115, so keep ahead to rise gently on the Prestastígur. The slopes are covered in black sand, where lyme grass thrives, and cairns march across a crest beyond post 120 at **Haugur**.

Cross a broad, shallow dip, pass a prominent pointed cairn at post 129 and continue undulating, gradually rising, over a broad crest at post 170, barely reaching 75m (245ft) at **Presthóll**. The descent leads to a road near a large **farm** at post 120 and a 'Prestastígur' signpost. Arrange a pick-up here, or turn right and follow the road to the little village of **Hafnir**.

WALK 6
Krýsuvík and Krísuvíkurbjarg

Start/Finish	Church at Krýsuvík or Vestarurlækur
Distance	12 or 16km (7½ or 10 miles)
Total ascent/descent	150m (490ft)
Time	3hrs or 4hrs
Terrain	Clear moorland tracks and coastal cliff paths
Map	1:50,000 'Reykjanes Activity Photomap'
Transport	None, but Krýsuvík is on the Salty Tours route

Before 2012 this walk started at Krýsuvík, which is still possible, but a new road now offers a starting point at Vestarurlækur, closer to Krísuvíkurbjarg. An easy walk along a rugged track leads to a splendid cliff walk popular with bird-watchers.

There was a farm at **Krýsuvík**, couched between Bæjarfell and Arnarfell. A small wooden church was built in 1857, but it burnt to the ground in January 2010. Carpenters at Hafnafjörður immediately launched a project to build an exact replica.

Follow the road from **Krýsuvík** as if for Grindavík. A signpost on the right points to Krísuvíkurbjarg and Selalda. Follow the stony track along and gently downhill, crossing a cattle grid and reaching a new road. Cross the road on a hump, where a stream runs through a culvert at **Vestarurlækur** and turn right to follow a track. ◄

Start here to save 4km (2½ miles) in total.

The track runs parallel to the road, pulls away from it and descends gently – soft, gritty and dusty. Wind across

a stony moor with areas of grass, heather and crowberry. Cross a cattle grid at a gap in a fence and cross a stream beyond, close to the hill called **Selalda**. Continue winding down a gentle moorland slope and pass a notice warning of rock-falls on nearby cliffs at **Hælsvík**.

Cliffs stretch away from Hælsvík, with views towards the end of Reykjanes

The track can be followed faithfully, with short, steep ascents and descents, to a small orange-and-red lighthouse on the cliffs of **Krísuvíkurbjarg**. Alternatively, the rugged cliff coast can be followed, with care where it has a crumbling or overhanging edge, to the lighthouse (this option is better for bird-watching). Views along the coast stretch to Eldey, off the end of Reykjanes, and inland to the broad plateau of Brennisteinsfjöll.

It is possible to continue along a grassy cliff path and cut inland to follow a road back to **Krýsuvík**, but the simplest way back is simply to retrace steps.

WALK 7
Seltún and Kleifarvatn

Start/Finish	Seltún
Distance	8km (5 miles)
Total ascent/descent	150m (490ft)
Time	3hrs
Terrain	Mostly gentle grassy or bare slopes, with some road walking
Map	1:50,000 'Reykjanes Activity Photomap'
Transport	None, but Seltún is on the Salty Tours route

Seltún features bubbling mud-pots and hot springs. The nearby lake of Kleifarvatn looks quite literally drained, as its level fell after an earthquake in 2000. A huge, vigorous geothermal pool is passed at Austurengjahver.

First, explore a short circular trail using board-walks and steps at **Seltún**, where there is a hut, toilets and car park. Most visitors drive away afterwards, but this walk explores further, first following the road towards Kleifarvatn. Tarmac gives way to a dirt road, and a gate on the right is marked 'Störi 1'. Next, a signpost on the right points to the hill of Stóra-Lambafell. Step over a fence and head for a wooden structure on a grassy plain. Keep right to follow a path, ford a murky stream and climb gently towards a little house called **Hverahlíð**. Keep left of it, stepping over a fence to pass a hot pool. There is a view of a sandy lake-bed, once covered by **Kleifarvatn**.

Turn right, either on grassy slopes or on the sand below, to reach a huddle of huts on a dry bay at **Hvammar**. Look for orange plastic marker posts bearing the letters DALAL and numbers. Follow these up a slope

that is pathless, although a path forms as the gradient eases. There are good views from post 44, and a steamy hollow is seen ahead on the fellside. Follow markers through a gap in a fence at post 37, then cross bare stones and earth, followed by wet, tussocky grass. Aim for the steamy hollow of **Austurengjahver**, which contains a big pool of boiling muddy water.

Keep left of it and follow markers over a stony crest, past post 23. Head down to a post tangled with old wire and drift right. At post 17 a blue-green lake is seen, and the route heads for it, going through a gap in a fence. The lake fills a crater formed by a single explosion and is called **Grænavatn**. Keep left of it, walk down to the road and turn right to return to **Seltún**.

An amazing large pool of boiling muddy water in a hollow on a fellside at Austurengjahver

WALK 8
Seltún and Djúpavatn

Start/Finish	Seltún
Distance	13km (8 miles)
Total ascent/descent	350m (1150ft)
Time	4hrs 30mins
Terrain	Rugged hills with some steep ascents and descents, as well as easy dirt roads
Map	1:50,000 'Reykjanes Activity Photomap'
Transport	None, but Seltún is on the Salty Tours route

This route explores rugged little fells using a combination of waymarked trails, a dirt road and short, unmarked, vague paths, revealing little lakes and rugged lava flows. Hot springs and bubbling mud-pots feature at the start.

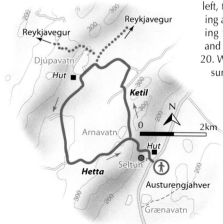

Leave the hut, toilets and car park at **Seltún** to follow the Ketilstígur trail, signposted straight up a stony slope, marked with orange plastic posts bearing the letters KETIL and numbers. The path traverses left, then keeps right of a valley, crossing a gap between fells at post 16, facing the tarn of **Arnavatn**. Keep right and cross a gap on a stony crest at post 20. Walk through a stony, dusty hollow surrounded by fells, passing left of gnarled outcrops. Markers lead over a broad, stony gap, where post 28 has the rocky peak of **Ketil** to the right.

The descent is steep and stony, passing right of a crater, and reaches post 38 at a 'Ketilstígur' signpost. Cross a dirt road and follow a vague path across moss-covered lava. Turn right at post

Duckboards allow safe access to hot springs and bubbling mud-pots at Seltún

41 along an old track, then left at post 46 along a dirt road on a broad, level, gravel plain. Moss lies to the left and bare lava to the right. When the road later swings left, there is moss on both sides. Keep left at a junction, making a rising traverse on a hillside. Catch a view of the lake of **Djúpavatn** on the right, but don't go down to it.

61

Follow the dirt road onwards through a gap, swinging right, and when it later descends, swing left and head south across level lava on the floor of a dale. Later still, it rises and swings right. Leave the road, heading left up a very shallow little valley, stony-floored, with grassy sides. Keep low while crossing a crest and look down to where two rocky valleys converge at a bare, ochre-coloured spur. Head for the furthest valley and turn left up it, following a narrow path past boulders to reach a broad and grassy area.

Turn right to climb steeply up a little side-valley, where a vague path reaches a gentler stony area. Walk across a very slight gap into another valley. The formidable rocky peak of **Hetta** is ahead, so turn left up the valley. A bouldery streambed becomes soft and sandy. Climb into another broad-floored valley, keeping left, but look up grassy slopes on the right to spot a couple of orange plastic marker posts. Turn left to follow these uphill and a vague path evolves.

Cross a fence and either walk down a grassy valley, as marked, or head left along a stony crest towards **Arnavatn**. Either way, turn right to pick up a path that was followed earlier in the day to return to **Seltún**.

WALK 9
Þingvellir and Skógarkot

Start/Finish	Service centre, Þingvellir
Distance	10km (6¼ miles)
Total ascent/descent	80m (260ft)
Time	3hrs 30mins
Terrain	Half along well-constructed paths and half along rugged paths
Map	'Gönguleiðir í Þingvallahrauni' map from the service centre
Transport	Reykjavík Excursions link Þingvellir with Reykjavík

Þingvellir can be described as a cultural and historic area in a fascinating geological landscape, possibly even 'sacred' to Icelanders. Settlers would travel here from all over Iceland, to formulate their laws and commit them to memory. The peculiar acoustics of the 'Law Rock' allowed one man to recite the laws so that thousands of people could hear them. It is a place of history and heritage, with cliffs, lakes, rivers, woods and fissured bedrock. Easy paths become more rugged later, crossing the low hill of Skógarkot.

Most tour buses allow a brief stop at the rugged Almannagjá, or 'everyman's gorge', and maybe a short walk. Anyone wishing to stay overnight can camp, enquiring at the service centre, where there is a café. Plenty of information illustrates the cultural significance of Þingvellir, so take this on board before starting. The route has frequent notice-boards full of interesting details.

Leave the **service centre** to follow a road signposted 'Þingvellir'. Pass two small car parks and camping areas, then a path heads right. Climb wooden steps and walk beside a fissure flanked by birch, willow, heather, crowberry, bilberry and bearberry. Pass small stands of conifers, and when a path junction is reached, turn right up to a junction in a rock-walled gorge.

Turn left along a board-walk flanked by horsetails. Keep right at a junction to reach a mass of boulders where the waterfall of **Öxarárfoss** enters the gorge. Double back to the previous junction and take the other board-walk to follow a stone-paved path and steps downhill. Keep right of a car park and take a broad path up into the gorge of **Almannagjá**, crossing a river and passing a pool where criminals were once drowned.

Walk through the gorge, veering left along a board-walk to the Law Rock, where Iceland's laws were spoken annually towards a cliff, which echoed the words back to people. Iceland is tearing apart at this gorge, and the land is slowly sinking. Go back onto the main path and climb

Almannagjá, where Iceland is slowly being torn apart, leaving a series of deep fissures

The lake of Þingvallavatn is seen to good effect.

to a viewpoint and **visitor centre** at the top of the gorge, then come back down the same path and turn right up flights of wooden steps. ◄

Go down steps and follow a path on a wooded slope to a car park, crossing a road bridge. Turn left alongside the river to a **church** and former hotel. Follow an access road up to a car park, crossing a couple of fissures filled with deep water, where people toss coins. Leave the car park for a nearby road and turn left, then quickly right as signposted 'Skógarkot'. The narrow path is very rugged, crossing broken ropy lava, deeply fissured in places, flanked by rich heath and increasing amounts of birch and willow. The path is uneven, but obvious throughout.

A complex junction of paths is reached, and the one to follow is the second left, signposted 'Hrauntún'. However, first climb straight up a low, grassy hill, where there are views from the ruined farm of **Skógarkot**. Retrace steps and take the Hrauntún path, but quickly turn left along a narrower path signposted 'Sandhólastígur', marked with red-tipped posts, and while it is often uneven, it is obvious throughout. When a sandy rise is crossed, reach a camping area, where a stony track leads to a road and the **service centre**.

Start/Finish	Hveragerði or Rjúpnabrekkur
Distance	10 or 17km (6¼ or 10½ miles)
Total ascent/descent	500m (1640ft)
Time	3hrs 30mins or 5hrs 30mins
Terrain	Mostly clear, well-marked valley paths, often gentle, but climbing and descending steeply at times
Map	1:50,000 'Hiking Trails in the Hengill Area'
Transport	Stræto bus 51 from Reykjavík or Selfoss to Hveragerði

This popular walk from Hveragerði visits several hot springs, bubbling mud-pots and fumaroles, and the town is surrounded by such features. The route combines a there-and-back walk through Reykjadalur with a circuit round a rugged fell at the dale-head.

Walkers arriving by bus must walk over 3km (2 miles) by road from **Hveragerði** to a car park. Cross a footbridge over a river, step over a hot stream and cross a cattle grid.

The route makes a circuit around a rugged fell at the head of Reykjadalur

A track passes a map-board and signpost at **Rjúpnabrekkur**, then a path marked by red-tipped posts crosses a couple of streams. Spot steaming vents while climbing slopes of grass or bare earth and stones. The gradient eases along a brow overlooking a river, Reykjadalsá, which features cascades. Further along the route is a ford, which some walkers avoid by following an unmarked path upstream here. But to make the most of this walk and its many geothermal sites use the ford.

Climb across slopes of grass and scree flanking **Reykjadalur**. Pass two little pools on a gentle simmer, then a huge and vigorous mud-pot at the foot of a grassy slope, belching sulphurous steam. Smaller mud-pots and hot springs are passed afterwards. The path later heads left, but misses some good sites, so ford the river, which is **hot**, to reach a signpost.

Turn left upstream, past iron-stained hot springs feeding the hot river. Either cross the river and climb as indicated by red posts, or first walk upstream to **Klambragil**, where there are hot springs, mud-pots and fumaroles near a rocky gorge. If making the detour, double back to the marked path, then climb until the gradient eases and a signpost is passed.

Cross gentle, grassy slopes and note plumes of steam to the left, but follow the path to another signpost. ◄ Keep right to follow blue-tipped marker posts over a grassy gap around

Walk 11 from Hellisheiði and Walk 12 from Ölfusvatn pass here.

400m (1310ft) at **Ölkelduháls**, passing more hot springs and mud-pots. Head down to another signpost and turn right downhill, following red markers. Cross a small stream, climb a little, then drop and pick a way carefully across a steep, bare slope. The path becomes easy and grassy down to **Dalasel**, where a fumarole roars noisily above. ▸

There used to be a hut here.

Continue down to a river, and either cross it or first head upstream to another vigorous mud-pot. The marked path reaches a signpost passed earlier in the day, so turn left, ford the hot river, and retrace steps through **Reykjadalur** to the road.

WALK 11
Ölfusvatn and Ölkelduháls

Start/Finish	Ölfusvatn, south of Þingvallavatn
Distance	21km (13 miles)
Total ascent/descent	500m (1640ft)
Time	7hrs
Terrain	Mostly gentle valley paths, sometimes vague, with one stretch through a rocky gorge
Map	1:50,000 'Hiking Trails in the Hengill Area'
Transport	None

An easy riverside walk leads to a more rugged circuit around a mountain. It can be linked with Walks 10 or 12 through Reykjadalur to Hveragerði, which may be easier than returning to Ölfusvatn, and there is the option of catching a bus at Hveragerði.

A car park, map-boards and signpost lie near a bridge at **Ölfusvatn**, around 125m (410ft). A campsite lies downstream, but this walk heads upstream beside **Ölfusvatnsá**. Blue-tipped posts appear later and the riverside sprouts heather, grass, birch and willow, speckled with flowers. Climb to avoid an eroded bank, pass a notice and climb away from the river, until markers lead back down.

67

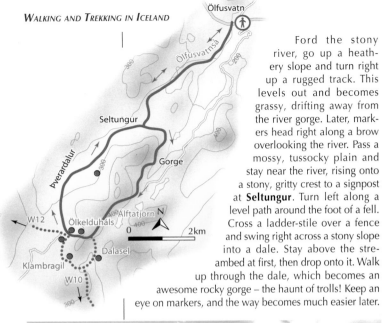

Ford the stony river, go up a heathery slope and turn right up a rugged track. This levels out and becomes grassy, drifting away from the river gorge. Later, markers head right along a brow overlooking the river. Pass a mossy, tussocky plain and stay near the river, rising onto a stony, gritty crest to a signpost at **Seltungur**. Turn left along a level path around the foot of a fell. Cross a ladder-stile over a fence and swing right across a stony slope into a dale. Stay above the streambed at first, then drop onto it. Walk up through the dale, which becomes an awesome rocky gorge – the haunt of trolls! Keep an eye on markers, and the way becomes much easier later.

The upper part of the Ölfusvatnsá, seen from the route near Seltungur

Keep right where two valleys converge, pass a cave cut into ash beds, and turn left up a steep, crumbling slope to follow a stone-strewn crest up and down. Go up another crumbling ridge to a signpost and turn right up a path. Continue along a rugged, stony track, which becomes grassy, with the shallow **Álftatjörn** well to the left. Cross a track and go under a pylon line while crossing a broad, grassy gap to a signpost. ▶ Keep straight ahead over another gap, passing mud-pots to another signpost. ▶

Turn right and follow blue-tipped markers left of a large hot pool and mud-pots. Go under a pylon line and cross a track, keeping right of a steam cap. The path runs down grassy slopes, keeping right to cross what is usually a dry streambed, followed by a mineralised stream, then a clear stream. Grassy slopes give way to stony slopes, and the path may be vague, then a lukewarm stream spills over a waterfall. The path drops gently into the grassy **Þverardalur** and crosses a stream. Continue gently downhill, with a river to the left, then climb around the foot of a fell, crossing a slight gap. A gentle descent leads to the signpost at **Seltungur**, where steps are retraced to **Ölfusvatn**.

Walk 10 heads left down to Hveragerði.

Walk 12 heads left down to Hveragerði.

WALK 12
Hellisheiði to Hveragerði

Start	Visitor centre, Hellisheiði
Finish	Hveragerði
Distance	19km (12 miles)
Total ascent	420m (1375ft)
Total descent	620m (2035ft)
Time	6hrs 30mins
Terrain	Some steep and rugged ascents and descents, but mostly gentle valley or moorland
Map	1:50,000 'Hiking Trails in the Hengill Area'
Transport	Stræto bus 51 from Reykjavík or Selfoss serves Hveragerði, and might stop on request at Hellisheiði

The Geothermal Visitor Centre at Hellisheiði (tel 4125800, www.orkusyn.is) shows how hot water and power is generated from subterranean hot-spots. Natural hot springs and mud-pots are passed on the way to Hveragerði.

Follow the access road to the **power station and visitor centre**, where there is a café. Keep straight ahead by road, take the second left and watch for blue-tipped marker posts revealing a broad, stony path up **Sleggjubeinsdalur** to a signpost on a gap around 5 0 0 m (1640ft).

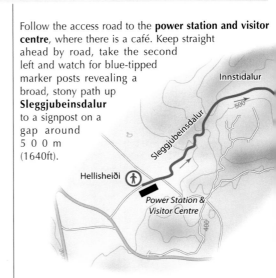

Keep right, gently down a stony track to a huge meadow surrounded by fells at **Innstidalur**. Head towards a distant hut, crossing an iron-stained stream and a clear one, then turn right downstream. Blue markers cross and recross the stream to a junction and signpost.

Turn right, undulating but generally falling to a lower meadow and signpost. Turn left along the edge of the meadow across four streams. Climb a little, then drop and walk parallel to the river, but well above it. Turn left uphill, then right as marked, steep and rugged, easing to pass a signpost on a slope. A gentle rising traverse leads to another signpost, continuing around the flank of **Kýrgilshnúkur**. Notice hot-spots and cross a broad, gritty, stone-strewn crest. Walk down a bare slope that gets lumpy when vegetated. Cross a track and note other nearby hot-spots while heading towards map-boards.

Follow blue-tipped markers over a slight rise, down to a pylon line, turning left up a track. Quickly leave it as marked uphill, spotting mud-pots off-route, and reach a signpost. ▶ Turn right to follow red-tipped markers gently downhill, then steeper above **Klambragil**

Walk 10 from Hveragerði and Walk 11 from Ölfusvatn pass here.

and its vigorous hot-spots. Ford a river and either turn left for the hot-spots or right downstream beside the river, passing iron-stained hot springs feeding into it.

When a signpost is reached, turn right to ford the river, which is hot, and follow an obvious path down through **Reykjadalur**. Small mud-pots and hot springs are

71

The warm water of the Reykjadalsá has to be forded on the way through Reykjadalur

followed by a huge and vigorous mud-pot at the foot of a grassy slope, belching sulphurous steam. Pass two little pools on a gentle simmer and cross slopes of grass and scree, descending to ford the river, Reykjadalsá.

Turn right and climb well above the river, looking down from a brow at its cascades. The path winds as it descends slopes of bare earth, stones or grass, crossing a couple of streams to join a track. Pass a map-board and signpost at **Rjúpnabrekkur**, cross a cattle grid, step over a hot stream and cross a footbridge over a river to reach a car park. Simply follow the road to **Hveragerði**.

WALK 13
Nesjavellir and Vörðuskeggi

Start/Finish	Nesjavellir
Distance	18km (11 miles)
Total ascent/descent	875m (2870ft)
Time	6hrs
Terrain	Rugged, hummocky moorland at the start and finish, with rough and rocky fellsides in the middle
Map	1:50,000 'Hiking Trails in the Hengill Area'
Transport	None

The highest point in the Hengill area is Vörðuskeggi, and its summit can be reached by a spur climbing from a rugged circular walk around Nesjavellir. A geothermal power station sits prominently in the middle of this route.

Roadside parking is available at prominent map-boards at **Nesjavellir**, and a nearby car park is for Hótel Hengill residents. The first part of this walk is exactly the same as the Reykjavegur trail (see Trek 1 Stage 1) as it heads from Nesjavellir over to **Dyradalur**, then climbs high on a rocky ridge to a sign-post. Turn left as sign-posted 'Köldulaugagil'.

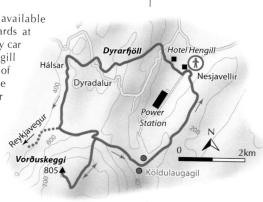

The rugged slopes of Vörðuskeggi are negotiated by following colour-coded markers and signposts

Looking down on the Hótel Hengill at Nesjavellir, with Þingvallavatn in the distance

Black-tipped marker posts climb the rugged mountainside, rising and falling, with cliffs above and below. Swing right up to a three-way signpost beneath overhanging rocks. The spur to the summit of Vörðuskeggi starts here, so turn right and climb, still following black-tipped markers up to another signpost. Turn right across a stony area, quickly reaching a final signpost. A short path heads right for **Vörðuskeggi**, climbing as a gritty zigzag to the summit at 805m (2641ft). Views stretch beyond Hengill to Reykjavík, Esja and Þingvallavatn. Retrace steps back downhill, passing one signpost to reach the previous one.

Turn right and follow black markers undulating across a rugged slope, reaching a point above a steam cap. Cross two stiles over a fence and pass between two hot-spots – one above and one below – at **Köldulaugagil**. A signpost points left down a ridge, and blue-tipped markers head for a stile over a fence. Keep to a brow overlooking the steaming valley, later dropping to a lower shelf. Stay high above the **power station**, crossing a rich heather moor before a final descent. Turn right as marked by green-tipped posts, then left at a huge climbing frame to return to the roadside at **Nesjavellir**.

TREK 1
The Reykjavegur

Start	Nesjavellir
Finish	Reykjanesviti
Distance	127km (79 miles)
Time	7 days
Terrain	Some stretches cross stony areas or rugged lava. Water is sparse and may need to be carried some distance between sources.
Facilities	Hotel at Nesjavellir. Coffee shop at Hellisheiði. The town of Hafnarfjörður and the village of Grindavík are off-route, but offer plenty of facilities.
Accommodation	Apart from one hut at Múlasel, wild camping throughout

The long-distance Reykjavegur trail was originally planned as a hut-to-hut trek, but most huts simply weren't constructed, so the only people who walk the trail are those prepared to wild camp along the way. Despite being close to Reykjavík the trail attracts very few walkers, and some stretches are far from water supplies, although with careful planning this can be overcome.

The route is blazed with blue markers and runs beside rugged fells at Hengill, passing a geothermal power station at Hellisheiði. The rugged low fells of Bláfjöll and Reykjanes are broken by extensive moss-covered lava flows, and drifts of black ash are crossed towards the end of the peninsula at Reykjanesviti. Don't be in a hurry to leave, as the cliff coast is dramatic and there is a notable geothermal hot-spot nearby.

Some parts of the Reykjavegur can be explored while enjoying easier day-walks on Walks 3, 4, 5, 8, 12 and 13. Salty Tours allows a couple of parts of the trail to be seen in advance, at Vatnsskarð (Stage 4) and Reykjanesviti (Stage 7).

STAGE 1
Nesjavellir to Múlasel

Start	Nesjavellir
Finish	Múlasel
Distance	11km (7 miles)
Total ascent	500m (1005ft)
Total descent	350m (1150ft)
Time	4hrs
Terrain	Well-marked paths, steep and rugged at times across mountain flanks
Map	1:50,000 'Hiking Trails in the Hengill Area'
Transport	Taxi from Reykjavík (expensive)
Accommodation	Free hut at Múlasel

This first stage of the long-distance Reykjavegur is a half-day walk, allowing time to reach Nesjavellir without the benefit of public transport. The route to a freely available hut at Múlasel is sometimes rough and rocky.

There are prominent map-boards at **Nesjavellir**, and a road runs towards the **Hótel Hengill**. Follow it and watch for a signpost down to the left. Green-tipped marker posts climb a few crude stone steps over a shoulder to another signpost. Head right, following red-tipped markers down, then up, a rugged

slope, easing among horsetails. Cross a road to a sign-post and climb a slope of lupins, and swing left to keep climbing. Miss the summit of **Dyrafjöll** and keep right at a signpost, following red markers down to a road.

Turn right and quickly leave the road to go down a path through a rocky defile marked by blue-tipped posts. Reach map-boards in a grassy hollow at **Dyradalur** and turn left to cross the road. Cross a ladder-stile and walk on grass and sand, then climb a stony slope and pumice scree. Cross a ridge and swing left, climbing over a bare rock gap at **Hálsar**.

All is bare rock beyond, and the route exploits horizontal ledges on a rocky peak, followed by loose red pumice. Continue along a rocky ridge, down across a broad, stony gap, with a crater to the left. Rise onto more red pumice and climb, with views across moorland to Reykjavík. Drop to a rocky gap, then climb and keep right of the ridge. Pass through a cleft between rocks and walk along a broad, rocky crest full of awkward holes. Go down a vegetated bouldery slope and pumice to reach a broad, sandy gap and signpost. ▶

Evening view from the little hut at Múlasel, looking back along the Reykjavegur

Walk 13 heads left here.

77

Turn right across sand, up a stony path and around a rocky shoulder. A rugged, mostly stony descent leads to gentle grass. Cross a rocky gap and drop down a steep, rocky, bouldery slope to the grassy **Marardalur** – a dale flanked by rocky slopes. Walk through it and leave across a gentle gap into another valley. Follow a stream through a boulder-choke and follow blue markers past a signpost. Trace the river downstream, crossing and recrossing as marked. A small hut appears at **Múlasel**, available free of charge, but with no facilities apart from a dry toilet.

STAGE 2
Múlasel to Bláfjallaskáli

Start	Múlasel
Finish	Bláfjallaskáli
Distance	31km (19¼ miles)
Total ascent	450m (1475ft)
Total descent	250m (820ft)
Time	11hrs
Terrain	Fairly well-marked, but sometimes vague path, often across rugged lava, with some steep and stony ascents and descents
Maps	1:50,000 'Hiking Trails in the Hengill Area'; 1:75,000 'Landmælinger Íslands – Suðvesturland'
Transport	None, apart from tour buses to the visitor centre
Accommodation	Wild camping only

This is a long stage, with no facilities apart from a visitor centre coffee shop. After crossing rugged lava flows, tents can be pitched beside a small tarn, or the walk can continue over the bleak and stony slopes of Bláfjöll to a ski resort.

Leave **Múlasel**, ford the river and turn right downstream, passing a couple of small streams. Join and follow a broad path, cross a steep-sided valley and drop to level moorland. A track heads for a distant farm, but follow the blue-tipped markers heading left, following parallel ruts trodden by horses. Eventually the path runs parallel to a dirt road. Either follow the blue markers, noting that the path becomes vague, or follow the road. Whichever is chosen, head for a large steaming building that incorporates the **power station and visitor centre** and a coffee shop (tel 4125800, www.orkusyn.is).

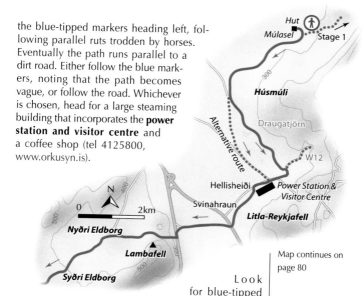

Map continues on page 80

Look for blue-tipped markers in front of the visitor centre and follow them across rugged lava, passing between a building and the foot of a grassy hill, **Litla-Reykjafell**. Cross a busy road and follow an abandoned, traffic-free stretch of the main road beyond. Blue posts run parallel on the left, and as the road rises towards a junction, the posts shortcut left to cross another road. Follow a stony track to a map-board and 'Reykjavegur' signpost.

Climb to a gap, with **Lambafell** to the left and small fell to the right. Drop to an extensive lava flow and follow markers onto it. The path winds, rises and falls, rugged underfoot, but softened by moss. Watch for holes and, apart from a noticeable dip, climb towards the cone of **Nyðri Eldborg** and keep left of it, then head for the cone of **Syðri Eldborg** and keep right of it. Signposts stand beside both cones, with another at the far side of the lava flow at **Leiti**.

Turn left to follow blue markers along the foot of the **Bláfjöll** massif, crossing stony, gravelly alluvial fans

Rugged lava slopes between Nyðri Eldborg and Syðri Eldborg, looking towards Bláfjöll

spreading from crumbling valleys. The path is occasionally used by motor-cyclists, sometimes at variance with the blue markers. Pass a small **tarn** (where tents can be pitched) to reach a signpost at **Fjallið eina**. Keep right, cross a stony streambed and make a steep and stony climb. The higher slopes are bouldery, and the path eventually disappears, so watch carefully for markers.

Climb above 600m (1970ft), almost to the top of **Kerlingarhnúkur**, then drop and cross level lava. Later, markers rise right and cross a stony crest, drifting down through a stony valley. Follow a line

Syðri Eldborg

Leiti

Bláfjöll

Tarn

Fjallið eina

Bláfjallaskáli

Stage 3

Breiðablik

Hengill

Kerlingarhnúkur

of street lights across a stony slope towards a road and a large building called **Hengill** – part of a ski resort. Turn left along the road to a big building called **Breiðablik**. There is nothing for walkers at these buildings at **Bláfjallaskáli**, but it may be possible to obtain water and camp.

Stage 3
Bláfjallaskáli to Kaldársel

Start	Bláfjallaskáli
Finish	Kaldársel
Distance	16km (10 miles)
Total ascent	100m (320ft)
Total descent	500m (1640ft)
Time	5hrs
Terrain	Mostly gentle slopes, often rugged underfoot, with some short, steep descents
Maps	1:75,000 'Landmælinger Íslands – Suðvesturland'; 1:50,000 'Reykjanes Activity Photomap'
Transport	Hafnarfjörður is a short taxi-ride from Kaldársel
Accommodation	Crude hut/cave at Valaból or wild camping

Apart from a short climb and a longer rugged descent from Stóribolli, most of this stage crosses level lava flows. As the route passes Helgafell there is an option to stay in a crude cave/hut, and the town of Hafnarfjörður is just off-route.

Look across the road from **Breiðablik** to spot blue-tipped marker posts. A vague path crosses rugged, vegetated lava full of holes. After an easy stretch over flat ropy lava, there is stony, mossy, grassy moorland. Note the aircraft wreckage to

Map continues on page 82

Thinly vegetated, bare lava flows between Bláfjallaskáli and Stóribolli

the right, but keep markers in view while admiring the rounded fells on all sides. A gentle fellside is reached, where the route swings left down a rocky edge into a gully.

Walk down a plain of sand and gravel, cross fissured lava, then climb rugged ground full of lava tubes. Pass left of **Stóribolli** and its crater, heading for a bare, rocky fell. Turn right down a cairned, crunchy pumice path, meandering across mossy lava, with views of Reykjavík and Esja beyond. Big holes gape beside the path, and an **emergency shelter** is passed before a dirt road and signpost are reached.

Cross the road and follow cairns and blue markers over bare lava flanked by moss. Later, there are stony and bouldery slopes, then jagged lava, giving way to flower-speckled moss, heather and crowberry. Go through a gate in a fence, under a power line and cross a track. Head gently down a rugged heather moor, cross a fissure and continue on grass. Blue markers drift to

Hafnarfjörður
Reservoir
Valaból
Kaldársel
Stage 4
Valahnúkar
200
Helgafell
Þríhnúkahraun
N
0   2km   Tvíbollahraun
■ *Emergency Shelter*

black ash slopes on **Valahnúkar**. Yellow-banded markers lead along a broad, clear ash path to a fenced woodland at **Valaból**. Grassy spaces are ideal for camping, and there is a crude hut in a cave, but no water.

Continue along the path and over a rise. There is a little **reservoir** nearby (securely fenced, so it doesn't count as a water source), and yellow-banded posts lead along a stony ash path, with rugged **Helgafell** rising beyond level lava. Turn right and head gently downhill, through a gap in a tall fence. A gravel path leads to signposts, and a building at **Kaldársel** is used for summer camps. ▶

A dirt road leads to Hafnarfjörður – 8km (5 miles) off route, with a full range of services.

STAGE 4
Kaldársel to Djúpavatn

Start	Kaldársel
Finish	Djúpavatn
Distance	19km (12 miles)
Total ascent	300m (985ft)
Total descent	175m (575ft)
Time	7hrs 30mins
Terrain	Rugged paths and tracks, beside forests and across lava flows
Map	1:50,000 'Reykjanes Activity Photomap'
Transport	None, but Salty Tours crosses Vatnsskarð, between Reykjavík and Grindavík
Accommodation	Wild camping only

There is minimal ascent and descent on this stage, but the ground is often rough and stony underfoot, although smoother lava flows are traversed towards the end. Level grass near the lake of Djúpavatn offers an ideal place to camp.

Leave **Kaldársel** as signposted 'Dalaleið' and 'Undirhlíðarvegur'. These trails are marked by orange plastic posts bearing the letters DALAL and UNDIR, and numbers. Blue-tipped 'Reykjavegur' posts go roughly the same way. Follow a winding gravel path and walk beside a forest of conifers and birch. If blue markers are followed the trail is rugged, but DALAL markers use a good path and track, with many opportunities to switch trails. The track eventually reaches a **picnic site**, but stay outside the forest to follow blue-tipped posts.

The path is flanked by lupins, later birch, and passes under a power line. UNDIR markers run concurrently with the path, and smooth lava gives way to a stony path beside rugged lava. Don't head into birch thickets, but veer right up an embankment to cross a road, dropping down the other side. Follow a wheel-marked track that becomes rough and stony, rising beside a forest. Conifers give way to birch, then clumps of willow. Markers drift left of the track, across tussocky vegetation.

On workdays a noisy quarry is heard near **Vatnsskarð**, and blue markers drift right from the UNDIR markers. Pick up and follow a stony track to a road. Turn quickly left and right and follow another stony track past old quarries, where blue markers reveal a path down blocky, mossy lava, crossing a track in a dip. The path rises awkwardly between blocky lava and a slope of patchy birch and willow, then becomes easier across grit and gravel. A stony, mossy, grassy slope leads fur-

ther up a dale and around the back of **Sandfell**.

A route marked by orange plastic posts joins from the left and leaves on the right, where the floor of the dale is level and mossy. Blue markers rise over a shoulder where there are wide-ranging views, stretching from

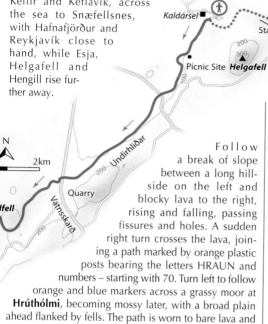

Keilir and Keflavík, across the sea to Snæfellsnes, with Hafnafjörður and Reykjavík close to hand, while Esja, Helgafell and Hengill rise further away.

Follow a break of slope between a long hillside on the left and blocky lava to the right, rising and falling, passing fissures and holes. A sudden right turn crosses the lava, joining a path marked by orange plastic posts bearing the letters HRAUN and numbers – starting with 70. Turn left to follow orange and blue markers across a grassy moor at **Hrúthólmi**, becoming mossy later, with a broad plain ahead flanked by fells. The path is worn to bare lava and

Djúpavatn has grassy areas nearby that are ideal for wild camping

85

can be covered quickly. Keep right where unmarked paths head left, eventually reaching a junction at post 26. A 'Ketilsstígur' signpost points ahead, but turn right to follow blue markers, crossing a mossy, messy track and turning right at the foot of **Hrútafell**.

The path becomes bare lava flanked by moss, and reaches a grassy, flowery plain at post 12. Drift right and follow a fence, passing a small stream. Cross a ladder-stile over the fence at post 6 and continue upstream. Reach signposts at the end of a track, where a flat grassy area before **Djúpavatn** is ideal for camping.

STAGE 5
Djúpavatn to Bratthals

Start	Djúpavatn
Finish	Bratthals
Distance	14km (8¾ miles)
Total ascent	125m (410ft)
Total descent	250m (820ft)
Time	5hrs
Terrain	Steep and stony ascent and descent at the start, then mostly gentle valley walking
Map	1:50,000 'Reykjanes Activity Photomap'
Transport	None
Accommodation	Wild camping only

More water comes in the form of little lakes and streams on this stretch of the Reykjavegur than on the rest of the route put together! The fells are impressive at the start, followed by a long walk through a broad dale.

Cross two streams at **Djúpavatn** – one flowing out of the lake and one flowing into it. Keep left of the latter, climb a stony slope and watch for blue markers above a gap. Keep left of light-coloured stony mounds to trace a narrow path across a slope. On the other side of the valley, pastel

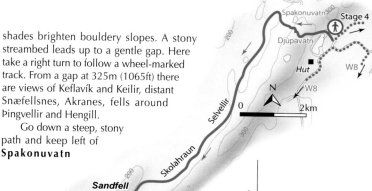

shades brighten bouldery slopes. A stony streambed leads up to a gentle gap. Here take a right turn to follow a wheel-marked track. From a gap at 325m (1065ft) there are views of Keflavík and Keilir, distant Snæfellsnes, Akranes, fells around Þingvellir and Hengill.

Go down a steep, stony path and keep left of **Spakonuvatn**

and a smaller tarn. There are no markers, but cross a stony gap and go steeply down a pumice track with a crater to the left. Swing around the crater, drop steeply and turn left down a rugged track to cross a small stream in a dip. Climb an ash-and-gravel track, fork left to cross a gap, then drop steeply, with a crater to the left. Keep right, not left uphill,

Looking down on Spakonuvatn and a smaller tarn, with the conical Keilir beyond

and note another crater to the right as the track undulates gently.

Follow wheel-ruts through grassy **Selvellir**, beside a small stream. The track rises gently and crosses another little stream. The grassy strip eventually gets pinched out at Þrengslin, where the slope rising left meets rugged lava on the right at a fence corner. Blue markers reappear as a path descends past boulders, rugged for a while, then grassy and easy again. Reach a gate, cross a ladder-stile over a fence, and continue, with the way grassy and easy.

The path becomes rugged, turning right to cross bare lava flanked by moss on **Skolahraun**. Rise gently and on more rugged ground, reaching a slope of pumice at the foot of **Sandfell**. Turn left and crunch along an ash path, which becomes stony, then cross a rugged gap and drift down the lower slopes of **Höfði** into another dale. Follow markers across pathless stones and gravel, sometimes vegetated. Orange plastic markers with the letters KRÝSU lead straight ahead. The path cuts across the dale at **Bratthals**, where the grass is good for camping beside an ash track.

STAGE 6
Bratthals to Þorbjörn

Start	Bratthals
Finish	Þorbjörn, near Grindavík
Distance	13km (8 miles)
Total ascent	100m (330ft)
Total descent	150m (490ft)
Time	4hrs 30mins
Terrain	A succession of short ascents and descents, often stony and rugged
Map	1:50,000 'Reykjanes Activity Photomap'
Transport	Reykjavík Excursions serves Grindavík and the Blue Lagoon, both off-route, from Reykjavík
Accommodation	Wild camping or a simple hut beneath Þorbjörn

This stretch is short, often rough and stony, with several short ascents and descents. At the end of the day, climbing Þorbjörn is possible, or bathing at the famous Blue Lagoon, or visiting the nearby village of Grindavík.

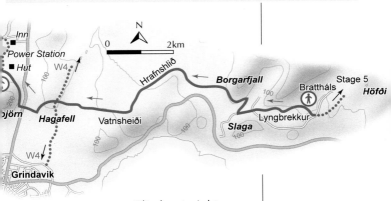

Climb straight up a short, steep, stony slope from **Bratthás**, watching for orange and blue markers across a stony slope. Drop into a broad, stony valley where a grassy area has been fenced at **Lyngbrekkur**. Pass a fence corner at post 18 and climb a stony slope. Note how 'stone stripes' change to 'stone polygons' at post 16 – caused by centuries of freeze/thaw action. Cross a stony gap and go down to a junction of tracks.

Keep straight ahead along the foot of **Slaga**, turning sharp right down another track. Another set of orange plastic posts bear the letters SAND. The track swings left along the foot of **Borgarfjall**, and, regardless of markers, stay on the track to climb, later levelling out. At post 29, blue Reykjavegur markers head left across rugged, pathless vegetated lava. Drift slightly left towards a road bend and cross an earth track. Veer right up a gentle grassy path, over a crest and down the rugged far side. Walk along the foot of **Hrafnshlíð** on grass and heather, and the path swings left towards a valley at Svartikrókur, then right to leave it.

89

A grassy area in a small forest at the foot of Þorbjörn has a small hut and picnic area

Blue markers rise up a rugged moor, where vegetation gives way to stony ground with fine stone polygons. Cross the broad, gentle gap of **Vatnsheiði**, drifting right on the way down to moss-covered lava. Cross a track at an orange marker (Walk 4 crosses here), but keep following blue markers over the low shoulder of **Hagafell**. Sheer cliffs and monstrous boulders are easily passed on the other side, and nesting fulmars can be seen. The path drops steeply and follows a heather-floored ravine.

Cross a busy road and turn right to follow a hot-water pipeline to a tank. Go down a track into coniferous forest, where there is a grassy slope, picnic site, basic hut, dry toilet, and possibly a tank of water, all at the foot of **Þorbjörn**.

Þorbjörn, Blue Lagoon and Grindavík

A grassy path climbs steeply from the picnic site onto Þorbjörn. A rugged path in the other direction crosses lava to a **power station**, where roads lead to the Northern Lights Inn and the incredibly popular hot-saltwater bathing at the **Blue Lagoon** (tel 4208801, www.bluelagoon. com). The fishing village of Grindavík and all its facilities are also nearby (see Walk 3).

STAGE 7

Þorbjörn to Reykjanesviti

Start	Þorbjörn
Finish	Lighthouse, Reykjanesviti
Distance	23km (14¼ miles)
Total ascent	125m (410ft)
Total descent	150m (490ft)
Time	8hrs
Terrain	Mostly low-lying, rugged lava, stones and sand, with tracks, paths and some pathless stretches
Map	1:50,000 'Reykjanes Activity Photomap'
Transport	None, but Salty Tours runs around Reykjanesviti
Accommodation	Wild camping only

The last stage of the Reykjavegur crosses lava fields and black sand to the end of the peninsula at Reykjanesviti. Don't be in a hurry to leave, as there are fascinating sights and features of interest to explore and enjoy.

Leave the picnic site, and walk to the end of the track and forest to follow a grassy path around the foot of **Þorbjörn**. This becomes rugged and reaches a road. Turn left, then right, dropping from the road into a grassy valley. A track crosses a gap, then blue markers head right along a vague path, linking with the **Skipsstígur** (Walk 3). Turn right to follow this and large cairns from post 43 to 50. Turn left to follow blue markers across rugged lava full of holes and fissures. Cross two tracks and keep straight

Map continues on page 92

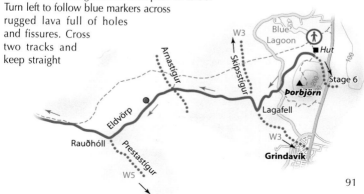

91

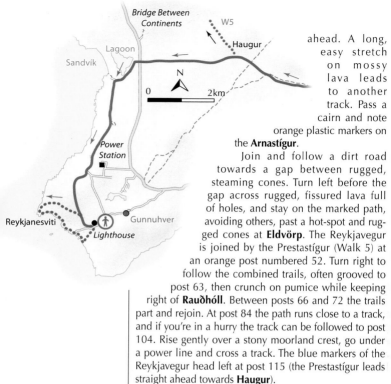

ahead. A long, easy stretch on mossy lava leads to another track. Pass a cairn and note orange plastic markers on the **Arnastígur**.

Join and follow a dirt road towards a gap between rugged, steaming cones. Turn left before the gap across rugged, fissured lava full of holes, and stay on the marked path, avoiding others, past a hot-spot and rugged cones at **Eldvörp**. The Reykjavegur is joined by the Prestastígur (Walk 5) at an orange post numbered 52. Turn right to follow the combined trails, often grooved to post 63, then crunch on pumice while keeping right of **Rauðhóll**. Between posts 66 and 72 the trails part and rejoin. At post 84 the path runs close to a track, and if you're in a hurry the track can be followed to post 104. Rise gently over a stony moorland crest, go under a power line and cross a track. The blue markers of the Reykjavegur head left at post 115 (the Prestastígur leads straight ahead towards **Haugur**).

Cross pathless moorland down a bouldery slope into a shallow valley, where vegetation thins among black sand. Climb a sandy slope and cross awkward stony, rocky ground with patches of lyme grass. Ahead are small rocky peaks, and the blue markers go through a gap, traversing awkward ground to reach and cross a road. A nearby metal sphere represents Saturn (part of the 'Power Plant Earth' exhibition). Cross sand and stones, turn left along a broad track and pass a stagnant **lagoon**, fringed by angelica and dunes covered in lyme grass. Rise a little and keep left at a junction. ◄

Right leads to a beach at Sandvík.

Rise through a bulldozed area and follow a sandy, stony track, rising and falling gently, flanked by jagged

92

slope rising left. A signpost on the left reads 'Suðurnámur'. Red peg markers run beside a stream then go straight up a vegetated spur to a shoulder. Keep climbing on grass, moss, crowberry and willow to a stony top with a cairn, around 730m (2395ft), and enjoy the view.

Looking down on the braided glacial river of Jökulsgilskvísl near Landmannalaugar

Go down to a gap and climb steep and stony ground to a bouldery cairned summit around 850m (2790ft). There is a slight gap beyond, then climb the stony ridge to the next summit, around 880m (2885ft). The ridge beyond is broad and rounded, and the red-pegged path crosses a couple of broad bumps. The highest part of **Suðurnámur**, over 910m (2985ft), is covered in black obsidian, and views stretch to Hofsjökull, Kerlingarfjöll and Langjökull.

The path drops to a gap on light-coloured gravel and swings left, down to a signposted junction. Trek 2 Stage 3 joins here, so turn left and follow it down to **Landmannalaugar**, the FÍ huts, campsite and mobile shop.

WALK 15
Landmannalaugar and Bláhnúkur

Start/Finish	Landmannalaugar
Distance	7km (4½ miles)
Total ascent/descent	450m (1475ft)
Time	2hrs 30mins
Terrain	Steep and stony fell with a river crossing on the ascent and descent
Map	1:25,000 'FÍ – Landmannalaugar Map of Hiking Trails', but get it corrected at the hut as many trails are shown incorrectly
Transport	Reykjavík Excursions serve Landmannalaugar from Reykjavík, Hveragerði, Selfoss, Skaftafell and Kirkjubærklauster. Trex (tel 5876000, www.trex.is) serves Landmannalaugar from Reykjavík, Hveragerði and Selfoss.

Bláhnúkur is very steep and stony on all sides, but well worth climbing as it is a notable viewpoint. This route includes geothermal areas and a peep through the gorge of Grænagil. The gorge provides a shortcut (omitting Bláhnúkur) if needed.

Leave **Landmannalaugar**, at 590m (1935ft), following the Laugavegur (see Trek 2 Stage 4) as far as a signpost beside a prominent steaming hot-spot at the foot

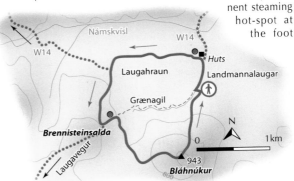

Landmannalaugar and the Fjallabak nature reserve are
immensely popular with walkers and trekkers

Walk straight ahead
here to shortcut
through Grænagil.

of **Brennisteinsalda**. Turn left for 'Grænagil', following white pegs down a slope of gravel onto rugged lava, reaching another signpost. ◄ Turn right to follow yellow pegs along a rugged path to a stony-floored valley. Either ford the river, Brennisteinsöldukvisl, or find a rocky constriction and jump across.

A path climbs steep and stony slopes, eventually following a ridge. Turn left at a higher level to follow another ridge to the summit of **Bláhnúkur**, a sharp ridge at 943m (3094ft). There is a view indicator, and outside the immediate colourful groups of fells views embrace Vatnajökull, Hofsjökull and Langjökull.

Pass the view indicator and turn left down a steep, winding, stony path. The ridge is obvious throughout, with one prominent hump, and is bare and stony all the way down. Turn right before reaching the steep and crumbling end of the ridge that leads onto a stony floodplain. Turn left and ford the river as it leaves the gorge of Grænagil, and simply walk straight back to **Landmannalaugar**.

WALK 16
Hvanngilshauser and Tangafoss

Start/Finish	Hvanngil
Distance	10km (6¼ miles)
Total ascent/descent	270m (885ft)
Time	3hrs
Terrain	Stony fells with and without paths, as well as rugged riverside paths. Small rivers need to be crossed.
Maps	1:100,000 'Mál og Menning – 4 Landmannalaugar Þórsmörk Fjallabak'; 1:100,000 'Ferðakort – Þórsmörk Landmannalaugar'
Transport	Occasional Reykjavík Excursions serve Hvanngil from Reykjavík, Hverageröi and Selfoss

Two short circular walks are combined in this route from Hvanngil. One walk climbs onto the fells and returns through a fine dale, and the other continues alongside two rivers, taking in a handful of splendid waterfalls.

Leave the FÍ huts at **Hvanngil** and follow the path signposted 'Þórsmörk' along an ash path over lava. Turn left at a junction signposted 'Hvanngilshauser', following red-tipped markers across level ash and lava. Cross a dirt road and climb a stony path on a rounded, mossy ridge. The top is quickly reached, crowned by a cairn, with a guestbook and fine views.

Turn left along the crest of **Hvanngilshauser** and cross a gap to reach the next rounded top. The route becomes rocky underfoot, reaching a broad, stony gap. Rugged peaks seen from the dale are not on the main crest, but lie to one side. Avoid a gentle summit to the right further along the crest, and climb straight to a higher summit, which is rocky on top. A steep descent leads to a stony gap, then a rocky ridge leads to another gap. Climb again as marked on grit, gravel and rock, weaving past grotesquely weathered rocks. Don't head for the top, but traverse right, then down across the slopes, swinging left down to a gap. Keep left to drop steeply into a dale flanked by fells.

Ford a stream and follow mossy, grassy wheel-marks through the dale, drifting gradually right. Ford another stream and note a cairn up to the right, which is an old shelter. White-tipped markers lead downstream along an

101

The hut at Hvanngil and the rugged ridge of Hvanngilshauser

easy path to a dirt road. Either turn left, crossing foot-bridges over two rivers to return to **Hvanngil**, or continue downstream to complete the remaining circuit.

The path downstream passes waterfalls at Hvanni and **Hvanngilsfoss**. Ford the river where marked and turn left to follow a bigger river upstream, squeezing between big boulders and a cliff. The river is in a rocky channel and the path climbs onto a crumbling edge, with a glimpse of **Súlufoss** ahead. Follow red markers upstream and later climb well above the river, overlooking the big fall of **Tangafoss**. The path runs upstream on a crumbling slope to a final fall, Faldur. Pull away from the river to follow a clear ash path to a junction, turning left to return to **Hvanngil**.

WALK 17
Þórsmörk and Valahnúkur

Start/Finish	Langidalur or Húsadalur
Distance	6km (3¾ miles)
Total ascent/descent	330m (1080ft)
Time	2hrs
Terrain	Clear paths through woods and steep fell paths
Map	1:25,000 'Útivist Göngukort – Þórsmörk og Goðaland'
Transport	Reykjavík Excursions and Trex serve Húsadalur and Langidalur from Reykjavík, Selfoss and Hveragerði

Valahnúkur is located in an ideal position in the Þórsmörk nature reserve, where it can be approached from huts at Langidalur, Húsadalur or even Básar. Although fairly small, surrounded by much higher fells, it is an ideal viewpoint.

Outside the hut at **Langidalur**, signposts point left for Valahnúkur and right for Húsadalur. Head right up a gentle grassy dale flanked by woods, crossing seven footbridges over a stream. Pass a cave called Skuggi and keep left, signposted 'Húsadalur'. ▶ A worn path leads to a gap, then a long flight of wooden steps drop into a wooded valley. A platform stands halfway,

To the right is the Laugavegur to Landmannalaugar.

103

The hut at Langidalur, looking across the Krossá river to Eyjafjallajökull

where an overhanging cliff bears a **cave** and centuries of carvings, including 'Gvðmvðvz Einázsson 1773'.

Go down more wooden steps, an ash path and log steps, then climb log steps to a grassy area. Keep straight ahead at a signposted junction. ◄ Reach a campsite, sauna, restaurant and huts at **Húsadalur**.

Again, to the right is the Laugavegur.

A signpost on the left points to a pool of warm water, with a board-walk running left. Follow it, go up a woodland path and fork right. A monstrous rocky tower rises to the right, and a signpost points straight ahead for Valahnúkur. Climb flights of log steps on a wooded slope to yet another signpost and turn right. There are more steep flights of logs steps, then chains alongside a rugged stretch.

The path climbs steep and stony ground, easing as the tree-line is passed, then a final steep and stony path climbs a slope of flowery grass, moss and willow. The summit of **Valahnúkur**, at 465m (1525ft), has a view indicator, and the vista extends from floodplains to Tindafjallajökull, along the Laugavegur, around to Mýrdalsjökull, Fimmvorðuháls and Eyafjallajökull.

Follow the path steeply down a ridge, with stone steps further down. There are stony slopes and sparse bushes, then taller trees and log steps. Cross a footbridge in the grassy dale to return to the hut at **Langidalur**.

WALK 18

Fljótsdalur and Þórólfsfell

Start/Finish	Fljótsdalur Youth Hostel
Distance	17km (10½ miles)
Total ascent/descent	500m (1640ft)
Time	5hrs 30mins
Terrain	A steep, pathless climb, followed by a long, winding descent on a track
Maps	1:100,000 'Mál og Menning – 4 Landmannalaugar Þórsmörk Fjallabak'; 1:100,000 'Ferðakort – Þórsmörk Landmannalaugar'
Transport	Occasional Reykjavík Excursions serve Fljótsdalur from Reykjavík, Hveragerði and Selfoss

Dick Phillips (www.icelandic-travel.com), who has organised treks in Iceland since 1960, uses the grass-roofed Fljótsdalur Youth Hostel as his base. Nearby Þórólfsfell offers a straightforward climb and is a fine viewpoint for Fljótsdalur and Þórsmörk.

Start from the **hostel** at Fljótsdalur. Walk down its steep access road, then turn right along a dirt road and left along another dirt road signposted 'Emstrur'. Pass notice-boards and a signpost for Þórólfsfell, and there should be a footbridge over a river. Follow the dirt road and cross a cattle grid near a signpost for a hut called **Fell**. Turn left to follow a path uphill, drift left, follow a fence and cross a grassy dip. Climb a stony and sparsely vegetated crest.

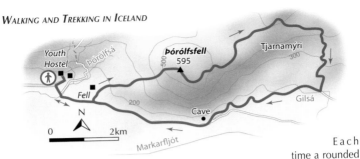

Each time a rounded hump is reached, drift left onto an adjacent crest, climb further, and repeat this move again. Eventually a steeper, more vegetated slope rises, then eases. A final steep slope has chunky stones underfoot, then the top of **Þórólfsfell** has broad, bouldery areas with grassy, stony hollows. A cairn supports a post at 595m (1952ft). Views take in nearby Tindafjallajökull and stretch to Mýrdalsjökull, Fimmvörðuháls, and Eyafjallajökull.

Spot nearby wheel-marks offering two descents. ◀ Turn left to follow the wheel-marks over a rise, later dropping down steep and stony terrain to

Turning right involves a very steep descent.

The grass-topped Fljótsdalur Youth Hostel contains a library of books about Iceland

windblown sand. Look for the continuation across a grassy plain at **Tjarnamýri**. Curve left and right, and cross stonier ground, rising and falling. Boulder-hop a stream and climb a grassy slope to a level, stony area.

The descent is stony, becoming more vegetated, winding all the way to the fell-foot. Turn right along a stony track, rising and falling, crossing a shallow stream. Rise and fall again and cross another stream, where either the track or a path can be followed. The next stream is in a bouldery gully, and the track beyond is very rugged. Pass a looming rock outcrop to join a dirt road, and turn right to follow it. Look out for an interesting **cave** under a pointed rock to the right; otherwise simply follow the dirt road and later retrace steps to Fljótsdalur.

WALK 19
Vestmannaeyjar – Heimaey

Start/Finish	Heimaey (harbour or airport)
Distance	9km (5½ miles)
Total ascent/descent	270m (885ft)
Time	9hrs
Terrain	Good roads, tracks and paths, as well as steep and stony slopes
Map	1:50,000 'Ferðakort – Vestmannaeyjar'
Transport	Eimskip ferries (tel 4812800) serve Heimaey from Landeyjahöfn, which is served by Sterna from Reykjavík, Hveragerði, Selfoss and Hvolsvöllur. Fewer ferries and bus connections serve Heimaey from Þorlákshöfn. Eagle Air flights serve Heimaey from Reykjavík (www.eagleair.is).

The island of Heimaey, the largest of the Vestmannaeyjar (Westman Islands), offers plenty of walking and bird-watching opportunities, and is notable for puffins. Many people explore the 'new' lava that increased the size of the island in 1973, and the volcano of Eldfell remains hot to this day.

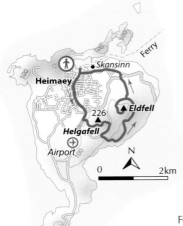

Start at the ferry pier and head into **Heimaey**, straight up Heiðarvegur, Strembugata and Dalavegur, as if for the airport (the alternative start/finish). Turn left as signposted for **Helgafell**, following a track straight towards the fell, climbing a narrow path on a grassy, flowery slope to the summit viewpoint at 226m (741ft). Descend a scant path on pumice, which becomes completely vegetated.

Turn right down a road to a notice-board and turn left along a gravel road signposted 'Haugasvæði'. Follow this towards the coast, swinging left

Puffins are often seen around the cliff coastline of Heimaey, particularly in the south

high above the sea and passing a basalt column. Drop to where an ash slope meets rugged lava and follow a loose ash path, rising gently. The ash bears patchy lyme grass, while the lava bears bulbous moss. Reach a gravel track and turn left to find a large cross planted in a black crater.

Turn left or right uphill. Left leads to a red crater and right leads onto the crater rim, and both paths join to crunch up red ash and pumice, passing an aircraft beacon to reach gnarled rocks on top of **Eldfell** at 221m (725ft). Look down on the town and harbour, around the island, then to the 1973 lava that spilled seawards. Retrace steps to the cross and follow the bendy track, turning left at a junction to reach a road. ▶

To the right is a hidden garden at Gaujulundur.

Cross the road to follow an ash and pumice path, heading left to run roughly parallel to the road. Cross a road near a junction and see how the lava almost closed the harbour mouth in 1973. Follow the road towards town, but note fine buildings down to the right at **Skansinn**, particularly the stave church. Either walk straight into town or explore a network of paths on rugged lava, where part of the town was buried in 1973. Notices abound showing details of buildings that were destroyed. Some excavation work has been completed at what is now being called 'Pompeii of the North'.

On 23 January 1973, **Eldfell** suddenly erupted. Lava and ash poured from a fissure and most of the population were quickly evacuated. A few people stayed behind and attempted to protect homes and businesses, but hundreds of buildings were destroyed and most were buried by ash. An enormous clean-up was required when the volcanic activity finally subsided in July. The story is told daily throughout the summer at the 'Volcanic Film Show', tel 4811045.

TREK 2
Hellismannaleið, Laugavegur and Skógar Trail

Start	Rjúpnavellir
Finish	Skógar
Distance	143km (88½ miles) – Hellismannaleið 59km (36 miles); Laugavegur 55km (34½ miles); Skógar Trail 29km (18 miles)
Time	9 days
Terrain	Easy at first on the Hellismannaleið, but hilly later. High and exposed on the Laugavegur, with some steep and stony slopes. Gentler later, but with increasingly difficult river crossings. A steep, rocky ascent on the Skógar Trail, with permanent ice on its high and exposed top. A long and gentle descent to Skógar.
Facilities	Huts. Small shop at Landmannalaugar and Langidalur. Restaurant at Husadalur. Shop, restaurant, hostel and hotels at Skógar.
Accommodation	Huts and/or camping throughout, though camping is not recommended at Fimmvörðuháls. Hostel and hotels available at Skógar.

The **Laugavegur** (Stages 4–7) is the most popular long-distance trek in Iceland, and some walkers feel it gets too busy. Certainly, the huts along the trail get booked well in advance, and the campsites alongside get very crowded. The trail from Landmannalaugar to Þórsmörk generally takes four days to walk, though marathon runners complete it in five hours!

It is well worth flanking this trail with two other trails. The three-day **Hellismannaleið** (Stages 1–3) offers a reasonably quiet and gentle hut-to-hut trek from Rjúpnavellir to Landmannalaugar. The **Skógar Trail** (Stages 8–9) offers a tougher two-day trek from Þórsmörk to Skógar. Together, all three trails combine to make a splendid nine-day trek.

As this area of South Iceland is a popular destination for walkers, there are good bus services to start and finish, as well as to many of the huts, from Reykjavík. Parts of the Laugavegur are walked on Walks 14, 15, 16 and 17.

Start	Rjúpnavellir
Finish	Áfangagil
Distance	19km (12 miles)
Total ascent	320m (1050ft)
Total descent	200m (655ft)
Time	6hrs
Terrain	Tracks, paths and pathless stretches, beside rivers and across stony, sandy slopes. Some short, steep ascents and descents.
Maps	1:100,000 'Mál og Menning – 4 Landmannalaugar Þórsmörk Fjallabak'; 1:100,000 'Ferðakort – Þórsmörk Landmannalaugar'
Transport	Reykjavík Excursions and Trex serve Rjúpnavellir from Reykjavík, Selfoss and Landmannalaugar
Accommodation	Huts at Áfangagil

The riverside walk from Rjúpnavellir to Fossabrekkur is delightful and easy, followed by stony and sandy slopes. A gentle hill-walk and steep descent leads to Áfangagil, where huts are couched in a remote valley.

Walk along an access track to huts at **Rjúpnavellir** (tel 8920409, www.rjupnavellir.is). Turn left as signposted for Áfangagil and Landmannalaugar, along a track flanked by young trees. White-tipped posts mark the whole of the Hellismannaleið. As trees thin out the moorland bears grass, moss and crowberry, speckled with flowers. Follow the posts as they drift right, overlooking

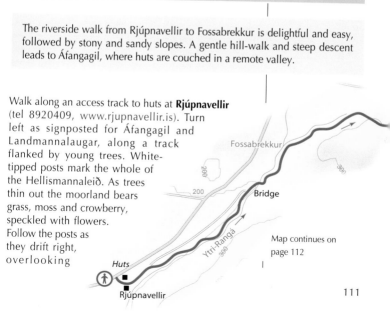

Fossabrekkur

Bridge

Ytri-Ranga

Huts

Rjúpnavellir

Map continues on page 112

The waymarked path descends a stony slope with fine views of Fossabrekkur

the **Ytri-Rangá**, with its islets and banks of angelica. (If time is pressing, follow the track.) Simply walk upstream and cross a **bridge**.

Climb above the river on black and white gravel, following white posts, with Hekla and Búrfell in view. Three side-valleys are crossed, all carrying streams, one of which must be forded. Continue high above the river then drop down a steep, loose slope with splendid views of **Fossabrekkur**. The river doesn't fall much, but is split by vegetated humps into a dozen waterfalls.

Continue upstream on grassy and bare slopes, with scree pushing walkers almost into the water. When there is a break in the cliffs above, the path climbs, then drops. Further upstream, the river is flanked by contorted rocks, so drift away

Áfangagil

Stac

Huts

Aldan

Landmannaleið

N

0   2km

Sauðafell

from it across bare pumice. Later, black sand bears clumps of lyme grass and a few flowers, but the overall aspect is desert-like. There is a distinct drift right as the markers rise and fall on slopes overlooking a shallow, dry valley. ▶ Rise and fall across black ash hills with rocks poking from them north of **Sauðafell**, and continue across black ash where jagged lava rises to the right. Drift left and head for a dirt road at **Landmannaleið**, and cross it. ▶

Pass a couple of ash-filled drystone enclosures, heading gently down and up over a broad, green slope. Go slightly down to cross a stony washout, then climb a bare, dusty, stony slope. Cross a nasty, loose, steep-sided gully, followed by an easy gully, around 400m (1310ft) on **Aldan**. Drift left downhill, and the slope becomes grassy as markers lead to a grass-roofed hut at **Áfangagil**, with a couple more huts nearby. Book in advance (hafseinn. hannesson@mast.is), although the door code to one hut can be gained by phoning 8959500, giving card details.

It is easier to walk through the valley, but keep an eye on the markers.

Bus services here.

STAGE 2
Hellismannaleið – Áfangagil to Landmannahellir

Start	Áfangagil
Finish	Landmannahellir
Distance	22km (13½ miles)
Total ascent	550m (1805ft)
Total descent	250m (820ft)
Time	8hrs
Terrain	Short, steep, stony ascents and descents, as well as broad ash and gravel plains, and some rugged lava
Maps	1:100,000 'Mál og Menning – 4 Landmannalaugar Þórsmörk Fjallabak'; 1:100,000 'Ferðakort – Þórsmörk Landmannalaugar'
Transport	Trex (tel 5876000, www.trex.is) serves Landmannahellir from Reykjavík, Selfoss, Rjúpnavellir and Landmannalaugar
Accommodation	Huts at Landmannahellir

The middle of the Hellismannaleið is a succession of rugged fell passes, separated by flat, dusty, stony plains. Lakes are seen towards the end of the day, and there is plenty of grass around Landmannahellir.

Leave the grass-roofed hut at **Áfangagil**, following a signpost for Landmannahellir, and climb a grassy and stony crest to a slight grassy gap. Climb right, as marked, up across a steep slope of ash and stones, turning left on top to reach around 420m (1380ft). Watch carefully for markers down a stony slope and walk straight across an ash plain.

Climb as marked through a dry ash valley flanked by small outcrops. There is thin vegetation further up. Then cross a stony gap and keep straight ahead over a patch of grass and willow towards another valley. The broad ash floor narrows, then broadens considerably, with boulders below **Valahnúkar**. Cross a very wide ash gap and head towards a distant conical fell, keeping left of a mudflat, then go right to cross a crest over 500m (1640ft). Go down a steep, stony slope, across an ash plain and up a stony slope as marked. To the left is the elongated, red-tinged crater of **Valagjá**. Continue along the path to a track and signposts.

Markers cross level ash, tinged green with vegetation, with rocks poking through. Cross a river and the rugged, mossy lava of **Lambafitjarhraun**. The path continues beside the lava, rising and falling across thinly vegetated ash slopes. After a short, steep climb, drift left into an ash valley, stony in places, passing occasional overhanging outcrops. The valley narrows and broadens, and the route runs between fells with mossy slopes, past rock and boulders, and over the stony crest of **Lambaskarð** at almost 580m (1900ft). To right and left are the lakes of Sauðleysuvatn and Hrafnabjargavatn, linked by a thin stream.

Drop to the stream and cross an ash plain and a track, climbing up the far side as marked on moss and stones. Swing right and

left, down to a stony gap, then steeply up to a stony fell around 670m (2200ft). Drop to a stony, mossy gap and

Stony fells are crossed before the route descends to Landmannahellir

climb a broad crest, drifting left across a moss-streaked slope to a broad, stony gap. Markers lead down to the lake of **Herbjarnarfellsvatn**. Join and follow a track that climbs steeply, descending to a stony plain that becomes grassy, where huts are seen at **Landmannahellir**. Check in at one of the furthest huts, marked with a large 'i' (tel 8938407, www.landmannahellir.is).

STAGE 3

Hellismannaleið – Landmannahellir to Landmannalaugar

Start	Landmannahellir
Finish	Landmannalaugar
Distance	17km (10½ miles)
Total ascent	550m (1805ft)
Total descent	540m (1770ft)
Time	6hrs
Terrain	A succession of fells, with some steep ascents and descents
Maps	1:100,000 'Mál og Menning – 4 Landmannalaugar Þórsmörk Fjallabak'; 1:100,000 'Ferðakort – Þórsmörk Landmannalaugar'; 1:25,000 'FÍ – Landmannalaugar Map of Hiking Trails'
Transport	Reykjavík Excursions serve Landmannalaugar from Reykjavík, Hveragerði, Selfoss, Skaftafell and Kirkjubæjarklaustur. Trex serves Landmannalaugar from Reykjavík, Hveragerði, Selfoss and Landmannahellir.
Accommodation	FÍ huts and campsite at Landmannalaugar

This stage starts with fells and lakes. After crossing a dirt road the fells become busier, the closer walkers get to Landmannalaugar. The quiet Hellismannaleið links with the popular and busy Laugavegur at Landmannalaugar.

Leave **Landmannahellir** from a horse corral, following a signpost for Landmannalaugar. Yellow and white markers

Morning mist clears from fells, seen from the gentle grasslands around Landmannahellir

climb an ash slope to the right of a little valley. A clear path is trodden through moss, grass and crowberry, sprinkled with flowers. Cross a gentle gap to a signpost, where yellow markers head left up Lödmundur, while white markers drop to the lake of **Löðmundarvatn**. Keep left of the lake, and the path easily crosses a very steep, grassy slope, with boulders beyond.

Fork right across level moss and grass, sometimes wet, crossing at least one small stream. Head left as marked by white pegs into a valley, keeping to the left, up a slope of grass, moss and crowberry. Swing right across a broad gap, pass a white-painted boulder and climb, drifting left to traverse a fellside at almost 700m (2300ft). Ranks of fells rise beyond **Lifrarfjallavatn**, and the path descends to a gap. Climb steeply and follow wheel-marks over a rounded, mossy hill, with stones and low rock outcrops on top. A gentle crest gives way to a stony descent to a dirt road at **Domadalsháls**. ▸

Bus services.

Drop from the road, turn left beside a deep, rocky gorge, and cross a stream. Climb to find wheel-marks rising steeply on a slope of moss, grass and crowberry. A lightly trodden path climbs from a shoulder, up moss and

117

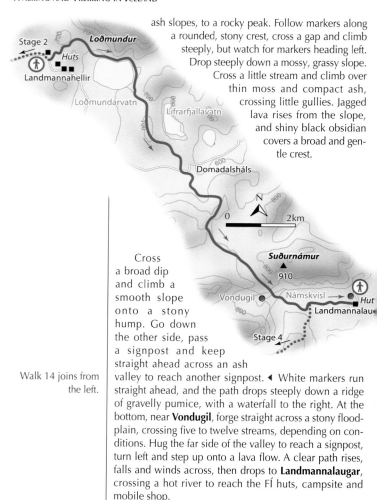

ash slopes, to a rocky peak. Follow markers along a rounded, stony crest, cross a gap and climb steeply, but watch for markers heading left. Drop steeply down a mossy, grassy slope. Cross a little stream and climb over thin moss and compact ash, crossing little gullies. Jagged lava rises from the slope, and shiny black obsidian covers a broad and gentle crest.

Cross a broad dip and climb a smooth slope onto a stony hump. Go down the other side, pass a signpost and keep straight ahead across an ash

Walk 14 joins from the left.

valley to reach another signpost. ◄ White markers run straight ahead, and the path drops steeply down a ridge of gravelly pumice, with a waterfall to the right. At the bottom, near **Vondugil**, forge straight across a stony flood-plain, crossing five to twelve streams, depending on conditions. Hug the far side of the valley to reach a signpost, turn left and step up onto a lava flow. A clear path rises, falls and winds across, then drops to **Landmannalaugar**, crossing a hot river to reach the FÍ huts, campsite and mobile shop.

STAGE 4

Laugavegur – Landmannalaugar to Hrafntinnusker

Start	Landmannalaugar
Finish	Hrfantinnusker
Distance	12km (7½ miles)
Total ascent	530m (1740ft)
Total descent	80m (260ft)
Time	4hrs 30mins
Terrain	Mostly climbing on bare, stony slopes, with gentle gradients and some short, steep climbs
Map	1:25,000 'FÍ – Landmannalaugar Map of Hiking Trails'
Transport	Reykjavík Excursions serve Landmannalaugar from Reykjavík, Hveragerði, Selfoss, Skaftafell and Kirkjubærklaustur. Trex serves Landmannalaugar from Reykjavík, Hveragerði and Selfoss.
Accommodation	Basic FÍ hut below Hrafntinnusker and nearby camping spots

The first day on the Laugavegur is quite literally uphill work – a mixture of gentle and steep climbs. The fells are amazingly colourful and there are notable mud-pots and hot springs, with permanent ice on the highest fells.

Leave **Landmannalaugar**, at 590m (1935ft), as signposted past the FÍ hut for the Laugavegur. Cross a hot river beside a lava flow and make a short climb, which is steep and rocky. The path eases, rising, falling and winding on **Laugahraun**, later leaving the lava to reach a signpost. ▸ Keep straight ahead uphill, following red-and-white pegs. Climb through a valley, with rugged lava on the left and steep, pastel-shaded slopes on the right. Climb a bouldery slope to steaming hot-spots and another signpost. ▸

Climb steeply and turn right along a gently steaming ridge, reaching the colourful stony slopes of **Brennisteinsalda** beneath a rock tower. Climb steeply, levelling out at a signpost. Keep left for a gentle descent marked by red pegs. ▸ A broad path crosses a slope of

Walk 14 joins from the right.

Walk 15 descends left.

Right is marked with green pegs, for Brennisteinsalda.

119

Looking down on the snow-bound hut on the upper slopes of Hrafntinnusker

thin moss, then climbs a rounded, stony ridge with hotspots to left and right.

Cross three light-coloured gravelly humps, then make a short, steep climb. As the gradient eases, look back towards Landmannalaugar, spotting the distant glaciers of Vatnajökull and Hofsjökull. Cross a broad, stony rise, descend gently to prominent markers held by mesh-bound cairns, and keep right for Hraíntinnusker. Look ahead to spot more markers across broad, stony, undulating terrain.

Descend towards a steaming valley at **Stórihver**, and either stay well left of it, as marked, or walk down through it and later turn left to rejoin the trail. (There are vigorous springs of boiling water.) Pass a sign on a gap and climb steeply, gradually easing, on a broad slope of stones and ash. Look back to see range upon range of fells, while ahead a broad gap is flanked by broad-topped fells. Traverse **Söðull** and cross a gap around 1060m (3475ft), following cairns. The FÍ hut lies below ice-capped **Hrafntinnusker**, reached after descending a slope of black, shiny obsidian. The hut is basic, with no showers, and heating comes from a hot-spot below it. Nearby camping spots are very rugged.

STAGE 5
Laugavegur – Hrafntinnusker to Álftavatn

Start	Hrafntinnusker
Finish	Álftavatn
Distance	12km (7½ miles)
Total ascent	130m (425ft)
Total descent	600m (1970ft)
Time	4hrs 30mins
Terrain	The highest parts are cut by awkward gullies, easier to cross early in the season when they are filled with snow. A steep, stony descent leads to a river that has to be forded.
Maps	1:100,000 'Mál og Menning – 4 Landmannalaugar Þórsmörk Fjallabak; 1:100,000 'Ferðakort – Þórsmörk Landmannalaugar'
Transport	Occasional Reykjavík Excursions serve Álftavatn from Reykjavík, Hveragerði and Selfoss
Accommodation	FÍ huts at Álftavatn

The walk from Hrafntinnusker can be splendid, with fine fell views, but only in good weather (in mist it requires careful navigation). Descending from the fells, there are wonderful views towards Álftavatn.

Leave **Hrafntinnusker** as marked, crossing black ash and broken obsidian. Early in the season, extensive snow

1060
Stage
Söðull
Hut
Hrafntinnusker
Rey
Jökulgil
Ford
Ford
Grashagakvísl
N
0   2km
Huts
Stage 6
Álftavatn

cover makes for easy walking, but marker posts are buried. As summer advances and the snow melts, crumbling gullies emerge, with rounded ridges between them, proving slow and tiring to negotiate. Keep an eye on the route across the foot of **Reykjafjöll**, note steam from hot-spots down to the right, and eventually climb to a rocky edge around 1020m (3345ft). ◄

The nearby peak of Háskerðingur is a notable viewpoint.

Turn right along the edge, where boulders have been nudged aside to form a gravel path. After passing a hot-spot, drop into a steep-sided valley and climb from it as marked, noting steam vents

Snow covers a succession of gullies, but hot-spots remain prominent because of their steam

all around. Descend to cross a stream above a waterfall spilling into **Jökulgil**. Climb steeply and turn right down a gravelly crest, passing hot-spots and crossing a little valley. Follow markers over a rise on Jökultungur. Enjoy views of shapely fells near Álftavatn, and the glaciers of Mýdalsjökull and Eyafjallajökull.

Descend steep and stony zigzags, which become more vegetated on the way down to a dale. The river **Grashagakvísl** has to be forded, although boulder-hopping is possible. There are three paths on the opposite bank, but only the last one is marked (all join up later). Walk over a gentle rise and cross a small stream to reach a gritty slope. Keep right at a fork, across ash and stones, becoming grassy, then ford a stream. A stony track leads to a huddle of FÍ huts at **Álftavatn**, where a lake is flanked by fine fells.

STAGE 6
Laugavegur – Álftavatn to Botnar/Emstrur

Start	Álftavatn
Finish	Botnar/Emstrur
Distance	16km (10 miles)
Total ascent	200m (655ft)
Total descent	270m (885ft)
Time	6hrs
Terrain	Three rivers need to be forded, while ascents and descents are mostly gentle. Vegetated slopes give way to bare ash and stony plains.
Maps	1:100,000 'Mál og Menning – 4 Landmannalaugar Þórsmörk Fjallabak'; 1:100,000 'Ferðakort – Þórsmörk Landmannalaugar'
Transport	Occasional Reykjavík Excursions serve Álftavatn, Hvanngil and Botnar/Emstrur from Reykjavík, Hveragerði and Selfoss
Accommodation	FÍ huts at Botnar/Emstrur

The first half of the day involves fording three rivers that become broader and deeper, then an ash and stony desert is flanked by shapely fells. The canyon of Markarfljótsgljúfur can be reached by a short detour at the finish.

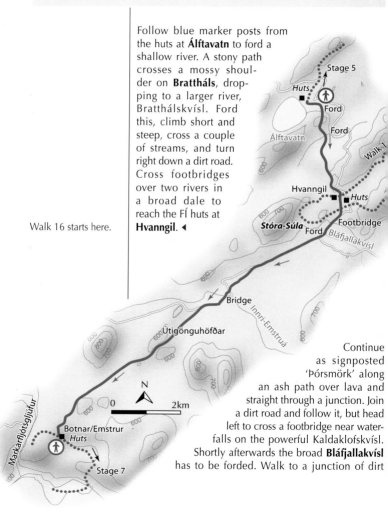

Follow blue marker posts from the huts at **Álftavatn** to ford a shallow river. A stony path crosses a mossy shoulder on **Bratthals**, dropping to a larger river, Bratthálskvísl. Ford this, climb short and steep, cross a couple of streams, and turn right down a dirt road. Cross footbridges over two rivers in a broad dale to reach the Fí huts at **Hvanngil**. ◀

Walk 16 starts here.

Continue as signposted 'Þórsmörk' along an ash path over lava and straight through a junction. Join a dirt road and follow it, but head left to cross a footbridge near waterfalls on the powerful Kaldaklofskvísl. Shortly afterwards the broad **Bláfjallakvísl** has to be forded. Walk to a junction of dirt

roads and continue as signposted 'Fljótshlíð'. The road is level or gently undulating, across bare ash and stones at the foot of **Stóra-Súla**, below 500m (1640ft). Watch for markers heading left along a path over gentle humps, later crossing a dirt road to reach a bridge over the **Innri-Emstruá**, where the riverbanks are green. ▶

Continue up, down and up the dirt road, turning left on top as signposted 'Botnar Emstrur'. The path undulates and rises gently towards a stony gap flanked by fells with mossy slopes at **Útigönguhöfðar**, around 600m (1970ft). Descend on boulder-strewn ash to a dusty valley. Drift left across a broad, stony ash plain, where flanking fells are covered in moss. Rise gently to a dirt road, either following it or using a parallel path, and switching between them if preferred.

Eventually, the path heads left of the track and descends a steep ash slope. Join a rough and stony track down to a huddle of FÍ huts at **Botnar/Emstrur**. However, before descending, it is worth crossing the dirt road at a battered sign and following a marked path to the awesome, deep, winding, rock-walled canyon of **Markarfljótsgljúfur**, where fulmars nest and soar.

A narrow path crosses ash and stones near the huts at Hvanngil

Go downstream to see a powerful fall with explosive spray!

STAGE 7
Laugavegur – Botnar/Emstrur to Þórsmörk

Start	Botnar/Emstrur
Finish	Langidalur or Húsadalur, Þórsmörk
Distance	15km (9½ miles)
Total ascent	350m (1150ft)
Total descent	600m (1970ft)
Time	6hrs
Terrain	Some gentle slopes, but also steep and rugged slopes, with areas of bare stones and ash, giving way to woods towards the end
Maps	1:100,000 'Mál og Menning – 4 Landmannalaugar Þórsmörk Fjallabak'; 1:100,000 'Ferðakort – Þórsmörk Landmannalaugar'
Transport	Reykjavík Excursions and Trex serve Húsadalur and Langidalur from Reykjavík, Selfoss and Hveragerði
Accommodation	FÍ hut at Langidalur; campsite and huts at Húsadalur

On the final stage of the Laugavegur, there are plenty of ups and downs, remarkable canyons, and a glacial river to ford. Dense woods are reached at Þórsmörk, where there is a choice of two finishing points – Langidalur or Húsadalur.

Read about the danger of flooding whenever the volcano Katla erupts beneath Mýrdalsjökull.

Leave **Botnar/Emstrur**, by crossing an adjacent valley and footbridge, climbing soft ash to a notice. ◄ A gentle path leads to a stream where angelica grows. Cross it and climb, then follow the path to a sudden steep drop in a gully of loose ash, stones and boulders. A rope leads to a footbridge over a sheer-sided canyon carrying the **Fremri-Emstruá**. Another bridge is fixed to a rock wall, and chains assist climbing.

The canyon of Markarfljótsgljúfur can be seen from here.

A gentler path continues over a stony area, rising and falling. Cross a stream where there is plenty of vegetation, and the path climbs onto a high, stony shelf. ◄ Climb past boulders onto a higher stony shelf, and note the prominent horned peak of Einhyrningur ('the unicorn'). Cross a

A footbridge spans the powerful glacial flow of Fremri-Emstruá

couple of rugged, steep-sided little valleys and streams, **Slyppugil** and **Bjórgil**, where willow is prominent.

Descend along the brow of a tightly winding canyon. The ground is mostly ash and stones, occasionally bare rock, becoming a gently sloping plain. Go through a little valley with a little cliff on the right and a bushy slope on the left, followed by a bushy slope on the right. Drift from the valley to follow an ash path over sparse grass to a river, the **Ljósá**, as it falls into a gorge. Cross a footbridge flanked by trees, then a moor of heather, crowberry, horsetails, creeping juniper and flowers.

127

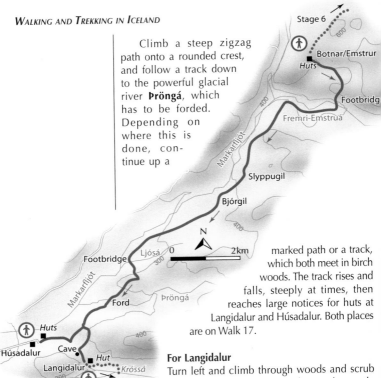

Climb a steep zigzag path onto a rounded crest, and follow a track down to the powerful glacial river **Þröngá**, which has to be forded. Depending on where this is done, continue up a marked path or a track, which both meet in birch woods. The track rises and falls, steeply at times, then reaches large notices for huts at Langidalur and Húsadalur. Both places are on Walk 17.

For Langidalur

Turn left and climb through woods and scrub onto a crest. Enjoy views and meander gently down through birch woods. Go down steep log steps to a signpost in a valley and turn left. There is a cave on the right at Skuggi, and the path crosses seven footbridges over a stream to reach the FÍ hut at **Langidalur**. ◄

Small shop and bus services.

For Húsadalur

Go along the track and turn left gently up a path to a cairn. Walk down a narrow path across crumbling slopes, passing wooded and grassy areas to reach a signpost in a valley. Turn right along a broad path, going gently down through the valley to reach the campsite and huts at **Húsadalur**. ◄ Walkers who intend to continue along the Skógar Trail need to walk to Langidalur to pick up the route.

Sauna, restaurant and buses.

STAGE 8

Skógar Trail – Þórsmörk to Fimmvörðuháls

Start	Langidalur or Básar
Finish	Fimmvörðuháls
Distance	13km (8 miles)
Total ascent	900m (2950ft)
Total descent	70m (230ft)
Time	5hrs
Terrain	Steep and rugged climbing, with some narrow, exposed ridges. Snow and ice on the highest parts.
Maps	1:100,000 'Mál og Menning – 4 Landmannalaugar Þórsmörk Fjallabak'; 1:100,000 'Ferðakort – Þórsmörk Landmannalaugar'; 1:25,000 'Útivist Göngukort – Þórsmörk og Goðaland'
Transport	Reykjavík Excursions and Trex serve Húsadalur, Langidalur and Básar from Reykjavík, Selfoss and Hveragerði
Accommodation	Basic hut at Fimmvörðuháls

The Skógar Trail, popular in its own right, is often added to the Laugavegur. The climb to Fimmvörðuháls is steep and rugged, with splendid views and amazing additions to the landscape since the 2010 Eyafjallajökull eruption.

Leave **Langidalur** by walking upstream on the broad shingle banks of the **Krossá**. Look ahead to spot two seasonal footbridges on wheels and cross them. Forge through thickets and turn left along a dirt road, crossing little footbridges near the Útivist huts at **Básar**. ▸ Before reaching the huts, walk straight along a rugged track as signposted 'Fimmvörðuháls'. Follow blue-tipped marker posts, crossing cobbles covered in low birch scrub.

Cross a footbridge over **Strákagil** and turn left to reach a toilet block. Afterwards, turn right up a few steps, past birch and willow bushes, and go up more steps, with fine canyon views. Keep right of a grotesque rocky

Save 2km (1¼ miles) by starting at Básar. There are several waymarked trails in this area.

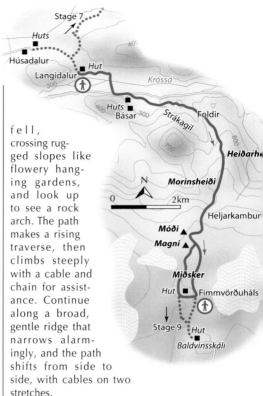

fell, crossing rugged slopes like flowery hanging gardens, and look up to see a rock arch. The path makes a rising traverse, then climbs steeply with a cable and chain for assistance. Continue along a broad, gentle ridge that narrows alarmingly, and the path shifts from side to side, with cables on two stretches.

Walk up a broad, vegetated ridge and enjoy views of surrounding fells. Cross a hump and a little gap, zigzag uphill, and climb straight up a broad crest on **Foldir**. Cross a gentle gap and note two paths on the steep right-hand slopes of **Heiðarhorn**, both climbing to a rocky gap. The gently sloping stony plateau of **Morinsheiði** has a signpost in the middle, and later there is a sudden steep-sided gap at **Heljarkambur**. Cross a narrow ridge and climb, holding a chain, across a crumbling cliff to reach safer slopes.

Prominent yellow marker posts held in mesh-bound cairns lead up a rocky, stony slope. Cross a shoulder

where the trail ahead was covered by lava in spring 2010 and was diverted right. Pass two new volcanic cones formed during the eruption – **Móði** and **Magni**. Some places are still hot and steaming, so take care and marvel at the vivid pastel colours.

Prominent yellow markers lead across a dip, then left of a fell called **Miðsker**. There are also smaller red-tipped markers right of the fell, leading more directly to the Útivist hut on a ridge at **Fimmvörðuháls**, around 1050m (3445ft). The hut is basic, with no showers, separate 'pee and poo' toilet arrangements, and water often has to be made by melting snow. For those who have followed the yellow markers, the route reaches a signpost where a right turn leads to the hut. Either way, there is a lot of barren black ash and ice around, and it is wise to tread carefully.

The colourful cone of Magni was formed only in spring 2010, diverting the Skógar Trail

STAGE 9
Skógar Trail – Fimmvörðuháls to Skógar

Start	Fimmvörðuháls
Finish	Skógar
Distance	16km (10 miles)
Total ascent	50m (165ft)
Total descent	1050m (3445ft)
Time	5hrs 30mins
Terrain	Mostly downhill, from black ash and stony slopes, along a stony dirt road, then beside a river down to grassy lowlands
Maps	1:100,000 'Mál og Menning – 4 Landmannalaugar Þórsmörk Fjallabak'; 1:100,000 'Ferðakort – Þórsmörk Landmannalaugar'; 1:25,000 'Útivist Göngukort – Þórsmörk og Goðaland'
Transport	Sterna serve Skógar from Reykjavík, Selfoss, Kirkjubæjarklaustur, Skaftafell and Höfn
Accommodation	Youth hostel and two hotels at Skógar

The descent from Fimmvörðuháls is long and gradual. The higher parts bear black ash from the 2010 eruption of Eyafjallajökull, but it becomes greener on the way down. Plenty of attractive waterfalls lead to the thrilling Skógafoss.

Skógafoss is a powerful and popular waterfall, but expect to get wet while approaching it

Leave **Fimmvörðuháls** either by dropping down ash slopes to pick up wheel-marks left by vehicles servicing the hut, or by walking to a signposted path junction and turning right to start the descent. Either way, there is black ash and ice underfoot, so tread carefully. Aim for the A-shaped FÍ hut of **Baldvinsskáli**. This fell into disrepair and there is a plan to replace it with a new model. Follow a dirt road from the hut, but quickly head right, passing marker posts on a slope of ash and stones. Rejoin the dirt road running gradually downhill, rising a little three times. When the road runs near the **Skógá** river, watch for a large waterfall.

Before reaching a vehicle ford, head right to cross a **footbridge**, then turn right to walk downstream. The river is a splendid guide, and if there is a path, use it, but if the ground is too steep, or there are cliffs, leave the river until it is safe to return. There are abundant waterfalls, with a couple of very impressive ones seen early, as well as smaller ones. Further down there are deep canyons, where only nesting fulmars can see into the depths.

Inflowing streams such as the Króksá and **Þvergil** are easily crossed, and as the surrounding slopes become greener, the river runs less through canyons and displays more waterfalls. The path rises and falls, and the river contains huge boulders and islands with trees on them. People are seen as the top of **Skógafoss** is approached, then hundreds of metal steps lead down to a level riverside meadow. Double back upstream to see and feel the full power of the 60m (200ft) waterfall, getting drenched in its spray! Walk through a campsite to its service hut and bus stop at **Skógar**, where there is a youth hostel, two hotels, restaurant with small shop, Icelandic Travel Market (tel 8942956) and folk museum.

133

3 SKAFTAFELL AND VATNAJÖKULL

The final part of the climb on Hvannadalshnúkur is criss-crossed with awkward crevasses (Walk 20)

Skaftafell, in South Iceland, is the most popular access point to the enormous Vatnajökull National Park. There is a busy campsite and visitor centre, with a small restaurant. Many visitors set their sights on Iceland's highest mountain, Hvannadalshnúkur (Walk 20), but remember that this involves glacier walking, as does neighbouring Hrútsfjall (Walk 21). The prominent peak of Kristínartindar (Walk 22) is steep and rocky, but easier to climb than the glaciated peaks. There are a number of short, easy and scenic signposted trails fanning out from the campsite, and some of these are used on Walks 23 and 24. Just outside the national park, on the road to Höfn, the amazing Jökulsárlón, or Glacier Lagoon, offers an easy and extremely scenic walk (Walk 25).

There are no long-distance treks in this area, but there are a surprising number of bus services that allow exploration of the area. In addition to the Sterna bus service linking Skaftafell with Reykjavík and Höfn, other buses run between Skaftafell and Jökulsárlón. Reykjavík Excursions offer a link with Landmannalaugar (Section 2), and the bus stops along the way to allow passengers to enjoy a short walk to a fine waterfall at Eldgjá. An interesting tour explores extensive lava flows around Laki, well to the west of Vatnajökull, dating from 1783–84. The bus stops three times and the driver explains about short waymarked walks that passengers can enjoy through remarkable volcanic landscapes.

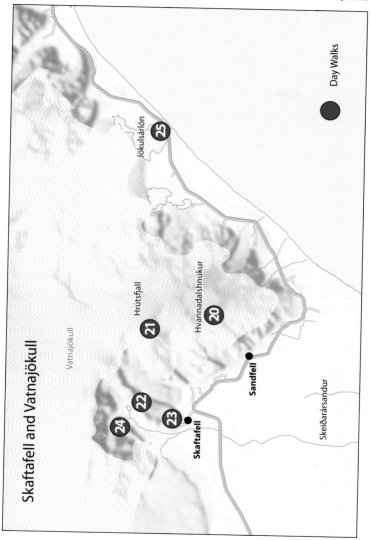

Skaftafell and Vatnajökull

Day Walks

Vatnajökull

Jökulsárlón

Hrútsfjall

Hvannadalshnúkur

Sandfell

Skaftafell

Skeiðarársandur

25

21

20

22

23

24

135

WALK 20

Sandfell and Hvannadalshnúkur

Start/Finish	Sandfell, near Skaftafell
Distance	23km (14¼ miles)
Total ascent/descent	2000m (6560ft)
Time	12hrs
Terrain	Steep, stony slopes, followed by glaciers. Start before 5am to avoid too much walking on soft, wet snow in the afternoon.
Maps	1:100,000 'Mál og Menning – 5 Skaftafell'; 1:100,000 'Ferðakort – Skaftafell'
Transport	Sterna and Reykjavík Excursions pass Sandfell between Skaftafell and Jökulsárlón, but not early enough for the ascent

Hvannadalshnúkur is the highest mountain in Iceland, on the rim of the huge Öræfajökull crater. Ascents require a minimum additional kit of ropes, ice axes, crampons and sunglasses, and previous experience of glacier walking.

There is a car park, ruined farm and graveyard at **Sandfell**, around 100m (330ft). Read a notice about the ascent of Hvannadalshnúkur, but there are no signposts or markers. Face the fellside and head left along a rugged track. Switch to a path and cross a stream, make a rising traverse and cross a smaller stream on **Sandfellsheiði**. The path zigzags up loose, dusty gravel near a slender waterfall.

Drift away from the stream, almost onto a ridge of loose, crumbling gravel. The path is clear until a cairn is reached at the edge of a bouldery, mossy slope. The summit dome is in view, although is soon lost. The path is scanty beside **Storalækjargljúfur**, so look around from time to time to be sure you can recognise the way back. ◀

When a large boulder is passed, take a good look around, as people often go astray here on the way back.

Rope up when the glacier is reached around 1000m (3280ft). Climb straight uphill, looking around to be sure of the way back. Around 1850m (6070ft), the slope eases and the ice flattens. The huge crater of **Öræfajökull** (which violently erupted in 1362) is full of ice, which creeps westwards. Small cracks become huge crevasses as an ice-fall develops, so don't aim straight for the summit, but trace a broad curve across the glacier.

The most awkward stretch is the final ascent, where the glacier pulls from the rocky rim of the crater, and the slope is criss-crossed with crevasses. (These became so wide in summer 2010 that guides stopped taking clients.) The summit dome of **Hvannadalshnúkur** varies in height as much as 10m (33ft), depending on accumulated snow and ice, but is

Hvannadalshnúkur
▲ 2110

Dyrhamar

Öræfajökull

N

0   2km

Storalækjargljúfur

Kotárjökull

Sandfellsheiði

Sandfell

Walking across the Öræfajökull towards Iceland's highest peak – Hvannadalshnúkur

137

generally quoted as 2110m (6923ft). Views stretch from the coast and campsite at Skaftafell, embracing all the mountains around Vatnajökull. If the sub-glacial volcano of Grímsvötn is active, as it was in 2011, part of the ice-cap may be black, rather than white. Retrace steps to **Sandfell**.

WALK 21
Svinafellsjökull and Hrútsfjall

Start/Finish	Svinafellsjökull, near Skaftafell
Distance	20km (13 miles)
Total ascent/descent	2000m (6560ft)
Time	11hrs
Terrain	Very steep and stony slopes, followed by glaciers. Start before 5am to avoid too much walking on soft, wet snow in the afternoon.
Maps	1:100,000 'Mál og Menning – 5 Skaftafell'; 1:100,000 'Ferðakort – Skaftafell'
Transport	Sterna and Reykjavík Excursions serve the main road between Skaftafell and Jökulsarlón, but not early enough for the ascent

Hrútsfjall is one of the highest peaks in Iceland, but is considerably shorter than neighbouring Hvannadalshnúkur. However, the ascent is rather more interesting, and includes a glacier crossing. If in doubt about your route-finding ability or glacier experience, hire a guide.

Start near the end of the dirt road to the glacier **Svinafellsjökull**. Instead of heading right to the glacier, go through a gap in a fence on the left and walk towards a steep and rugged slope, picking a way along its base. Heather, crowberry and bearberry grow among boulders, and there are grassy strips. Pass bare moraine at the snout of

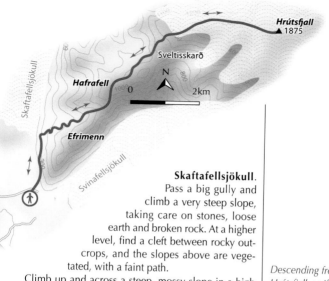

Skaftafellsjökull.
Pass a big gully and
climb a very steep slope,
taking care on stones, loose
earth and broken rock. At a higher
level, find a cleft between rocky outcrops, and the slopes above are vegetated, with a faint path.

Climb up and across a steep, mossy slope in a high
valley. Cross a number of gullies, one of which has a
stream. Aim for a gap at the head of the valley, below

*Descending from
Hrútsfjall, as if
heading for the fell of
Efrimenn*

There is a view across Svinafellsjökull to Hvannadalshnúkur.

Efrimenn, over 600m (1970ft). ◄ Turn left to follow a ridge up to a broad slope of stones and moss, and continue up another ridge on Hafrafell.

Don't climb to the summit, but head left on a falling traverse across a stony slope, following a faint path. Pass between enormous boulders, then climb, not to the gap of **Sveltisskarð**, but beside a stream on a slope of rubble and boulders, through a rocky breach. Continue up a slope of rubble to the foot of a glacier. Rope up and use ice axes and crampons to climb, hoping that crevasses above have adequate snow-bridges. There are cliffs above and below the glacier, so beware of stones from above, and don't go low as there is an ice-fall.

There are four summits on this mountain, so miss the first one and head for a gap, then continue up a ridge of snow to the top of **Hrútsfjall**, at 1875m (6152ft). Enjoy the views, taking in nearby mountains and an extensive part of Vatnajökull, then retrace steps to the bottom.

WALK 22
Skaftafell and Kristínartindar

Start/Finish	Visitor centre, Skaftafell
Distance	20km (12½ miles)
Total ascent/descent	1075m (3525ft)
Time	7hrs
Terrain	Mostly well-trodden paths; easy and wooded at the bottom, but steep, stony and rocky at the top
Maps	1:50,000 'Mál og Menning – 5 Skaftafell'; 1:25,000 'Ferðakort – Skaftafell'; national park map from the visitor centre
Transport	Sterna and Reykjavík Excursions serve Skaftafell from Reykjavík, Selfoss, Kirkjubærklaustur, Landmannalaugar and Höfn

Kristínartindar rises high above Skaftafell, flanked by the glaciers Skaftafellsjökull and Morsárjökull. It is a splendid viewpoint for the higher mountains, and signposted trails on the lower slopes allow all kinds of variations to the route.

Leave the visitor centre at **Skaftafell** and follow a broad tarmac path, not the road, through the campsite. Reach a junction, where a well-signposted gravel path climbs, making a zigzag to a junction. Turn right across the wooded slope above the campsite, going up and down, often on wooden steps. Birch scrub is lower at **Hrútagil**, and the path bends left and right, climbing steeply and stone-paved. The gradient eases as the path climbs to a junction at **Sjónarnípa**.

Keep straight ahead up a gentle slope, where low willow, flowers and grass give way to moss, crow-berry and stony patches. The peg-marked path climbs steeper, easing along a stony shoulder. The pegs make a sharp left turn, while the path climbing higher is unmarked, but well-trodden. ▶ Climb a steep, stony slope streaked with moss above **Mosvellir**. Turn right at a cairn and traverse from stony to mossy ground. Turn left up towards a rugged crag, then turn right on a rising traverse beneath it. Walk from a steep, mossy slope onto a broken rock and stones. Turn left round a corner and reach a gap over 900m (2950ft) between two peaks.

Follow the peg-marked path via Flár to omit Kristínartindar.

141

Looking across Skaftafellsjökull to Hrútsfjall on the ascent of Kristínartindar

Turn right, but note a path down to the left, used later for the descent. Zigzag up a steep and stony slope, continuing up a broken rock ridge to the top of **Kristínartindar**, which is bare rock at 1126m (3694ft). Splendid views stretch from Vatnajökull and Hvannadalshnúkur down to an immense floodplain. Descend by doubling back to the gap, then taking the other path down across scree.

Turn right to follow the peg-marked path across a mossy, grassy slope and small stream. Continue along a broad crest, rising and falling over **Nyrðrihnaukur** and **Fremrihnaukur**. After a short, steep, rugged drop, keep left of a pool surrounded by bog cotton on a broad gap. The path swings left gently down to a stream. Willow scrub develops downstream, and a footbridge spans a ditch. Dense, tall willow is followed by low, mixed scrub, then a stony crest. Bear left at a view indicator at **Sjónarsker**, and go down a stony slope to a signposted junction.

Turn right down through birch scrub to another junction, and walk ahead down a broad, stony path. At the next junction, turn right down a broad, stony track for **Sel**, and at yet another junction, turn left to pass interesting grass-roofed buildings. (If the door is open, look inside.) Walk down to a road and turn left through a car park. Turn right down a winding woodland path, with waterfall views. Flights of wooden steps reach tall pines at Lambhagi. Don't enter a car park, but turn left across footbridges to return to the **campsite** and visitor centre.

The visitor centre shows film footage of the eruption of **Grímsvötn** – a sub-glacial volcano beneath Vatnajökull. Towards the end of 1996 the volcano was particularly active, melting vast areas of the glacier, which caused devastating floods and damage to the Ring Road. At one stage the volume of water flowed at a rate second only to the mighty Amazon!

WALK 23
Skaftafell and Svartifoss

Start/Finish	Visitor centre, Skaftafell
Distance	8km (5 miles)
Total ascent/descent	300m (985ft)
Time	2hrs 30mins
Terrain	Well-signposted paths on wooded and open slopes, mostly gentle but occasionally steep
Maps	1:50,000 'Mál og Menning – 5 Skaftafell'; 1:25,000 'Ferðakort – Skaftafell'; national park map from the visitor centre
Transport	Sterna and Reykjavík Excursions serve Skaftafell from Reykjavík, Selfoss, Kirkjubærklaustur, Landmannalaugar and Höfn

Most casual walkers visiting Skaftafell follow an easy path up to Svartifoss, where a waterfall spills down a cliff of basalt columns. There are other waterfalls, as well as fine viewpoints, on this short and easy circular walk.

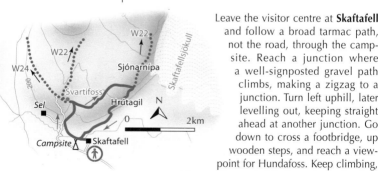

Leave the visitor centre at **Skaftafell** and follow a broad tarmac path, not the road, through the campsite. Reach a junction where a well-signposted gravel path climbs, making a zigzag to a junction. Turn left uphill, later levelling out, keeping straight ahead at another junction. Go down to cross a footbridge, up wooden steps, and reach a viewpoint for Hundafoss. Keep climbing, reaching another waterfall viewpoint and a signposted junction. Turn right up a grassy slope to a bare, stony area with a view of **Svartifoss**. Go down for a closer look, but return to the bare, stony area afterwards.

Looking down on the snout of Skaftafellsjökull on the way back down to the campsite

Follow a path signposted 'Sjónarnípa', climbing gently and crossing duckboards on wet ground. Drop to cross a footbridge above a waterfall in Eystragil, and climb to another signposted junction. ◄ Turn left up through low scrub and cross another duckboard, later dropping as marked by pegs on a gentle, stony slope. Reach **Sjónarnípa**, where Skaftafellsjökull can be seen from a steep brow, with Hrútsfjall and Hvannadalshnúkur rising beyond.

Turn right to shortcut downstream to the campsite.

Turn right and follow a peg-marked path downhill, which becomes steeper and stone-paved later, turning left and right through low birch scrub at **Hrútagil**. Continue, often on wooden steps, up and down, across a wooded slope above the campsite. Reach a junction, turn left down to the **campsite**, and left again to return to the visitor centre.

WALK 24

Skaftafell and Morsárdalur

Start/Finish	Visitor centre, Skaftafell
Distance	28km (17½ miles)
Total ascent/descent	300m (985ft)
Time	8hrs
Terrain	Well-marked paths on wooded slopes, mostly gentle, becoming unmarked and less well trodden
Maps	1:50,000 'Mál og Menning – 5 Skaftafell'; 1:25,000 'Ferðakort – Skaftafell'; national park map from the visitor centre
Transport	Sterna and Reykjavík Excursions serve Skaftafell from Reykjavík, Selfoss, Kirkjubærklaustur, Landmannalaugar and Höfn

This route visits the popular waterfall of Svartifoss, then crosses a wooded hillside to reach the broad dale of Morsárdalur. A there-and-back walk visits Kjós, getting close to colourful mountains in a remote valley.

Leave the visitor centre at **Skaftafell** and follow a broad tarmac path, not the road, through the campsite. Reach a junction where a well-signposted gravel path climbs, making a zigzag to a junction. Turn left uphill, later levelling out, keeping straight ahead at another junction. Go down to cross a footbridge, up wooden steps, and reach a viewpoint for Hundafoss. Keep climbing, reaching another waterfall viewpoint and a signposted junction. Turn right up a grassy slope to a bare, stony area with a view of **Svartifoss**. Go down to cross a footbridge, climb chunky stone steps and follow a path to a junction.

Turn right for Morsárdalur up a broad, stony path. Pass a low drystone wall and fork left as marked by pegs. The path narrows, with short duckboards, winding through willow scrub and grass. Birch becomes dominant, and the ground is rugged towards the bottom. Turn left and cross a suspension **footbridge** over the glacial Morsá. Walk straight across sand and gravel, reaching birch, willow and lupins. The peg-marked path veers left into dense birch woods, so watch for a trodden path on the right beforehand to proceed through **Morsárdalur**.

Walk across gravel and grassy areas near the edge of the dale, avoiding birch and willow scrub. There are little clumps of flowers, and damper areas feature swathes of arctic riverbeauty. Ahead, the dale is choked by masses of rubble, completely covering Morsárjökull. Turn left into a narrower dale, where there is hardly any vegetation. Fells rise steep, rocky and stony in pastel shades. Head as far into **Kjós** as you wish, then retrace steps to the suspension **footbridge**.

Don't cross the bridge, but walk downstream on gravel and black sand, following a yellow-pegged track to another

The floor of Morsárdalur is broad and stony, offering easy, but sometimes pathless walking

bridge. Cross over and follow a gravel path downstream, climbing over flood embankments, following a track on top of the second one. Drop to a car park, avoid cabins beyond and follow a dirt road and tarmac road to a car park. Cross duckboard footbridges over rivers and follow a path through woods to return to the **campsite** and visitor centre.

WALK 25
Jökulsárlón – Glacier Lagoon

Start/Finish	Café at Jökulsárlón
Distance	16km (10 miles)
Total ascent/descent	100m (330ft)
Time	4hrs
Terrain	Easy, low-level, hummocky gravel moraine, with some tracks and paths
Map	1:100,000 'Mál og Menning Atlaskort 23 – Öræfajökull'
Transport	Sterna serve Jökulsárlón from Reykjavík, Selfoss, Kirkjubæjarklaustur, Skaftafell and Höfn. Reykjavík Excursions serve Jökulsárlón from Skaftafell. For boat trips, tel 4782222, www.jokulsarlon.is.

A full circuit of the 'Glacier Lagoon' isn't possible, as the adjacent glacier, Breiðamerkurjökull, is heavily crevassed. Out-and-back shore walks are offered, with the option to take a boat trip around icebergs featured in the James Bond film *Die Another Day*. If you intend to walk one arm only, halve the distance and time accordingly.

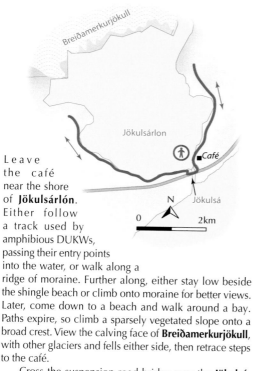

Leave the café near the shore of **Jökulsárlón**. Either follow a track used by amphibious DUKWs, passing their entry points into the water, or walk along a ridge of moraine. Further along, either stay low beside the shingle beach or climb onto moraine for better views. Later, come down to a beach and walk around a bay. Paths expire, so climb a sparsely vegetated slope onto a broad crest. View the calving face of **Breiðamerkurjökull**, with other glaciers and fells either side, then retrace steps to the café.

Cross the suspension road bridge over the **Jökulsá**. The river is short and slightly tidal. Icebergs get stuck and have to melt and break before they reach the sea. Go through a car park to the shore of **Jökulsárlón** and follow any path, either along the shore or over hummocky

149

Amphibious DUKWs weave around the icebergs, generally taking 30mins

moraine for more extensive views. Paths eventually expire at a distant bay, but walk around it and cross a floodplain. The shore leads to a point, but it is best to climb straight up a pathless slope onto a broad crest. Again, there is a view of the calving face of **Breiðamerkurjökull**, with other glaciers and fells either side. Retrace steps to the café.

4 SNÆFELL AND LÓNSÖRÆFI

The wonderfully remote Snæfellsskáli at the foot of the snow-capped Snæfell

Snæfell is an eye-catching, ice-capped fell that often pops up in view around East Iceland. The ascent of Snæfell allows walkers to see part of the remote and challenging Lónsöræfi Trail (Trek 3). Although the fell lies in a remote part of the country, access is much easier than it used to be, following the construction of a road servicing the enormous Hálslón reservoir and Kárahnjúkar hydro-electric power plant.

However, transport into this area, a remote part of the Vatnajökull National Park, needs careful planning. It takes 1½ days to travel by bus from Reykjavík to Egilsstaðir, but the approach can be speeded up considerably by flying the distance with Air Iceland. Jeeptours, www.jeeptours.is, tel 8982798, will transport groups of walkers from Egilsstaðir to Snæfellsskáli by arrangement, as there are no bus services.

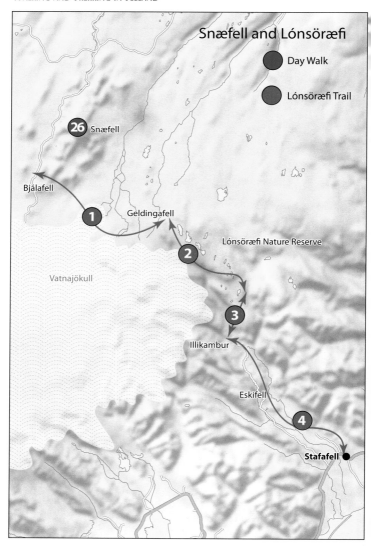

Snæfell and Lónsöræfi

Day Walk

Lónsöræfi Trail

26 Snæfell

Bjálafell

1

Geldingafell

2

Lónsöræfi Nature Reserve

Vatnajökull

3

Illikambur

Eskifell

4

Stafafell

WALK 26

Snæfellsskáli and Snæfell

Start/Finish	Snæfellsskáli
Distance	16km (10 miles)
Total ascent/descent	1050m (3445ft)
Time	6hrs
Terrain	An easy track and path are followed by steep and stony slopes, with snow and ice on the final climb to the summit
Map	1:50,000 'Mál og Menning – 6 Lónsöræfi Snæfell'
Transport	Jeeptours will transport groups from Egilsstaðir to Snæfellsskáli

Snæfell is the highest fell in Iceland that is not part of a glacier, but it has its own summit ice-cap. It is a prominent landmark throughout eastern Iceland and bears a waymarked path most of the way up its flanks.

Snæfellsskáli is a wonderfully remote Fĺ hut at almost 800m (2625ft). ▶ Leave the hut to continue along the dirt road signposted 'Eyjabakkajökull'. Cross a couple of streams and follow the track almost to a river.

Turn left up a path marked by red-tipped posts, climbing gradually as vegetation dwindles. Cross a rugged little **canyon** and climb a stony slope. The path is clear, and the slope steepens, becoming rocky. Although the peak of **Axlartindur** rises above, the path keeps well to the left, traversing a stony slope, descending a little to cross gullies, then climbing past outcrops and boulders. **Axlarjökull** lies to the left as the path reaches the ridge of Uppgönguhryggur, around 1300m (4265ft).

Turn left, without the benefit of further posts, although there are cairns. The path climbs a very steep and stony slope. When the stones suddenly change to a lighter shade the gradient eases a little. Snow and ice are reached around

If you have to walk the 12km (7½ miles) dirt road to the hut, the scenery is worth the effort.

Although many people climb without ice axe and crampons, it is best to use them.

1500m (4920ft). ◄ If there are abundant footprints all climbing the same way, they might be trusted, but keep away from steep slopes. There are a couple of false summits before the true summit of **Snæfell** is reached at 1833m (6014ft). Extensive views embrace Vatnajökull, while Herðubreið is prominent north-west. Much of eastern Iceland is in view, and the first day's terrain on the Lónsöræfi Trail (Trek 3) can be studied.

High on the slopes of Snæfell, looking towards Axlartindur and distant Vatnajökull

TREK 3
The Lónsöræfi Trail

Start	Bjálafell
Finish	Stafafell
Distance	85km (52¾ miles)
Time	4 days
Terrain	One of the more difficult trails, starting in a very remote, pathless area and including two glacier crossings and several river crossings. It becomes easier later, with waymarks and trodden paths, and finishes with a dirt-road walk.
Facilities	Basic huts
Accommodation	Huts and/or camping; hostel and campsite at Stafafell

Before planning to walk the Lónsöræfi Trail, note that this is one of the tougher, more remote treks in Iceland. It was more difficult to reach a few years ago, but reservoirs and hydro-electric power plants have been constructed and new roads serve the area. The Lónsöræfi Trail is unmarked and untrodden for half its length, so prospective trekkers must be competent navigators. The first day on the trail involves crossing glaciers – the large Eyjabakkajökull and the smaller Kverkkvislarjökull – as well as rivers. This cannot be recommended for anyone without glacier-walking and river-crossing experience. Basically, trekkers have to 'read' the terrain and take care with every step, and some maps of the trail are woefully inadequate. There are likely to be few or no other trekkers, and some of the huts are not staffed by wardens.

In the event that walkers start this trail only to realise that it is beyond their capabilities, then turn back while there is still time and retreat to Snæfellsskáli (Walk 26). In any case, it is wise to heed any advice about current conditions that the wardens at Snæfellsskáli offer, and they may ask you to leave your name and contact details before you start the trail. Beyond the halfway point, there are waymarks and trodden paths, as well as an option to finish early at Illikambur, on Stage 4.

Jeeptours will transport groups of walkers, by arrangement, from Egilsstaðir to the start of the Lónsöræfi Trail on the slopes of Bjálafell. Once committed to the trek, an early finish can be arranged with Stafafell Travel, who offer pick-ups on a dirt road at Illikambur. The final stage is long, but half of it follows a dirt road, and if necessary it can run into an extra day. Once Stafafell is reached, Sterna buses run to Egilsstaðir in one direction, and in the other direction to Höfn, where it is possible to stay overnight and continue to Reykjavík the following day.

Descending Leiðartungur to reach the glacial river of Jökulsá í Lóni (Stage 3)

STAGE 1

Bjálafell to Geldingafellsskáli

Start	Bjálafell
Finish	Geldingafellsskáli
Distance	25km (15½ miles)
Total ascent	400m (1310ft)
Total descent	480m (1575ft)
Time	10hrs
Terrain	Pathless stony slopes, glacier crossings and glacial rivers to ford. The trail is neither trodden nor marked.
Map	1:50,000 'Mál og Menning – 6 Lónsöræfi Snæfell'
Transport	Jeeptours transport groups from Egilsstaðir to Snæfellsskáli and Bjálafell
Accommodation	Basic hut at Geldingafellsskáli

The Lónsöræfi Trail starts rugged, remote and pathless, beside the Vatnajökull ice-cap. Glaciers are crossed at Eyjabakkajökull and Kverkkvíslarjökull. Some walkers start from Snæfellsskáli, which makes this a very long day.

From Snæfellsskáli there is a walk of 12km (7½ miles) along a dirt road, and finally a climb over a gap beside **Bjálafell**. Doing this invariably means having to camp before the end of this stage. Groups can be dropped by Jeeptours around 860m (2820ft) on the dirt road, where sprawling, gently sloping stony plains rise to the edge of Vatnajökull.

The initial direction to walk is roughly eastwards, gradually drifting south-east to reach the glacier **Eyjabakkajökull**. As there are no paths or markers, careful navigation is required. There is an overall slight descent, and if a small, shallow **tarn** is seen, or its dry bed is spotted, keep well to the right of it. Throughout this area, stony slopes feature a few little streams with mossy streaks alongside, and when climbing from the tarn, avoid awkward boulders. The gently sloping hill

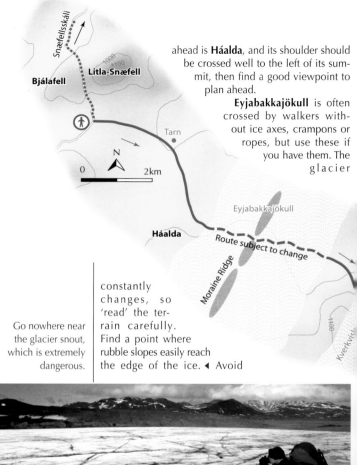

Snæfellsskáli

Bjálafell

Litla-Snæfell

1000

1100

Tarn

N

0   2km

Háalda

Eyjabakkajökull

Route subject to change

Moraine Ridge

1100

Kverkvísl

ahead is **Háalda**, and its shoulder should be crossed well to the left of its summit, then find a good viewpoint to plan ahead.

Eyjabakkajökull is often crossed by walkers without ice axes, crampons or ropes, but use these if you have them. The glacier

Go nowhere near the glacier snout, which is extremely dangerous.

constantly changes, so 'read' the terrain carefully. Find a point where rubble slopes easily reach the edge of the ice. ◄ Avoid

Admiring Eyjabakkajökull from a moraine ridge only halfway across

holes and crevasses, and when a steep-sided rubble ridge is reached in the middle of the glacier, cross using a gap. Parts of the glacier have collapsed, revealing a sub-glacial river, so keep away from any parts that look unstable. Pick a good point to leave the ice safely.

Climb up masses of moraine, crossing a couple of little streams. When a crest is reached, turn right uphill, admiring waterfalls in a rocky valley. A tongue of ice – **Kverkkvíslarjökull** – feeds into the valley and is crossed at around

1000m (3280ft), with splendid views northwards. Maintain height across stony slopes drained by small streams, and descend gradually into a broad, stony depression, dotted with boulders, well below **Kvíslarjökull**.

Ford a couple of small glacial rivers and ascend gradually on mossy and bare moraine. Ford glacial streams and cross a gap behind **Dökkafell**. Keep well right of the fell, then turn left across rock-strewn slopes to head downhill. Ford the river **Blanda** to reach the little FÍ hut, around 780m (2560ft), at **Geldingafellsskáli**. The hut is basic, with no showers, and water is from the river.

STAGE 2
Geldingafellsskáli to Egilssel

Start	Geldingafellsskáli
Finish	Egilssel
Distance	20km (12½ miles)
Total ascent	530m (1740ft)
Total descent	680m (2230ft)
Time	8hrs
Terrain	Pathless stony slopes over to a steep-sided, rugged valley. More rugged, pathless slopes to a lake.
Map	1:100,000 'Mál og Menning – 6 Lónsöræfi Snæfell'
Transport	None
Accommodation	Basic hut at Egilssel

The Lónsöræfi Trail climbs over remote and rugged terrain, passing close to the glacier Vesturdalsjökull. It is worth dropping into Vesturdalur to see a powerful waterfall, then make a rising and falling traverse to the hut at Egilssel.

Cross over the jeep track serving **Geldingafellsskál** enter a shallow valley and walk up it, keeping we above the river. The direction is roughly south-ea and height is gained on stony slopes, crossing shallov gullies. ◄ Eventually, cross a very broad and stony cres below 900m (2950ft) at **Vesturdalshraun**, where there ar hummocks and pools. Keep high and aim for the edg of **Vesturdalsjökull** to see a splendid rocky canyon an where a stream goes under the glacier.

Watch for reindeer throughout the day.

Pick a way over rock and stones to leave, an wander along a rugged brow overlooking the glacie snout, where a river surges through the rugged valley **Vesturdalur**. Look very carefully to pick a safe way dow steep slopes, avoiding rocky outcrops and gullies, ar follow the river Jökulsá í Lóni downstream on a vegetate shelf. Cross streams and climb a little, then, with litt warning, a **waterfall** plunges over a cliff into an awesom gorge, landing with explosive spray in a deep, dark canyon. ▶

Climb a steep, vegetated slope on a faint path, drifting right

Alternatively, any walkers not interested in visiting the waterfall should traverse high across the slopes.

up and across a gully. Continue up a ramp that becomes stony and bouldery, leading along a brow high above the valley. Head into a side-valley where rivers converge at waterfalls, and ford them upstream. Make a rising traverse across the stony, bouldery slopes of **Kollumúlaheiði**,

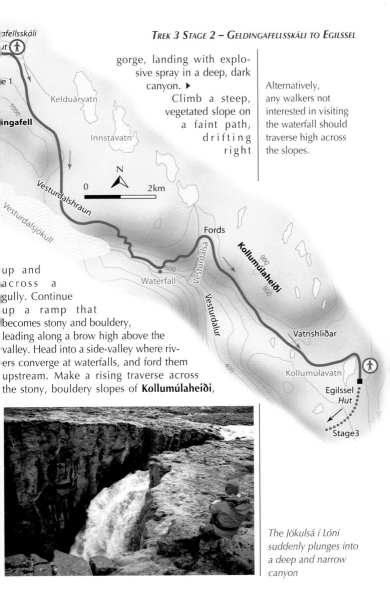

The Jökulsá í Lóni suddenly plunges into a deep and narrow canyon

161

A long and slender
waterfall is seen
across Vesturdalur.

touching 800m (2625ft), then drift gradually down-wards, looking ahead to spot small tarns in a side-valley. ◄ Swing right into the side-valley, crossing streams and rugged spurs between them, to see the large tarn of **Kollumúlavatn**. The little FÍ hut of **Egilssel** is perched on a crest above the tarn. The hut is basic, with no showers and water is from the lake or river.

STAGE 3
Egilssel to Múlaskáli

Start	Egilssel
Finish	Múlaskáli
Distance	10km (6¼ miles)
Total ascent	150m (490ft)
Total descent	580m (1900ft)
Time	4hrs
Terrain	Gentle uplands with paths and markers, then a long descent, steep and stony at times. Chain-assisted scrambling above a glacial river.
Map	1:100,000 'Mál og Menning – 6 Lónsöræfi Snæfell'
Transport	None
Accommodation	Múlaskáli hut

After two very remote and rugged days, the Lónsöræfi Trail features trodden paths and marker posts. There are dramatic viewpoints and colourful fells, and some remarkably rugged scrambles towards the end of the day.

Walk down from **Egilssel** to ford the outflow from **Kollumúlavatn**. Follow a peg-marked path along a mossy, stony crest. Climb a slope flanked by columnar cliffs that break to form curious columnar 'scree'. Walk up a stony slope with less vegetation, bouldery in places, and level out on a stony top. Either follow pegs onwards, gently down and later turning right, or turn right and climb gen-tly along the broad, stony, unmarked mossy crest. The

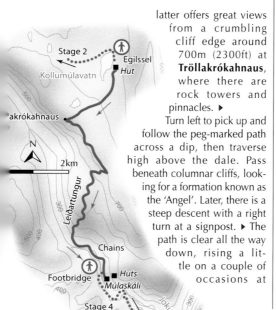

latter offers great views from a crumbling cliff edge around 700m (2300ft) at **Tröllakrókahnaus**, where there are rock towers and pinnacles. ▸

Turn left to pick up and follow the peg-marked path across a dip, then traverse high above the dale. Pass beneath columnar cliffs, looking for a formation known as the 'Angel'. Later, there is a steep descent with a right turn at a signpost. ▸ The path is clear all the way down, rising a little on a couple of occasions at

A precarious promontory viewpoint on crumbling cliffs at Tröllakrókahnaus

Even better views are available from a promontory.

Left leads down to slender waterfalls.

163

Leiðartungur, then steepening beside a gully. Pass patches of flowery heath and go down a little valley flanked by scree.

Creeping juniper and willow appear, along with bilberry, heather, crowberry and flowers. Continue down to the river **Jökulsá í Lóni**, where birch scrub becomes tall and gnarled. Cross a stream and walk through woods, then cross another stream with a broad, bouldery bed. Rise across a birch slope and cross another stream, and climb high above the river to a wall-like dyke. Use a **chain** to drop into a rocky gully between waterfalls. Climb steeply on scree, using another **chain** around a rocky edge. Zigzag down steep, loose scree to the bouldery riverbed.

Turn left downstream, linking paths on birch slopes and crossing streambeds and scree, sometimes close to the river. A rising traverse leads to a well-vegetated shelf, dropping to gates and signposts. Go into a fenced enclosure to find two huts. The lower one is the FÍ hut of **Múlaskáli**, around 200m (655ft).

STAGE 4
Múlaskáli to Stafafell

Start	Múlaskáli
Finish	Stafafell
Distance	30km (18½ miles)
Total ascent	400m (1310ft)
Total descent	580m (1900ft)
Time	10hrs
Terrain	A succession of steep ascents and descents, with sometimes steep, stony slopes. Tracks and a dirt road are easily covered.
Map	1:100,000 'Mál og Menning – 6 Lónsöræfi Snæfell'
Transport	Stafafell Travel minibus serves Illikambur from Stafafell and Höfn (tel 6996684). Sterna serve Stafafell from Höfn and Egilsstaðir.
Accommodation	Accommodation and campsite at Stafafell

This is a long day's walk – difficult at first, then becoming easier. But there are two other options. First, a minibus pick-up can be arranged at Illikambur, for an early finish. Second, the distance can be broken by using a hut at Eskifell.

Double back from Múlaskáli to the gates in the fence, and cross a suspension footbridge over the river. A rope assists on scree, then turn left downstream, high above the river. ▶ Cross a stream, followed by two broad, bouldery streambeds. A peg-marked path climbs steep, stony zigzags on a rocky ridge. The gradient eases at information boards at the end of a dirt road at **Illikambur**, around 300m (985ft). ▶

Go up and down the dirt road to a dip where there is a sheep-fold and

signpost on the left. Follow a peg-marked path rising and falling, on scree and vegetated slopes, with barely a glimpse of the river due to hummocks alongside. Pass a couple of little pools and later use zig-zag scree paths across a

Signposts indicate routes to the fells, for future visits.

Stafafell Travel minibus pick-up point.

Map continues on page 167

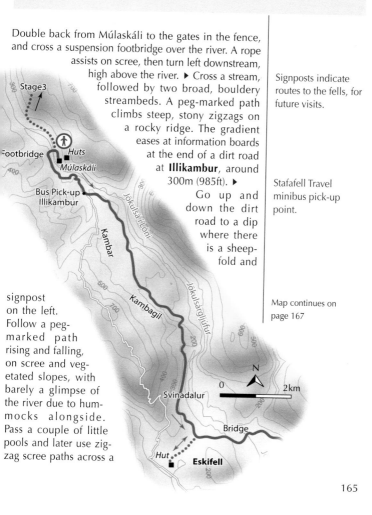

165

A hut is available off route at Eskifell, if it proves necessary to split this long day's walk

confluence of side-valleys. Climb over to another valley, which has a grassy floor, at **Kambagil**.

Walk down the valley and keep left of a bouldery stream, later switching right. Cross loose scree while passing attractive little waterfalls. Switch to the left at a confluence of valleys, but watch for the path crossing back to the right, rising, falling and rising on scree and vegetated slopes. The glacial river is seen in the gorge of **Jökulsárgljúfur**, then the path swings down into a side-valley with steep scree slopes. Climb from it and cross a little gap beyond. Keep climbing to cross another gap, then drop steeply into another valley.

Walk down through the valley and watch for markers crossing the broad floor and a stream, then climb and cross another stream. Climb on scree and follow a stony terrace, narrowing, onto scree perched above a cliff. Cross carefully and enjoy views through **Svínadalur**. Reach a signpost and drop to the left, crossing a stream and later keeping left of a small pool. Go down scree paths, past birch bushes, to a hummocky gap and signpost. ◄

Turn right to reach a hut at Eskifell, 1 km (½ mile) off route, operated by Stafafell Travel.

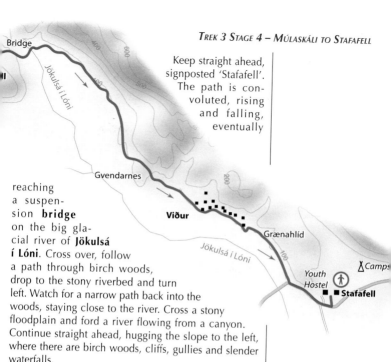

Keep straight ahead, signposted 'Stafafell'. The path is convoluted, rising and falling, eventually reaching a suspension **bridge** on the big glacial river of **Jökulsá í Lóni**. Cross over, follow a path through birch woods, drop to the stony riverbed and turn left. Watch for a narrow path back into the woods, staying close to the river. Cross a stony floodplain and ford a river flowing from a canyon. Continue straight ahead, hugging the slope to the left, where there are birch woods, cliffs, gullies and slender waterfalls.

A big, stony alluvial fan spreads from the biggest gully, and a rough, stony track runs onwards, meandering in and out of birch woods, rising and falling, and becoming easier. There are other tracks, so stay on the clearest one, rising and falling over stony, bushy hills. Cross a broad, stony riverbed where a canyon lies to the left, then climb a steep, stony, bushy slope at **Gvendarnes**. Descend through a valley with pastel shades of scree, crossing a stony plain to reach cabins at **Viður**.

The track almost reaches the river, then climbs, later running beside the river. Go up through a rock cutting, down across a bridge, then rise and fall close to the river at **Grænahlið**. Rise gently to a cattle grid and turn left along the main road to reach the church, accommodation and campsite at **Stafafell**. ▶

Stafafell Travel is based here (tel 4781717 or 4782217, **www.eldhorn.is/stafafell**).

167

5 EGILSSTAÐIR AND THE EASTFJORDS

Cairns and telegraph poles mark the way across a snow-bound Hjálmárdalsheiði (Víknaslóðir, Stage 1)

Egilsstaðir is a modern and fairly nondescript service town in East Iceland, offering access to the Eastfjords, which are well worth exploring. However, keep an eye on the weather forecast, as these fjords attract more mist, low cloud and fine drizzle than many other parts of Iceland. On clear days the Eastfjords are breathtaking, but on misty days it is best to choose walks with strong and interesting features. Fortunately, Egilsstaðir is ideally placed amid some fine waterfalls and woodlands that could be enjoyable even in wet weather. Climbing into fells, however, should be reserved for a fine day.

It takes 1½ days to travel by bus from Reykjavík to Egilsstaðir, but the approach can be speeded up considerably by flying the distance with Air Iceland. There are also buses from Akureyri and Mývatn to Egilsstaðir, for anyone already travelling through North Iceland. Alternatively, anyone arriving on the ferry from Denmark to Seyðisfjörður can literally step ashore and start walking. There are a few local bus services that aren't widely known, so check timetables at the tourist information office in Egilsstaðir or Seyðisfjörður.

Egilsstaðir and/or Seyðisfjörður are likely to be visited by walkers heading for the Víknaslóðir (Trek 4), and a number of walks are accessible from the towns. Even without transport, fine waterfalls and interesting woods can be visited from the centre of Egilsstaðir (Walk 27). Buses link Egilsstaðir and Seyðisfjörður, offering access to several waterfalls (Walk 28). A useful bus service links a waterfall walk at Hengifoss (Walk 29) with a woodland walk at Hallormsstaður (Walk 30). A bus between Egilsstaðir and Bakkagerði passes the start of a rugged walk to a jumble of massive boulders at Stórurð (Walk 31).

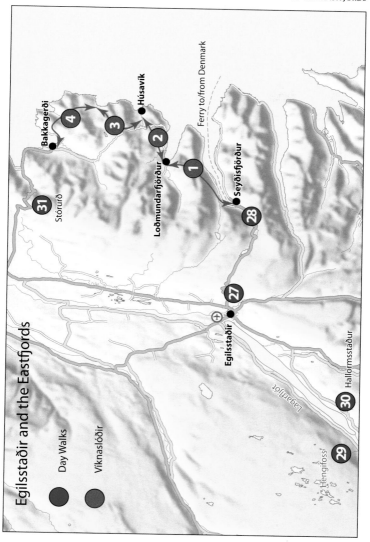

Egilsstaðir and the Eastfjords

Day Walks

Víknaslóðir

WALK 27
Egilsstaðir and Fardagafoss

Start/Finish	Tourist information office, Egilsstaðir
Distance	16km (10 miles)
Total ascent/descent	400m (1310ft)
Time	5hrs
Terrain	Roads, tracks and paths – steep and rugged near the waterfall, but gentle on lower slopes and in woods
Map	1:75,000 'Víknaslóðir – Trails of the Deserted Inlets'
Transport	Sterna serve Egilsstaðir from Höfn and Mývatn, while local buses arrive from most East Fjord villages

Two short, interesting walks from Egilsstaðir are combined here. One is a there-and-back walk to the waterfall of Fardagafoss, and the other is a short circular walk through woods on the outskirts of town.

Leave the tourist information office in **Egilsstaðir** and follow the road for Seyðisfjörður, until a bridge crosses the river of **Eyvindará**. There is a car park and access to a woodland walk at Selskógur (explored later). Cross an old road bridge next to the main road bridge, and continue up the old road, flanked by young trees and lupins. Join the main road, walk along it and turn right – not the turning for Miðhús, but the next one, marked as a dead-end.

Keep right of an electricity transformer, and go over a rise and down to a junction, where the farm of **Steinholt** lies to the right. Keep straight ahead up a grassy slope to join and follow the old gravel road, then continue up the main road from a waterfall. There are

Fardagafoss is the highest of a series of waterfalls easily reached from Egilsstaðir

two signs on the right – one for Árningasteinn, and the next for Fardagafoss at a small car park. Cross a little footbridge and climb a rugged slope. Walk up a moorland slope with low birch scrub and wet areas. Stay on the clearest path and look right to see a waterfall in a crooked gorge. The path continues climbing towards the bigger fall of **Fardagafoss**.

Either admire the waterfall from the slope or use a chain to go down a steep and rugged path to a guest-book. It is possible to climb to the waterfall, and even go behind it into a substantial cave, but expect to get wet. After exploring, retrace steps back to the road bridges and car park, and look at notice-boards explaining about woodland walks at **Selskógur**.

Walk up a tarmac path into the woods, which becomes gravel, with occasional river views. Turn right from the river, then left up a woodchip path, as if heading towards a power line. However, suddenly swing right along the woodchip path, rising and falling, but mostly rising. Avoid paths to the left, where buildings are seen, and follow a bendy path downhill to return to the car park. Retrace steps back into **Egilsstaðir**.

WALK 28
Neðri-Stafur and Seyðisfjörður

Start	Neðri-Stafur
Finish	Seyðisfjörður
Distance	8km (5 miles)
Total ascent	100m (330ft)
Total descent	520m (1705ft)
Time	2hrs 30mins
Terrain	A riverside walk, steep at times, followed by a climb onto a rugged slope and a steep descent
Map	1:75,000 'Víknaslóðir – Trails of the Deserted Inlets'
Transport	Bus service between Egilsstaðir and Seyðisfjörður (tel 4721515)

Enjoy splendid views from Neðri-Stafur, then walk down past a succession of fine waterfalls. A short climb offers a bird's-eye view of Seyðisfjörður at the end. The town becomes quite animated when the Norröna ferry arrives from Denmark.

Arrive by bus and start from a road bend and monument at **Neðri-Stafur**, where there is a splendid view downdale to Seyðisfjörður. Cross a metal footbridge over a little gorge and turn left downstream beside the **Fjardará**. There are a few waterfalls in the gorge, then watch for marker pegs, which prove useful whenever there are rock outcrops near the river. The waterfalls come in all shapes and sizes, and after a placid stretch there is a big fall at **Gufufoss**. After another placid stretch there are more falls.

Peaceful Seyðisfjörður gets very busy when the Norröna ferry arrives from Denmark

173

Pass a small dam and drift well away from the river to avoid a ravine. Later, the peg-marked path drops to the river and crosses a footbridge to reach a hydro-electric **power station**. ◄ Follow the access road away, staying close to the riverside to pass corrugated farm buildings. Join the road just below a golf club hut – **Hagavöllur** – and turn right down the road a short way.

This is the oldest operational hydro-electric power station in Iceland, built in 1913.

Turn left up a track, which becomes grassy and is fenced beside the golf course. Keep an eye on markers while climbing towards the base of a cliff, where grassy slopes are littered with fallen rocks. Cut across the slope, watching carefully for markers, as there is barely a path where the route makes a steep descent. However, pass what looks like a barrier – actually a sign bearing the name **Seyðisfjörður**. Cross a ladder-stile over a fence and follow a road into town. ◄

Full range of facilities, including a ferry to the Faroe Islands and Denmark.

WALK 29
Litlanesfoss and Hengifoss

Start/Finish	Southern end of Lagarfljót
Distance	6km (3¾ miles)
Total ascent/descent	250m (820ft)
Time	2hrs
Terrain	An ascent on a good path beside a ravine
Map	Free East Iceland map from tourist information offices
Transport	Tanni Travel buses serve Hengifoss from Egilsstaðir (tel 4761399)

This is one of the most popular short walks in eastern Iceland, visiting two waterfalls. The aim is to climb to Hengifoss, but don't neglect Litlanesfoss on the way. Hengifoss falls 118m (387ft). It is the longest waterfall in this guidebook and the third longest in Iceland.

Hengifoss is the third longest waterfall in Iceland, at 118m (387ft)

Start at the southern end of **Lagarfljót**, where the lake is heavily silted. There is a car park with toilets and map-boards. Go through a gate and climb over 50 wooden steps. Continue up a clear path through another gate, catching a glimpse of a waterfall spilling into a ravine. Further uphill are two paths – one near the ravine, where you cannot afford to slip, and one set back at a safe distance. Cross a footbridge over a little stream and enjoy views of **Litlanesfoss**, which is flanked by attractive basalt columns.

Walk up through another gate, cross a footbridge over a stream and climb a bouldery slope. Go down to a notice-board above a narrow gorge and follow a path upstream, crossing a little stream with a dainty waterfall. Stony and grassy areas reach an abrupt end at a guestbook, where **Hengifoss** is seen pouring into a rocky amphitheatre. Enjoy the spectacle and retrace steps to the car park.

WALK 30
Hallormsstaðaskógur

Start/Finish	Hallormsstaður
Distance	8km (5 miles)
Total ascent/descent	250m (820ft)
Time	2hrs 30mins
Terrain	Woodland tracks and paths, with colour-coded markers
Map	1:25,000 'Hallormsstaðaskógur Gönguleiðir' – free map from tourist offices
Transport	Tanni Travel buses serve Hallormsstaður from Egilsstaðir (tel 4761399)

Forests of tall trees are rare in Iceland, and Hallormsstaðaskógur is well worth exploring, using colour-coded trails. A variety of tree species from around the world thrive on the slopes rising from Lagarfljót.

A little Shell filling station stands beside the road at **Hallormsstaður**, where a road is signposted 'Hótel Hallormsstaður' and 'Hússtjórnarskóli'. Turn left at a junction marked by a boulder for the latter and reach a car park. This walk combines trails marked blue and green into a single circuit. Climb steeply among birch, rowan and conifers, and fork left as marked blue. Later, beneath a power line, avoid a footpath sign pointing left and stay on the undulating track, which is bendy as it descends, with masses of angelica in open spaces between trees.

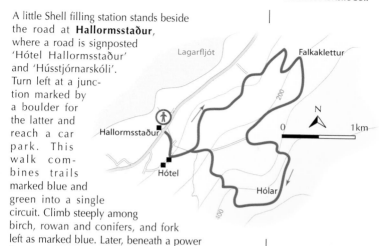

Turn right at a junction, as marked blue, up a grassy track, passing a clearing where tall grass is tangled with vetch. The track levels out, and some trees are labelled with their species and country of origin. Turn right at a junction, left at a higher junction, then right at an even higher one. There is a view of Lagarfljót from the rocky brow of **Falkaklettur**. Climb a stony track, which eases as a rutted grass or earth track, and

Well-marked paths wander through wonderfully mixed woodland at Hallormsstaður

177

walk ahead, as marked blue, until a junction with other colours is reached. ◄ Turn left up a grassy track marked green and orange. The trees thin, and grassy, flowery spaces develop. The orange trail runs ahead towards cliffs, so turn right along the green trail, which is a vague grassy path at **Hólar**.

Wander around boulder-studded mounds beneath cliffs, past trees and dwarf birch, through grass, bilberry and crowberry. Pass a muddy hollow and the path runs downhill. Cross a level grassy area to reach a ridge of broken rock, where there is a view of buildings below. Turn right, winding, rising and falling among trees. Turn left down a winding, vegetated track and left down a clearer track. When two tracks head right, go down the second one, the least grassy, which is marked with three-coloured posts, returning to the car park and exit road.

Turn right here for a shortcut downhill.

WALK 31
Vatnsskarð and Stórurð

Start/Finish	Vatnsskarð
Distance	20km (12½ miles)
Total ascent/descent	480m (1575ft)
Time	7hrs
Terrain	Marked paths cross the fells, descending to a mass of boulders. An easy valley walk returns to a dirt road, leading back to the start.
Map	1:75,000 'Víknaslóðir – Trails of the Deserted Inlets'
Transport	Weekday bus links Egilsstaðir with Vatnsskarð and Borgarfjörður (tel 8948305)

This popular circuit starts on the pass of Vatnsskarð, follows an upland crest and drops to Stórurð. Here an amazing jumble of monstrous boulders can be explored using a circular path, then another route returns to Vatnsskarð.

Start at the top of **Vatnsskarð**, where there is an emergency shelter around 430m (1410ft). Across the dirt road is a signpost for Stórurð and a map-board. The path has marker pegs and climbs a steep, stony, mossy slope, becoming gentler, and reaches the top of **Geldingafjall** at 634m (2080ft). Views stretch west across an enormous flood-plain with snaking rivers.

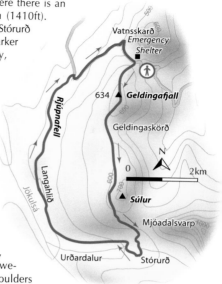

Go down to a gap at **Geldingaskörð** and continue beside a hummocky, stony crest. Keep right of **Súlur**, passing a rock with a yellow 'T' on it. Walk ahead and down to a path junction at **Mjóadalsvarp**, at 558m (1831ft). Turn right down a steep path overlooking the massive boulder-jam at Stórurð, and marvel at the Dyrfjöll and awesome 'U'-shaped gap where the boulders originated.

One of the scenic little tarns in the chaotic boulder-jam of Stórurð

A junction of peg-marked paths has signs reading – (left) 'Efri leið um urð Hólaland' and (right) 'Neðri leið um urð Ósfjall'. Go upstream and cross the little glacial river to follow pegs across level moss. An interesting circuit around Stórurð passes boulders and a boulder-bound tarn. Keep right at a junction and cross a rounded moraine to see a stream erupting from boulders. Cross over to another tarn, which has a cave on its far side. Cross a level lawn, passing a guest book, and watch for pegs while crossing a river erupting from boulders. Reach another junction, turning left as marked for Ósfjall.

A small cave beneath monstrous boulders beside a small tarn at Stórurð

The grassy slopes are like a lawn, with few rocks, so the way down through **Urðardalur** is easy. Follow the markers, keeping well away from the river, crossing small streams and possibly fording a larger one. There is a slight ascent onto a shelf at **Langahlíð**, then continue gradually downhill below the crest of **Rjúpnafell**. Cross a stream and climb to a parking space at a bend on a dirt road, where a signpost points back for Stórurð. Turn right and walk up the dirt road back to **Vatnsskarð**.

TREK 4
The Víknaslóðir

Start	Seyðisfjörður
Finish	Borgarfjörður
Distance	74km (46 miles)
Time	4 days
Terrain	Mostly easy and largely along dirt roads, but there are some steep and vague paths at the start and finish that need more care
Facilities	Shops, restaurants and guest houses at Seyðisfjörður and Borgarfjörður; huts in between
Accommodation	Hostels and guesthouses at Seyðisfjörður and Borgarfjörður; huts and/or camping in between

This four-day hut-to-hut trail is mostly easy going and would appeal to those walkers who want to attempt a trek without having to get into very remote country.

'Víknaslóðir' isn't the name of a designated trail, but is taken from a local map title and means 'trails of the deserted inlets'. A series of three huts at the head of three formerly inhabited inlets are connected by dirt roads that are easy to follow on foot. Starting from the ferryport village of Seyðisfjörður, a narrow path is followed over the fells to the first hut at Loðmundarfjörður. From there, the easy dirt roads lead through gaps in the fells to huts at Húsavík and Breiðavík over the next two days. The fourth and final day's walk leads along narrow paths through the fells to reach Borgarfjörður and the village of Bakkagerði.

Transport is better in the Eastfjords than most visitors realise. Although it takes 1½ days to travel by bus from Reykjavík to Egilsstaðir, the approach can be speeded up considerably by flying the distance with Air Iceland. The start and finish of the trail can be reached using local buses between Egilsstaðir and Seyðisfjörður, and between Bakkagerði and Egilsstaðir. Anyone arriving on the ferry from Denmark to Seyðisfjörður can literally step ashore and start walking the trail immediately.

STAGE 1
Seyðisfjörður to Loðmundarfjörður

Start	Seyðisfjörður
Finish	Loðmundarfjörður
Distance	23km (14¼ miles)
Total ascent/descent	650m (2130ft)
Time	9hrs
Terrain	Easy road-walking, followed by a steep and rugged climb. A river needs fording on the descent, and the walk is easy at the end.
Map	1:75,000 'Víknaslóðir – Trails of the Deserted Inlets'
Transport	Bus service between Egilsstaðir and Seyðisfjörður (tel 4721515)
Accommodation	Hut at Loðmundarfjörður

The first day on this trail follows a dirt road from Seyðisfjörður, alongside the fjord of the same name. A high crest is crossed and the route descends to another fjord, Loðmundarfjörður. Scattered buildings include farms, a hut and a church.

Leave **Seyðisfjörður** in the direction of the youth hostel, up a tarmac road and down a dirt road. The dirt road climbs past a junction for Vestdalur. Continue along the coastal road past a few ruins, crossing a bridge over the **Vestdalsá**. ◄ Pass a boarded-up building, go up the road and pass farm buildings at **Dvergasteinn** and **Sunnuholt**, where there are many abandoned vehicles.

Look upstream to see waterfalls.

Either follow the dirt road up to a small notice on the left or fork left up a grassy track, passing above the notice, then turn left. Look for orange marker pegs, head towards a little waterfall, then swing right. Mixed vegetation gives way to birch scrub on **Skógarhjalli**. Climb and cross a stream, then cross a stony slope with views of the fjord. The rising traverse later goes up a grassy shelf between steep slopes. Climb and swing left into **Kolsstaðadalur**. Keep left of a stream and its waterfalls, climbing steep and rocky ground. A big, single-leap waterfall is seen ahead, and the stream has to be forded below it.

Follow the path carefully to reach the high brow above. Watch for marker pegs and old cairns with wooden posts in them. A cairn on the highest part of the route, around 600m (1970ft) on **Hjálmárdalsheiði**, contains a guestbook. Head gradually downhill from cairn to cairn, past a cairn holding down bales of cable. There is a view down to Loðmundarfjörður, and a line of old telegraph poles heads straight down **Hjálmárdalur**.

The poles lead down to a river, but don't follow them across. Stay on the right-hand side and the poles later cross back. Continue down the path and pass waterfalls, then

The inlet of Loðmundarfjörður is seen on the descent from Hjálmárdalsheiði

The grassland is used by nesting eider in spring, and their down is harvested.

ford the river as marked, near where the poles cross. There is more vegetation, and the path stays well above the river. Both the path and the poles drift left, dropping down a rugged slope to the head of the fjord. Reach sand, shingle and driftwood, with fenced-off grassland beyond. ◄

Walk towards the farm at **Sævarendi** and cross a couple of little footbridges beyond, then cross a bridge over the **Fjarðará**. Turn left along a dirt road and cross a bridge over another river. Later, turn right for the FÍ hut at **Loðmundarfjörður**, which has showers, or cross a footbridge to visit a diminutive church first.

Start	Loðmundarfjörður
Finish	Húsavík
Distance	15km (9½ miles); extension to Húsavík church adds 8km (5 miles)
Total ascent	500m (1640ft)
Total descent	400m (1310ft)
Time	5hrs; extension to Húsavík church adds 2hrs 30mins
Terrain	Clear and obvious dirt roads crossing a pass between fells
Maps	1:75,000 'Víknaslóðir – Trails of the Deserted Inlets'
Transport	None
Accommodation	Hut at Húsavík

This day's walk is simply a matter of following dirt roads alongside the fjord and over a pass. It is likely to be completed quickly, so an extension is suggested to a little church beside a rugged bay at Húsavík.

Leave the hut at **Loðmundarfjörður** and walk back along the track, reaching a cross-roads and small map-board near **Sævarendi**. Turn left to follow a stony dirt road up to a junction, where the farm of **Stakkahlíð** lies to the left. Turn right and follow the track high above the fjord, later crossing a wooden bridge over the **Hrauná**, with its fine waterfalls. Cross over to the next river, which is culverted, then two other streams have to be jumped or forded.

Map continues on page 186

The dirt road climbs higher, crossing two culverted streams which run to the summer house of **Nes**.

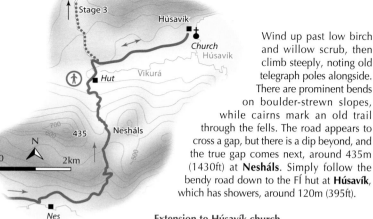

Wind up past low birch and willow scrub, then climb steeply, noting old telegraph poles alongside. There are prominent bends on boulder-strewn slopes, while cairns mark an old trail through the fells. The road appears to cross a gap, but there is a dip beyond, and the true gap comes next, around 435m (1430ft) at **Nesháls**. Simply follow the bendy road down to the FÍ hut at **Húsavík**, which has showers, around 120m (395ft).

Extension to Húsavík church

Walk down the dirt road from the hut and cross a wooden bridge over a cascade. Climb past a fine waterfall, then the road bends right to a junction. Follow a track straight ahead gently downhill, fording a small river. The track rises and falls, crossing another stream, then climbs and becomes grassy as it reaches a couple of buildings and small **church** at Húsavík. The rugged bay is worth exploring before retracing steps to the hut.

A waterfall on the Hrauná, seen while following a dirt road from hut to hut

Start	Húsavík
Finish	Breiðavík
Distance	15km (9½ miles)
Total ascent	400m (1310ft)
Total descent	500m (1640ft)
Time	5hrs 30mins
Terrain	Clear and obvious dirt road crossing a pass between fells, then a more rugged track through a dale
Maps	1:75,000 'Víknaslóðir – Trails of the Deserted Inlets'
Transport	None
Accommodation	Hut at Breiðavík

A dirt road is followed from dale to dale, over a pass between fells. Its continuation leads straight for Borgarfjörður for a quick exit, but this route follows a more rugged track to a hut near the sea at Breiðavík.

Walk down the dirt road from the Húsavík hut and cross a wooden bridge over a cascade. Climb past a fine

Evening view of Sólarfjall, near the coast, from the hut at Breiðavík

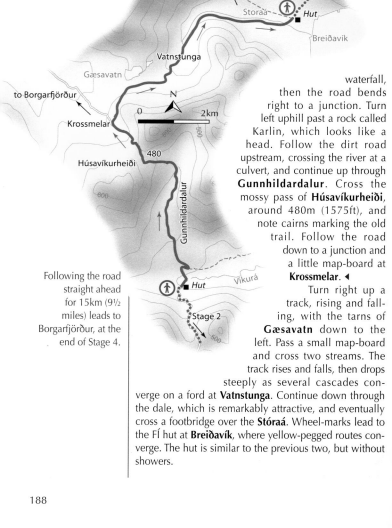

waterfall, then the road bends right to a junction. Turn left uphill past a rock called Karlin, which looks like a head. Follow the dirt road upstream, crossing the river at a culvert, and continue up through **Gunnhildardalur**. Cross the mossy pass of **Húsavíkurheiði**, around 480m (1575ft), and note cairns marking the old trail. Follow the road down to a junction and a little map-board at **Krossmelar**. ◄

Turn right up a track, rising and falling, with the tarns of **Gæsavatn** down to the left. Pass a small map-board and cross two streams. The track rises and falls, then drops steeply as several cascades converge on a ford at **Vatnstunga**. Continue down through the dale, which is remarkably attractive, and eventually cross a footbridge over the **Stóraá**. Wheel-marks lead to the FÍ hut at **Breiðavík**, where yellow-pegged routes converge. The hut is similar to the previous two, but without showers.

Following the road straight ahead for 15km (9½ miles) leads to Borgarfjörður, at the end of Stage 4.

Start	Breiðavík
Finish	Bakkagerði, Borgarfjörður
Distance	21km (13 miles)
Total ascent/descent	800m (2625ft)
Time	8hrs
Terrain	Mostly clear paths over gaps in the fells, but sometimes vague. One river to ford in the middle. Road-walking at the end.
Map	1:75,000 'Víknaslóðir – Trails of the Deserted Inlets'
Transport	Weekday bus links Borgarfjörður and Egilsstaðir (tel 8948305)
Accommodation	Bakkagerði

After easy walking along dirt roads on previous days, the route follows less obvious paths through the high fells. Bear in mind that there is also a rugged, high-level dirt road leading more directly to Borgarfjörður over the pass of Gagnheiði, which could be used as a bad-weather alternative.

Cross a footbridge over a little river beside the hut at **Breiðavík** and follow yellow marker pegs uphill. The

Footbridge and huts at Breiðavík, with the misty fells of Gagnheiði beyond

189

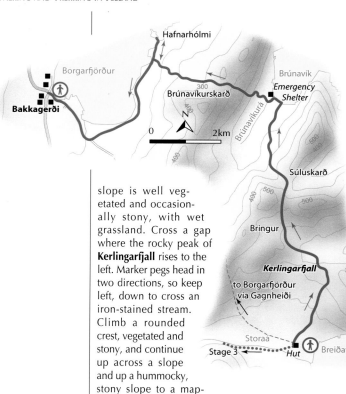

slope is well vegetated and occasionally stony, with wet grassland. Cross a gap where the rocky peak of **Kerlingarfjall** rises to the left. Marker pegs head in two directions, so keep left, down to cross an iron-stained stream. Climb a rounded crest, vegetated and stony, and continue up across a slope and up a hummocky, stony slope to a map-board at **Bringur**.

Marker pegs head in four directions, each of them named – follow those climbing straight ahead, marked for Súluskarð. A broad gap, over 400m (1310ft), has a slight hump in the middle, which the path crosses. Walk downhill and keep left across scree to reach the gap of **Súluskarð**. Markers head two ways, so turn left, down across a vegetated slope. When a couple of little streams are crossed, a footbridge can be seen far below, spanning **Brúnavíkurá**. ◄ Follow the marked path onwards, rising to cross a stream, then avoid other paths. Cross stony

This footbridge could be used to avoid a ford later.

Little waterfalls are seen on the climb from Brúnavík to Brúnavíkurskarð

hummocks and drop to a beach at **Brúnavík**. Turn left and ford a river to reach an emergency shelter.

Climb above the hut, keep left of some ruins, cross a stream and zigzag up past attractive waterfalls. Traverse left, then the path is wet in places as it winds uphill. Pass a cairn on the gap of **Brúnavíkurskarð**, over 350m (1150ft), between tall and small rocky peaks. Wind downhill and don't cross a stream, but later cross a smaller one. Walk down to a ladder-stile and cross a fence to reach a car park. ▶

Turn left to follow the road over a rise, then down and around the head of **Borgarfjörður** to reach the village of **Bakkagerði**. ▶

Turning right here leads to a harbour, Hafnarhólmi, and a popular viewpoint for puffins.

Accommodation, shop, restaurants and buses to Egilsstaðir.

191

6 JÖKULSÁRGLJÚFUR

The red slopes of Rauðhólar, seen from the lower summit bearing a tuft of grass (Walk 33)

The small Jökulsárgljúfur National Park, established in north-east Iceland in 1978, merged with the enormous Vatnajökull National Park in 2008. The centrepiece of this area is the torrential, murky glacial river of Jökulsá á Fjöllum, with its powerful waterfalls – Selfoss, Dettifoss, Hafragilsfoss and Réttarfoss. Naturally, the focus of all walks in this area is on the river and its nearby cliffs and canyons. Generally, the slopes are gentle, and any steep ascents and descents are short-lived. Waymarking and signposting is good, and the river provides a natural guide. Three easy and interesting walks are offered, at Ásbyrgi (Walk 32), Vesturdalur (Walk 33) and Dettifoss (Walk 34). If you are prepared to walk and camp, then consider the two-day trek downstream, following the Jökulsárhlaup (Trek 5).

There is good access to Jökulsárgljúfur by bus, though it would take 1½ days to reach this area from Reykjavík. Buses serve Ásbyrgi, Vesturdalur and Dettifoss from the major town of Akureyri and the smaller settlements of Húsavík and Reykjahlíð (Mývatn). If travelling from Reykjavík, it is possible to fly to Akureyri with Air Iceland before switching to buses. Take very careful note of the times buses serve various places if intending to commute to Jökulsárgljúfur on a daily basis, or play safe and stay on one of the campsites.

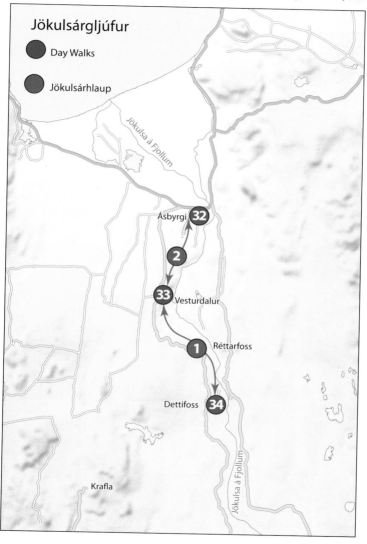

WALK 32
Ásbyrgi and Áshöfði

Start/Finish	Visitor centre, Ásbyrgi
Distance	8km (5 miles)
Total ascent/descent	100m (330ft)
Time	2hrs 30mins
Terrain	Rough and rocky moorland, wooded in places, with some short, steep climbs
Maps	1:50,000 'Mál og Menning – 8 Akureyri Mývatn Dettifoss'; 1:50,000 'Jökulsárgljúfur', from the national park visitor centre
Transport	SBA Norðurleið buses serve Ásbyrgi from Akureyri, Mývatn and Húsavík

A waymarked trail, the Áshöfðahringur, makes a circuit around the fell of Áshöfði. The route crosses rugged moorland, enjoys views of Jökulsá á Fjöllum in a canyon, and passes a wooded tarn towards the end.

Start at the visitor centre at **Ásbyrgi**, following a path signposted 'Tófugjá', marked with yellow pegs across a golf course. Continue through rough grass and willow scrub along the base of cliffs, reaching a signpost at **Tófugjá**. ◄ Turn left up about 50 wooden steps and an eight-rung ladder, then scramble with the aid of two ropes, climbing a metal staircase with 16 steps to a cliff-top.

This can be reached from a roadside map-board at a corner of the nearby campsite.

Turn right past dense birch to a signpost, turning left to rise gently through woods. There is a large hayfield to the left, then cross a rugged horse-riding trail. Keep straight

Tent pitched on the campsite at Ásbyrgi

ahead, cross another hayfield, then rise and fall over rugged ground, passing bushes and lush vegetation. Reach a signpost and small map-board at **Gilsbakki** and turn left. Follow the edge of a curved, partly wooded valley, drop into it and climb the other side, continuing through woods.

A sudden view of a canyon reveals the grey, glacial **Jökulsá á Fjöllum**. Follow a level heathery shelf, keeping straight ahead at a signposted junction. ◄ Walk down through patchy woods, past rocks, with views of a white suspension bridge and small tarn. The path passes the tarn, then drifts left from the bridge through woods. Reach a three-way signpost and small map-board, keep right to walk down through the woods, and go left at a fork to reach **Ástjörn**.

Go left here for a short detour to the 143m (469ft) summit of Áshöfði.

Follow the wooded shore path, with duckboards across wet areas, and cross a step-stile over a fence. The path runs parallel to a road, reaching the access track for the farm of **Ás**. Either head straight for a filling station, where there is a shop and café, or turn left along the track, right down steps, and head back to the visitor centre at **Ásbyrgi**.

WALK 33
Svinadalur and Rauðhólar

Start/Finish	Vesturdalur
Distance	13km (8 miles)
Total ascent/descent	200m (655ft)
Time	4hrs
Terrain	Tracks and paths, waymarked and well-trodden, across rugged moorland, through woods, then rising and falling on rocky slopes
Maps	1:50,000 'Mál og Menning – 8 Akureyri Mývatn Dettifoss'; 1:50,000 Jökulsárgljúfur, from the national park visitor centre
Transport	SBA Norðurleið buses serve Vesturdalur from Akureyri, Mývatn, Húsavík, Ásbyrgi and Dettifoss

Two short circular walks from Vesturdalur are combined here. The first is quiet, while the second is popular, rugged and scenic. Both walks link with the Jökulsárhlaup, which follows the glacial river Jökulsá á Fjöllum downstream.

Start from the information office at the **Vesturdalur** campsite. Follow a track barred to vehicles, signposted 'Svinadalur', passing overhanging cliffs at **Eyjan**. ▶ A narrow path marked by yellow pegs heads right past bushes, rejoining the track later to cross a rise. The path then heads left of the track, climbing near a waterfall, along a boardwalk and past a little rock tower. Walk up broad moorland dotted with pools to rejoin the track. When the track splits, keep left, but look right at the ruined farmstead of **Svinadalur**. The track leads down to a sign, where a left turn leads to **Kallbjarg**. At this point follow Trek 5 Stage 1 to a car park at Vesturdalur, then Trek 5 Stage 2 towards Rauðhólar.

This fell makes a worthwhile objective for a separate short walk.

When a path junction is reached, where Ásbyrgi is straight ahead and red ash slopes rise right, turn right. Although there is a path up an ash crest towards the 220m (720ft) summit of **Rauðhólar**, this is closed due to erosion. Double back along the crest to a lower summit, which has a tuft of grass. Walk down a steep ash path as if for the river, past a rocky hump. Go further down, using wooden steps past a rugged crater, and go down a short ladder.

Wander past lumpy rock towers, catching a glimpse of the river. Pass the bulging buttocks of a big rock tower and go down stone steps to a junction. Keep left, down more stone steps, and note the big cave of **Kirkjan** to the right, which is worth inspecting. Continue along the path, rising and falling, following markers and keeping out of roped-off areas around **Hljóðaklettar**.

A large cave called Kirkjan, beneath an arch formed from basalt columns

There is some scrambling required while marvelling at rock formations – especially basalt columns. Pass a rock tower near the river and continue as if returning to the car park. However, before that point, take a peg-marked path that heads right into woods, avoiding the dirt road, and leads through the campsite at **Vesturdalur**.

WALK 34
Selfoss and Dettifoss

Start/Finish	Dettifoss car park
Distance	6km (3¾ miles)
Total ascent/descent	80m (260ft)
Time	2hrs
Terrain	Mostly easy paths, with some scrambling. It is wet and slippery near the waterfalls.
Maps	1:50,000 'Mál og Menning – 8 Akureyri Mývatn Dettifoss'; 1:50,000 'Jökulsárgljúfur', from the national park visitor centre
Transport	SBA Norðurleið buses serve Dettifoss from Akureyri, Mývatn, Húsavík, Vesturdalur and Ásbyrgi

This simple circular walk links the powerful waterfalls of Selfoss and Dettifoss, exploring away from the river afterwards. Dettifoss is incredibly powerful and very popular, but other paths are quiet, crossing desert-like areas.

Leave the car park on a broad, clear, obvious path, generally running downhill. Turn right along a sandy path and walk upstream beside the **Jökulsá á Fjöllum**. Crowberry and willow grow on the right, with a cliff dropping into the river on the left, and the powerful waterfall of **Selfoss** ahead, where water pours over columnar cliffs from both sides of a gorge.

Walk downstream, following the cliff edge to a viewpoint for the powerful and noisy **Dettifoss**. A metal stairway drops to lower paths, which are always wet, and the spray is like rain, but carries grains of sand and mud. The longer you stay, the wetter and dirtier you

The murky waterfall of Dettifoss completely dwarfs visitors at a viewpoint

Selfoss pours from both sides of a rocky gorge, only a short walk upstream from Dettifoss

People on the other side of the fall are 70km (45 miles) away by road!

get! With the sun in the right direction, rainbows play among huge plumes of spray. Climb back up the metal stairway to the upper path, turn right and expect to get sprayed even while walking high above the river. ◄

The path climbs and follows the edge of a rocky plateau above a canyon. Cross wet and vegetated ground which dries to become barren and rocky, with sandy and stony paths. Follow yellow pegs, which lead down into a dry side-valley flanked by rock walls at **Sanddalur**, reaching a map-board. Turn left, signposted 'Vesturdalur', climbing steeply and scrambling up chunky rock-steps. Follow a level, easy path along a broad terrace of willow and crowberry, then climb more chunky rock-steps. There is another rugged terrace, then more climbing onto a bleak plateau. Follow pegs straight ahead, and turn left when another set of pegs is seen. Pass a secluded 'walkers only' camping area to return to the car park.

TREK 5

The Jökulsárhlaup

Start	Dettifoss
Finish	Ásbyrgi
Distance	34km (21 miles)
Time	2 days
Terrain	Easy going, following reasonably clear and gentle paths parallel to the river, only rarely rising and falling for short distances. Water is sometimes left in a large container near Dettifoss for campers, but is not guaranteed, so take supplies.
Facilities	Shop at Ásbyrgi
Accommodation	Very basic campsite near Dettifoss, for walkers only. Campsites at Vesturdalur and Ásbyrgi.

'The Jökulsárhlaup' is actually the name of an annual marathon event from Dettifoss to Ásbyrgi, which some runners complete in less than 2½ hours. The route offers walkers a simple two-day trek downstream beside the glacial river Jökulsá á Fjöllum. Given that most of the paths are gentle, and the signposting and waymarking is good, it makes an ideal introduction to easy backpacking in Iceland.

There are campsites along the trail, but note that the one near Dettifoss is very basic, with no guaranteed water supply, and it is for walkers only. Motorists are expected to drive to one of the other campsites – at Vesturdalur or Ásbyrgi. These have more facilities, including toilets and showers.

Access to this short trek is exactly the same as described in the introduction to Section 6. It is worth having the times of local bus services to hand, so that anyone attempting this as their first-ever trek is aware of options to bail out if it proves difficult. Parts of the route can be sampled in advance by walking Walks 32, 33 and 34.

The Jökulsá á Fjöllum becomes constricted at Katlar, below Hólmatungur

Start	Dettifoss car park
Finish	Vesturdalur
Distance	20km (12½ miles)
Total ascent	150m (490ft)
Total descent	350m (1150ft)
Time	6hrs 30mins
Terrain	Mostly easy, well-marked paths, with little ascent or descent. Most streams have footbridges, but one river has to be forded.
Maps	1:50,000 'Mál og Menning – 8 Akureyri Mývatn Dettifoss'; 1:50,000 'Jökulsárgljúfur', from the national park visitor centre
Transport	SBA Norðurleið buses serve Dettifoss and Vesturdalur from Akureyri, Mývatn, Húsavík and Ásbyrgi
Accommodation	Campsite at Dettifoss (no facilities and may lack water)

The walk downstream from Dettifoss, beside the canyon of Jökulsá á Fjöllum, is fairly easy. There are views of splendid waterfalls, and the initial barren landscape gradually becomes wooded before Vesturdalur.

Buses reach Dettifoss in the middle of the day. ▶ Leave the car park on a broad, clear, obvious path, generally running down to a viewpoint for the powerful and noisy **Dettifoss**. A metal stairway drops to lower paths, which are always wet. Climb back up the metal stairway to the upper path, turn right and expect to get sprayed even while walking high above the river.

The path climbs and follows the edge of a rocky plateau above a canyon. Cross wet and vegetated ground which dries to become barren and rocky, with sandy and stony paths. Follow yellow pegs, which lead down into a dry side-valley flanked by rock walls at

Walkers either hurry downstream or use a basic campsite nearby, enjoy Walk 34, then walk to Vesturdalur the following day.

Alternative route
Turn right for a steep, rocky descent, a precarious riverside path to Hafragilsfoss, and a steep and rugged climb to the main route beyond.

The very rugged alternative route rejoins here.

Sanddalur, reaching a map-board. ◄ Turn left, sign-posted 'Vesturdalur', then climb steeply and scramble up chunky rock-steps. Follow a level, easy path along a broad terrace of willow and crowberry, then climb more chunky rock-steps. There is another rugged terrace, then more climbing onto a bleak plateau. Follow pegs straight ahead, pass a map-board and cross a track.

Stony ground leads to the head of a narrow canyon. Climb, turn right and walk along the rim, reaching a map-board high above **Hafragilsfoss**. ◄ Continue along the main canyon rim, across vegetated and rocky areas. Later, the path drifts away from the river, overlooking **Réttarfoss** and turbulent channels. Reach a car park at **Hólmatungur** and go down past tall, dense birch and willow, crossing a footbridge over a stream. Keep ahead at one junction and stop at the next. ◄ Keep left to continue, and the river

Turning right leads to a rugged area near the river at Katlar, for a short, circular walk.

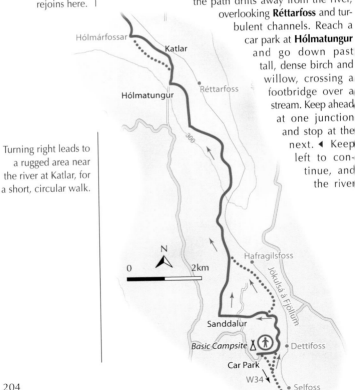

204

*The twin rock towers
of Karl og Kerling
stand beside the river*

is flanked by rubble, rather than cliffs, with plenty of heather.

Climb a well-vege-
tated slope, keeping
right to cross two
broad, wooden
bridges near a con-
fluence of cascades
at **Hólmárfossar**.
Walk down past tall
birch trees, down
steps beside a water-
fall, and continue
along a sandy path
with a river on the left.
Watch for basalt columns
that have fallen to form
curious columnar 'scree'.
Marker pegs indicate a ford
through the river, then climb past

lumpy outcrops. A signpost for **Gloppa** reveals a cave beneath one outcrop. Further along, cross two streams using footbridges, and the path continues to a signposted junction. ◄

Walk 33 joins here.

Kallbjarg lies just to the right – a cliff-top viewpoint – otherwise keep ahead and downhill to cross duckboards over wet ground. Wander through birch scrub, bilberry and heather to reach another signpost. ◄ Keep ahead, and when the path splits, left is easy while right enjoys river views. Either way, a broad path leads to a car park and map-board. Turn left up a dirt road to find a campsite at **Vesturdalur** and, further up, a small information office.

Turning right offers a view of two rock pillars by the river – Karl og Kerling.

STAGE 2
Vesturdalur to Ásbyrgi

Start	Vesturdalur
Finish	Ásbyrgi
Distance	14km (8½ miles)
Total ascent	100m (330ft)
Total descent	150m (490ft)
Time	5hrs
Terrain	Mostly easy paths, but with rugged ground alongside. At the end there is a steep, rocky descent.
Maps	1:50,000 'Mál og Menning – 8 Akureyri Mývatn Dettifoss'; 1:50,000 'Jökulsárgljúfur', from the national park visitor centre
Transport	SBA Norðurleið buses serve Vesturdalur and Ásbyrgi from Akureyri, Mývatn, Húsavík and Dettifoss
Accommodation	Campsite at Ásbyrgi

The riverside route continues downstream, though there are other popular walks intersecting with it around Hljóðaklettar and Ásbyrgi. These give walkers the option to use other routes and include other nearby features of interest.

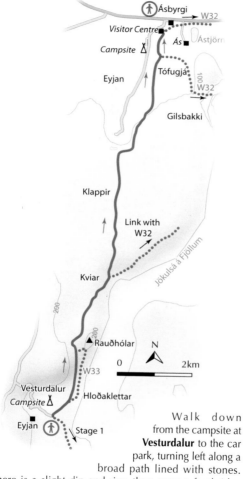

Walk down from the campsite at **Vesturdalur** to the car park, turning left along a broad path lined with stones. There is a slight dip and rise, then cross a footbridge over a little stream, passing a signpost. Continue towards a rock tower, to another signpost, and take the left for 'Rauðhólar' and 'Ásbyrgi' at **Hljóðaklettar**. ▶ Climb

Right is also possible, but more rugged, by reversing the end of Walk 33.

207

gradually through a little valley, and near the top the red ash slopes of **Rauðhólar** lie to the right. However, walk ahead as signposted 'Ásbyrgi'.

The path crosses a bare, gritty slope, aligns itself with a fence, then drifts downhill for a while. Follow the fence again and drift from it again through low vegetation. Wander across a hillside to reach a canyon rim overlooking the grey, glacial **Jökulsá á Fjöllum** near a map-board. ◄

Turning right here to walk along the canyon rim is possible, and later links with Walk 32 to reach Ásbyrgi.

Walkers step across the lip of a former waterfall above an echoing cliff

Turn left along a trodden path over level moorland at **Kviar**, later with a cliff edge to the left. Further along pass bushy patches and, later still, wet grassy areas and pools – all that remains of a long-vanished river. Keep right of a large pool and cross a ladder-stile over a fence. Later, the wet grassy area is noticeable to the left. Further along, in an area of hummocky rock, the route crosses the old riverbed at **Klappir**. The bed becomes clearer where it drops as a series of water-filled potholes to an abrupt cliff at the head of a canyon. ▶

Below, people yell at the cliffs to hear the echo!

Turn right to walk along the cliff edge, across a dip in the rocks, past a sign for Ásbyrgi. The path winds and undulates on rocky, hummocky moorland, crossing a ladder-stile over a fence and a rocky streambed. Pass through bushy and rocky areas, followed by easy moorland. Pass a cairn on a rocky brow, with more rock beyond, then go in and out of birch woods. Keep ahead at a signpost, then go down the cliff, using a metal staircase with 16 steps, scrambling with the aid of two ropes, then descend an eight-rung ladder and about 50 wooden steps to **Tófugjá**. Either walk straight to a campsite or turn right to the visitor centre at **Ásbyrgi**.

The prominent Eyjan is remarkably easy to climb from the campsite at Ásbyrgi

7 AKUREYRI AND EYJAFJÖRÐUR

View of Hrísey from the ferry on Eyjafjörður

Akureyri is the second largest settlement in Iceland after the city of Reykjavík, but with a population a little over 15,000 it is really only a small town. However, it has abundant services and is a major transport hub for exploring North Iceland.

The conical peak of Súlur dominates the town and is often streaked with snow. A walk to the summit (Walk 35) is a popular local route that can be attempted even from the town centre. Most people return the same way, but an alternative descent is described here. Eyafjörður is a very long fjord and one of its highlights is the low-lying island of Hrísey, which can be explored using easy nature trails (Walk 36). Far beyond the mouth of the fjord, the rugged little island of Grímsey can be visited (Walk 37), and the northern part of the island is the only part of Iceland that lies within the Arctic Circle.

Sterna and SBA Norðurleið bus services converge on Akureyri from both sides of the Ring Road encircling Iceland, as well as trundling along the Kjölur Track through the bleak and barren centre of Iceland. However, it takes all day to reach the town from Reykjavík, and two days if bus services are taken via Egilsstaðir, around East Iceland. Some visitors prefer to fly with Icelandair from Reykjavík to Akureyri to save time. Local bus services run to Litli Árskógssandur (linking with a short ferry ride to Hrísey) and to Dalvík (for a longer ferry to Grímsey). It is also possible to fly with Icelandair from Akureyri to Grímsey. SBA Norðurleið buses also head east of Akureyri, serving Mývatn (Trek 7), Ásbyrgi and Dettifoss (Section 6). On Mondays a splendid three-day bus tour leaves Akureyri for Kverkfjöll and Askja (Section 8).

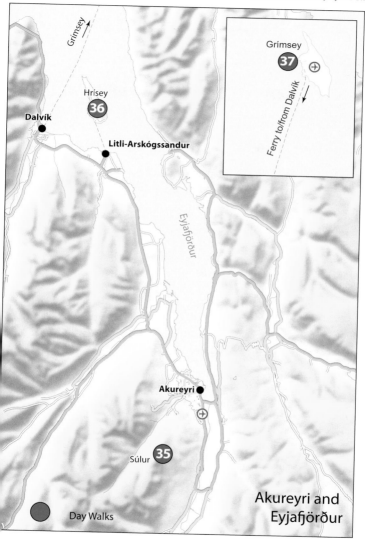

Grímsey

37

Ferry to/from Dalvík

Grímsey

Hrísey

36

Dalvík

Litli-Arskógssandur

Eyjafjörður

Akureyri

Súlur **35**

Day Walks

Akureyri and
Eyjafjörður

211

WALK 35

Akureyri and Súlur

Start/Finish	Akureyri
Distance	20km (12½ miles)
Total ascent/descent	1200m (3940ft)
Time	7hrs
Terrain	Roads at the start and finish. The ascent uses a steep and stony path. The descent is less trodden and boggy in places.
Map	1:120,000 'Mál og Menning – 8 Akureyri Mývatn Dettifoss'
Transport	Sterna, Reykjavík Excursions and SBA buses serve Akureyri from as far away as Reykjavík and Egilsstaðir

Súlur rises proudly from the suburbs of Akureyri and can be climbed from the town centre. Most walkers return the same way, but a waymarked route offers a less trodden and sometimes boggy descent to a campsite.

Using a street plan, leave **Akureyri** by following Þingvallastræti gently uphill. The road levels out, and a signpost points left along Miðhúsabraut for 'Glerárdalu' and 'Súlur'. Pass a dairy, turn right up Súluvegur, and th tarmac gives way to a dirt road. Keep right of a tip t reach a **car park** at 240m (790ft), about 4km (2½ mile from the town centre. Follow a track across a stream, tu left and climb briefly and steeply up a path to battere signs for Súlur and Lambi.

Cross a ladder-stile over a fence for Súlur, follow ing a narrow, clear path and crossing a couple of litt streams and gullies, sparsely marked by posts. Lush a varied vegetation gives way to steep, stony, boulde strewn slopes, where the path is less clear. ◄ Clin steeply onto a ridge, which is stony all the way to t top of **Súlur**, at 1144m (3753ft), where there is a cai and guestbook. Views extend around Glerárdalu beyond Akureyri, through Eyjafjörður, taking in rang of fells. ◄

Snow lingers long here, and if the path and posts are buried, follow footprints.

The ridge can be followed to a summit at 1213m (3980ft), if desired.

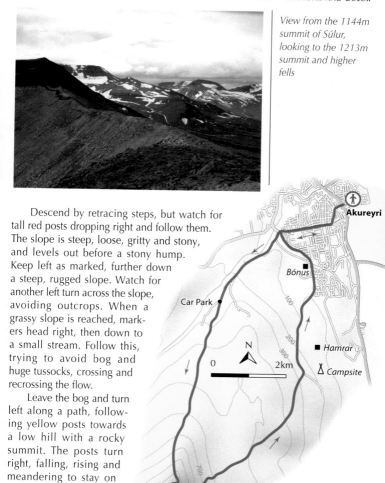

View from the 1144m summit of Súlur, looking to the 1213m summit and higher fells

Descend by retracing steps, but watch for tall red posts dropping right and follow them. The slope is steep, loose, gritty and stony, and levels out before a stony hump. Keep left as marked, further down a steep, rugged slope. Watch for another left turn across the slope, avoiding outcrops. When a grassy slope is reached, markers head right, then down to a small stream. Follow this, trying to avoid bog and huge tussocks, crossing and recrossing the flow.

Leave the bog and turn left along a path, following yellow posts towards a low hill with a rocky summit. The posts turn right, falling, rising and meandering to stay on firm ground. Go down a vegetated and stony slope and note the posts drift left into a

213

slight valley, which leads downhill. Eventually cross a fence and pass between a cabin and its toilet hut. Walk down to a forest and turn left along a clear path. Don't cross a footbridge, but turn right over a rise and drop down steep and rugged ground, between trees, to a track above a campsite at **Hamrar**.

Turn left along the track, rising, falling and meandering through forest. Leave the forest at a barrier and a mapboard. Follow the track, with a golf course to the left, and cross its access road to reach a **Bónus** supermarket. Keep right of it and use a pedestrian crossing on a busy road. Turn left on a cycle path parallel to the road, then veer right, later passing the dairy seen earlier in the day. Turn right to follow Þingvallastræti back into **Akureyri**.

WALK 36
Eyjafjörður and Hrísey

Start/Finish	Harbour, Hrísey
Distance	7km (4½ miles)
Total ascent/descent	100m (330ft)
Time	2hrs 30mins
Terrain	Rugged moorland and coast, but easy walking on marked paths
Map	1:120,000 'Mál og Menning – 8 Akureyri Mývatn Dettifoss'
Transport	Sterna serve Litli Árskógssandur from Akureyri, then Sævar ferry to Hrísey (tel 6955544)

Walking on Hrísey is limited to nature trails with informative notices on the southern half of the island. The northern half is a reserve for ptarmigan, and the island is also used to quarantine imported Belted Galloway cattle.

Leave the harbour at **Hrísey**, following the road called Ægisgata, side-stepping the village to a crossroads. Walk

Attractive church in the village on Hrísey, seen at the end of the walk

straight up Hjallavegur to a dirt crossroads beside a football pitch. Turn left at a walking sign, and masses of angelica grows beside the road. Turn right at a walking sign, up a track between fish-drying frames. Rise on heather, bilberry and crowberry moorland, with conifers dotted around. Bear left along wheel-marks from a notice about ptarmigan. Little flag markers lead up to a moorland crest, passing lupins, reaching a rock called **Háeyjarsteinn**, over 60m (195ft). Views encompass the fells flanking Eyjafjörður, and the villages of Dalvík and Grenivík.

Descend to the rugged shore, reaching a signpost indicating a short path to **Borgarbrík**, where there is a narrow inlet. Double back along a path set back from the coast, passing a notice about a deserted farm – **Hvatastaðir**. When the trail splits later, keep left along the coast, but beware cliff edges. Eventually drift uphill, linking with a broad sand and gravel path. Turn left to follow it gently downhill. ◄ Pass a curious scrap-sculpture in a shallow valley and pass 'The Fountain of Energy' sculpture.

Go up onto a little rocky crest, then down a path overlooking a marsh at **Langamýri**. Turn right into a forest and later look down on houses along the shore. Leave the forest and walk down a dirt road, turning right along a coastal road past houses. The road is brick-paved as it returns to the village, which is attractive and interesting.

Turning right here leads to a picnic site on top of Háaborð.

216

WALK 37
Grímsey

Start/Finish	Sandvík or the airport
Distance	12km (7½ miles)
Total ascent/descent	200m (655ft)
Time	3hrs 30mins
Terrain	Easy roads and tracks, with the option to use more rugged cliff paths
Map	From the gallery on Grímsey
Transport	Sterna serve Dalvík from Akureyri, then Sæfari ferry to Grímsey (tel 4588970). Air Iceland from Akureyri to Grímsey.

The island of Grímsey was named after its first settler, Vestfjarða-Grímur Sigurðsson. The Arctic Circle divides the uninhabited north from the inhabited south. A walk around the island's cliffs reveals Arctic terns, puffins, fulmars and gulls.

Leave the harbour and go into **Sandvík**, turning left to follow the road towards the tiny airport. Before reaching it, head left along a track near cliffs where puffins stand sentinel. Further along the track, before the end of the airport runway at Básar, the Arctic Circle is crossed. The track splits beyond a cattle grid, so keep left to enjoy good views over the bay of **Básavík**. When a slight dip is reached, the track splits. ▶ Turn left across a gentle rise, and the track descends to the northernmost point on the island at

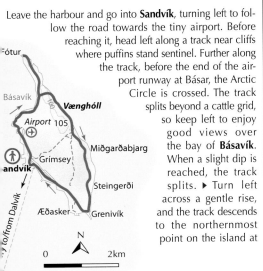

Turn right here for a shortcut.

217

A little lighthouse at Grenivík at the southern end of Grímsey

Fótur. There are fine views of the cliffs, and a small cairn looks out across the Arctic Ocean.

Double back along the track and turn left at the junction passed earlier, or follow narrow, uneven paths, high on the cliffs, later linking with the track. The grassy track offers a few glimpses over the cliffs, and is easier than the tussocky grass either side. It runs near **Vænghóll**, the highest point on the island at 105m (345ft), and drifts inland towards communication masts and a junction. Stay on the rough grass on the cliff-tops at **Miðgarðabjarg** by keeping left along the track, undulating, but generally descending. The cliff-top is rugged at first, but better later, climbing a little to join the track at **Steingerði**. Walk down to a lighthouse at **Grenivík** and perhaps onto the rugged southernmost point.

The church was built of driftwood in 1867 and renovated in 2002.

Follow a gravel road away from the lighthouse, either linking with a tarmac road at a couple of houses or first following a cliff-top route overlooking the islet of **Æðasker** and a huddle of rocky stacks. The road leads past a prominent little church and other buildings at Miðgarðer. ◄ Follow the road back to **Sandvík** and the harbour.

8 KVERKFJÖLL AND ASKJA

A series of four easy nature trails can be explored near the huts at Herðubreiðarlindir (Walk 39)

Kverkfjöll and Askja, deep in the central highlands of Iceland, seem very remote on maps, but they are also surprisingly busy. At Kverkfjöll, visitors can see glaciers and geothermal hot-spots in the same place (Walk 38). Climbing the glacier to Hveradalur requires experience and equipment, but guided walks and equipment are available from the hut at Sigurðaskáli. If weather conditions are bad, it may still be possible to enjoy shorter, easier walks. On the way towards Askja, for example, there are four inter-linked nature trails at the 'oasis' of Herðubreiðarlindir (Walk 39).

There are options for long-distance treks in this area. The remote and challenging Askja Trail (Trek 6) is a hut-to-hut route across vast lava landscapes, where water can be scarce. It has two completely different finishing points, which need to be considered when

making plans. The Mývatn Trail (Trek 7), which is of the author's imagining, is altogether easier (it doesn't even require a backpack to be carried) and is offered as an introduction to trekking.

Many visitors to Iceland assume that they need their own 4WD vehicles to venture into the central highlands, but there are jeeps, buses and tours available. On Mondays a splendid three-day bus tour leaves Akureyri for Kverkfjöll and Askja, stopping to sample short walks and allowing all day Tuesday for Walk 38. Various jeep tours offer access on a daily basis, at a hefty price, and these are only worth the expense if weather conditions are good. In mist, the journey is quite pointless! With a good weather forecast promised, it is worth travelling one-way into this area, with a view to completing the long-distance Askja Trail.

219

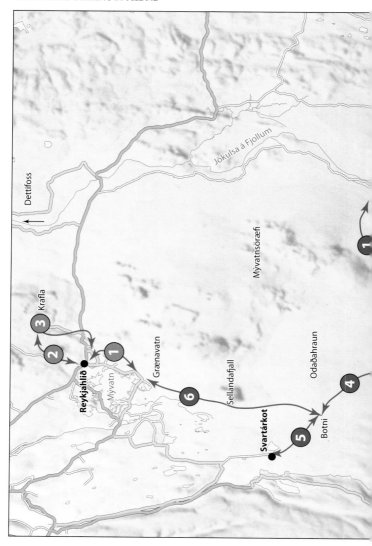

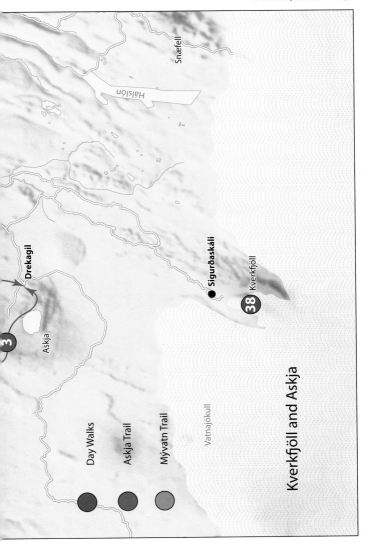

Kverkfjöll and Askja

Day Walks

Askja Trail

Mývatn Trail

Vatnajökull

Snæfell

Hálslón

Drekagil

Askja

Sigurðaskáli

Kverkfjöll

38

3

A glacier calves into a crater lake in a geothermal area at Kverkfjöll

WALK 38
Kverkfjöll and Hveradalur

Start/Finish	Car park beyond Sigurðaskáli
Distance	20km (12½ miles)
Total ascent/descent	1000m (3280ft)
Time	8hrs
Terrain	Steep, stony moraine and glacier walking, requiring ropes, ice-axes and crampons
Maps	1:100,000 'Mál og Menning – 7 Askja Herðubreið Kverkfjöll'; 1:100,000 Askja and Kverkfjöll national park map, available from the Sigurðaskáli hut
Transport	SBA Norðurleið buses operate each Monday from Akureyri and Mývatn to Kverkfjöll, where the glacier walk can be joined on Tuesday

Kverkfjöll seems inaccessible to walkers without 4WD vehicles, but bus and jeep tours reach it, and guides lead groups onto the glacier. This is a remarkable area, where glaciers sit on top of extensive geothermal hot-spots.

Leave the hut, **Sigurðaskáli**, and drive for 3.5km (2¼ miles) along a dirt road to park around 860m (2821ft). ▶ Follow blue pegs down a stony path, crossing two streams and a footbridge over a big river flowing from the glacier snout and **ice cave**.

Walk downstream and follow red pegs over hummocky moraine, crossing small streams. Turn left up a valley, and views develop as the path steepens. Look down onto the jagged glacier

Note the warnings about a nearby ice cave, which collapsed in 2010 and reformed in 2011, then a visitor was killed by falling ice.

Map continues on page 224

Roped-up walkers take a break while climbing the glacier to Kverkfjöll

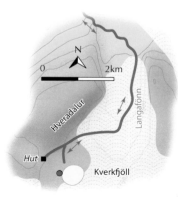

of **Kverkjökull** as the path climbs steep zigzags. Cross a significant dip on a narrow gap between glaciers. Walk to the one on the right, **Langafönn**, around 1200m (3940ft), and rope up to climb it. The ice is steep, but walkable, and the idea is to climb straight to a gap between rocky areas scoured by ice, around 1700m (5580ft). The gradient eases and it is necessary to drift right, watching carefully for crevasses. Look ahead to spot a bare, rocky ridge with a prominent triangle marker on top. It may be safe to come off the rope and remove crampons here.

Explore downhill, looking at steam vents around **Hveradalur**, maybe waiting for a glacier to calve icebergs into a crater lake. A small hut overlooks the lake, and by climbing the rugged crest above, there is a view down to another lake, while clouds of steam rise from several hot springs and mud-pots. After exploring, retrace steps back to **Sigurðaskáli**. ▶

If conditions aren't good for this walk, there are short waymarked trails on Virkisfell and Biskupsfell.

WALK 39
Herðubreiðarlindir

Start/Finish	Herðubreiðarlindir
Distance	10km (6¼ miles)
Total ascent/descent	50m (165ft)
Time	3hrs 30mins
Terrain	Easy nature trails on rugged lava
Maps	1:100,000 'Mál og Menning – 7 Askja Herðubreið Kverkfjöll'; 1:100,000 Askja and Kverkfjöll national park map, available from the wardens' hut at Herðubreiðarlindir
Transport	SBA Norðurleið buses operate each Monday from Akureyri and Mývatn, stopping briefly at Herðubreiðarlindir. Other daily tours from Mývatn.

Herðubreiðarlindir is one of a handful of 'oases in the desert', where vegetation thrives on barren lava. Four short nature trails are here combined into a half-day's walk in the shadow of the mighty fell of Herðubreið.

▶ Start at the wardens' hut at **Herðubreiðarlindir**, where staff are also national park rangers. Face the hut and head right, following orange-tipped marker posts past big boulders and over bare lava to

For those arriving on a tour, there might be time for only one trail.

Colour-coded trails appear to head towards Herðubreið

the grey glacial river of **Jökulsá á Fjöllum**. Turn left downstream to a confluence with the Kreppa. Drop onto gravel and continue downstream. A vegetated strip between the river and lava leads back to the wardens' hut.

Walk towards the FÍ hut of Þorsteinsskáli, studying a map-board at a car park before crossing a footbridge. Keep left of the hut, walk upstream and follow markers bearing green, red and yellow. Step up onto lava and turn left, marked only by red-tipped posts. Step down and continue upstream, past interlinked pools fringed by angelica. The largest is **Álftavatn**, where the path swings left. Continue mostly on black ash close to a dirt road, and return to the car park.

Cross the footbridge, keep left of the hut, and walk upstream, but this time step onto the lava and stay on it, following green-and-yellow markers. The rolling lava is ropy in places, with mounds, slabs and cracks. Watch for green-tipped markers heading right, following winding paths or little gullies. Reach a junction where blue-tipped markers head left, but first turn right to the tiny ruin of **Eyvindarkofi**. ◀

The outlaw Eyvindur Jónsson lived here through the winter of 1774–75.

Retrace steps and follow blue-tipped markers, passing willow thickets where water gushes from the lava. A stony stretch is followed by a sudden sharp right turn, down from the lava to cross two footbridges over an island in the river Lindaá. Turn right to follow the blue-tipped markers across cobbles to return to the car park at **Herðubreiðarlindir**.

TREK 6
The Askja Trail

Start	Herðubreiðarlindir
Finish	Grænavatn
Distance	96 or 121km (59¾ or 75¼ miles)
Time	5 days (with a choice between a short or long final day)
Terrain	Rugged lava flows at first, with steep and stony slopes in the middle, ending with long, easy walking along dirt roads. Water is scarce on many parts of the route.
Facilities	Huts and/or camping
Accommodation	Huts and/or camping

The Askja Trail wanders across smooth and broken lava flows, areas of light-coloured, lightweight pumice, stony ground and fine dark ash. Most of this material erupted from the enormous Askja caldera, and the massive crater contains a large lake today. This is a fascinating area for those who want to appreciate volcanic landforms, but is quite rugged underfoot in places.

It has to be remembered that water is often very scarce on this trek, so the situation at each hut is explained. Before leaving Herðubreiðarlindir, ask about the availability of water at the Bræðrafell hut, and be prepared to carry adequate supplies.

Despite the rugged terrain on some stretches, the final couple of days follow easy dirt roads, where the only limit is how far you can comfortably walk towards the end. The trail has two alternative end points at Svartárkot and Grænavatn. Very keen walkers could also link with the Mývatn Trail (Trek 7), though that is really intended as an easy introduction to long-distance trekking.

Transport to and from the Askja Trail needs careful planning. The cheapest deal is to catch the SBA Norðurleið bus, on Mondays only, from Akureyri or Mývatn to Herðubreiðarlindir. Jeeps are much more expensive, but if operators are struggling to fill seats, they may be willing to offer a deal. Bear in mind that most bus and jeep tours also visit Drekagil and Víti, so there are other options for starting the trail later or finishing earlier. Once the remote hut of Botni is reached, there is a choice of routes to finish. If taking the short option (Stage 5) to Svartárkot, a pick-up needs to be arranged. If taking the long option (Stage 6) to Grænavatn, it is possible to keep walking to find lodgings, or arrange a pick-up with a local taxi and head for Reykjahlíð.

Herðubreiðarlindir to Bræðrafell

Start	Herðubreiðarlindir
Finish	Bræðrafell
Distance	18km (11 miles)
Total ascent	180m (590ft)
Total descent	40m (130ft)
Time	7hrs
Terrain	Mostly gently sloping lava, stones and sand, but often quite rugged and pathless underfoot
Maps	1:100,000 'Mál og Menning – 7 Askja Herðubreið Kverkfjöll'; 1:100,000 Askja and Kverkfjöll national park map, available from the hut
Transport	SBA Norðurleið operate each Monday from Akureyri and Mývatn, linking Herðubreiðarlindir and Drekagil. Other daily tours from Mývatn.
Accommodation	Basic hut at Bræðrafell; water may be scarce or absent

The first day on the Askja Trail involves very little climbing, but there are rugged, broken lava fields, and the lower slopes of Herðubreið are stony and sandy. Herðubreið can be climbed, but its steep, rocky slopes are unstable.

Start from the wardens' hut at **Herðubreiðarlindir**, and walk to the FÍ hut of Þorsteinsskáli, crossing a footbridge to reach it.

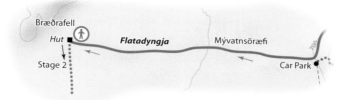

Keep left of the hut and follow a path upstream, following markers bearing green, red and yellow. Step up onto lava and follow only markers bearing yellow. ▶ The rolling lava is ropy in places, with mounds, slabs and cracks, and it is important to keep the yellow posts in view as they head towards the mighty fell of **Herðubreið**.

Turn right at the base of the fell on sand and stones washed from the slopes. Climb gently, crossing a couple of small streams and a boulder-strewn slope, followed by more lava. Brown ash beds rise left, heavily eroded to brown sand. Watch as the posts rise left through a gap,

Red markers head left, and green later head right – both on Walk 39.

The little hut at Bræðrafell, looking back along the trail to Herðubreið

229

and continue along the sandy trail between steep ash and level lava. Cross stony mounds and slopes of stones and ash, crossing a stream around 600m (1970ft).

The slope becomes boulder-strewn, so walk on nearby ash and follow markers across stony ground to a **car park** at the end of a dirt road. Turn right to follow the Askja Trail and yellow posts. ◄ Cross the rugged **Mývatnsöræfi** lava, which becomes a little easier while passing a mangled mass of eruptive lava. Pass similar features, followed by a mass of boulders at 676m (2217ft) on **Flatadyngja**. A gap on the right reveals a rugged crater.

A little hut is seen ahead, and left of it is a fell with a rock tower. Views extend from Herðubreið to Askja and Kverkfjöll. A gentle descent leads to the FÍ hut at **Bræðrafell** (small and basic, no showers, with water from rain barrels – if the barrels are empty, obtain water by looking for lingering snow.)

A notice explains how to climb Herðubreið, 'Queen of Icelandic Mountains', on steep, unstable slopes, from 700m (2295ft) to the 1682m (5518ft) summit.

STAGE 2
Bræðrafell to Drekagil

Start	Bræðrafell
Finish	Drekagil
Distance	20km (12½ miles)
Total ascent	280m (920ft)
Total descent	100m (330ft)
Time	7hrs
Terrain	Mostly gently sloping; often rocky, stony, sandy or pathless
Maps	1:100,000 'Mál og Menning – 7 Askja Herðubreið Kverkfjöll'; 1:100,000 Askja and Kverkfjöll national park map
Transport	SBA Norðurleið operate buses each Monday from Akureyri and Mývatn, linking Herðubreiðarlindir and Drekagil. Other daily tours from Mývatn.
Accommodation	Huts at Drekagil

Few walkers are likely to be seen on this stage, which becomes increasingly desert-like. However, vehicles will probably come and go on a dirt road leading to a huddle of huts at the mouth of a canyon at Drekagil.

Walk southwards from the **Bræðrafell** hut, following the yellow posts with ease until jagged lava is reached. Weave through, cross smaller broken rocks, then climb a little on ash and pumice on the left side of a fell. ▶ Drop steeply a short way on ash, then rise and fall through increasingly rugged terrain. Jagged lava gives way to a stony slope, and the route follows the margin between a slope and lava flow. Turn a corner to see brown ash beds forming cliffs and boulders beneath **Dyngjufjallaháls**. Shift onto lava, which is easy at first but becomes more rugged while rising gently. Another pumice slope is crossed and the ground gets rougher.

Follow a track over ash and stones, with rugged slopes rising right and gentler lava stretching left. Cross a stony plain at the foot

The trail enters the Vatnajökull national park here.

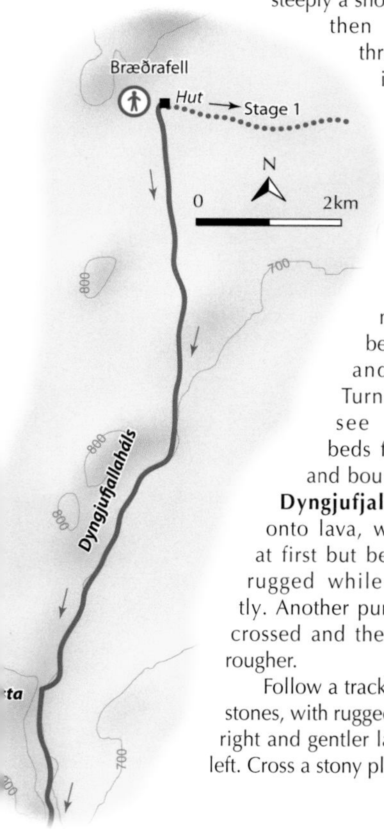

Map continues on page 232

Bræðrafell
Hut → Stage 1
N
0   2km
700
800
800
Dyngjufjallaháls
800
ta
700
800

231

of **Stórakista**, where big boulders have come to rest. The track later swings left, but follow the yellow posts that run straight ahead, rising and falling gently on stones and sand. Rise to the foot of bare, stony fellsides, keeping rugged lava to the left, all the way to the foot of **Litlakista**, around 780m (2560ft).

Watch carefully for marker posts swinging left onto moss-covered lava. A good path is flanked by thousands of rocky stumps. The way ahead is gentle, apart from short, steep drops and climbs. Increasing amounts of lightweight, light-coloured, gravelly pumice occur on **Vikrahraun**. Eventually it looks like a desert, with little vegetation. Don't be distracted by wheel-marks, but watch for marker posts while passing tongues of black lava. There is no discernible path later, but head for a dirt road, reaching it at a little notice for Bræðrafell.

Light-coloured gravelly pumice creates desert-like conditions on Vikrahraun

Turn right up the road, levelling out with huts seen ahead. Two rivers are crossed, and the first may need to be forded. Reach the well-equipped FÍ huts at **Drekagil**, at 800m (2625ft), which are often very busy. ▶

Have a look inside the rugged canyon beyond, although steps have to be retraced.

STAGE 3
Drekagil to Dyngjufell

Start	Drekagil
Finish	Dyngjufell
Distance	23km (14¼ miles)
Total ascent	750m (2460ft)
Total descent	900m (2950ft)
Time	9hrs
Terrain	Steep ascents and descents over fells. Muddy around Víti, followed by gentle ash and rugged lava. Another climb and a long descent to the finish, often pathless.
Maps	1:100,000 'Mál og Menning – 7 Askja Herðubreið Kverkfjöll'; 1:100,000 Askja and Kverkfjöll national park map
Transport	SBA Norðurleið operate buses each Monday from Akureyri and Mývatn, linking Drekagil and Askja. Other daily tours from Mývatn.
Accommodation	Basic hut at Dyngjufell

This stage of the Askja Trail involves the most ascent and descent, in and out of a vast lake-filled volcanic caldera. The little crater at Víti is often busy, but the route to Dyngjufell is usually very quiet. Vegetation is almost completely absent.

Leave the huts at **Drekagil**, around 800m (2625ft), keep right of the canyon, and climb up a slope of lightweight, light-coloured pumice, passing a sign for Askja. Climb a path marked by yellow posts, cross a slight dip, then climb further onto soft sand, followed by stones. Cross

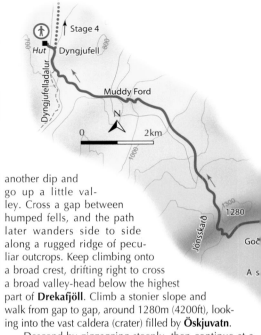

Stage 4

Hut Dyngjufell

Dyngjufelladalur

Muddy Ford

N

0   2km

1280

Jónsskarð

Goč

A s

another dip and go up a little valley. Cross a gap between humped fells, and the path later wanders side to side along a rugged ridge of peculiar outcrops. Keep climbing onto a broad crest, drifting right to cross a broad valley-head below the highest part of **Drekafjöll**. Climb a stonier slope and walk from gap to gap, around 1280m (4200ft), looking into the vast caldera (crater) filled by **Öskjuvatn**.

Lukewarm murky water in a crater at Víti tempts people to bathe

Descend by zigzagging steeply, then continue at a gentler gradient beside a valley where multi-coloured boulders lie on light-coloured pumice. Cross a little

valley and note hot-spots on a slope. Later, cross gullies
and jagged black lava at **Bátshraun**. Take care on a short,
steep, crumbling slope, and aim for the little crater of
Víti, turning right to climb above it. Marker posts lead
across black ash, rising gently later, then down to a car
park at **Vikraborgir**.

A signpost on the left reads 'Dyngjufell', and the route
crosses jagged, broken lava towards a fell called **Tanni**.
Turn left at a signpost on a hump of lava and walk along
the foot of the slope. Keep lava flows to the left, while the
slope rising right can be rocky, bouldery, stony or ash. Rise
gently, but watch for marker posts climbing steeply to
the right on rugged pumice. Reach the gap
of **Jónsskarð**, around 1280m (4200ft), and
look back across the Askja caldera.

Follow the yellow posts as
there is no path. Walk down
to a level area, cross stony
hummocks and go down a
stony slope, later drop-

ping more steeply. Veer right, as marked, to follow a
river, crossing inflowing streams. The gradient is gentle,
but the ground is stony, with barely a trodden path. Drift
right from the river, following posts and cairns while
dropping from one level to another. There is a sudden
steep descent past grotesque outcrops, continuing down
a dusty, gravelly path onto a desert-like plain threaded
by a river. The river is shallow, but unpleasantly muddy
when forded.

Walk across the plain and over a bouldery rise. A sand and gravel path leads over a hump and down a ridge to a signpost below a grey-banded fell. Turn right to follow a track across a stream. The small FÍ hut at **Dyngjufell** lies across a muddy river. The hut is basic, with no showers. Water is drawn from the muddy river to settle in a barrel.

STAGE 4
Dyngjufell to Botni

Start	Dyngjufell
Finish	Botni
Distance	20km (12½ miles)
Total ascent	50m (165ft)
Total descent	250m (820ft)
Time	6hrs 30mins
Terrain	A long, gentle track through stony, sandy desert, followed by a rugged track over broken lava
Map	1:100,000 'Mál og Menning – Atlaskort 21 Mývatnsöræfi'
Transport	None
Accommodation	Basic hut at Botni

Route-finding along a dirt road is very easy, but needs a little more care towards the end of the route. After crossing sparsely vegetated, desert-like terrain, there are pools, springs and lush greenery around Botni, on the edge of the national park.

Leave the hut at **Dyngjufell** and follow the track downstream on barren gravel. The dale broadens, and a few large boulders have fallen from cliffs on the right. The gradient is imperceptibly downwards, through there is a slight rise over coarse stones, with a view back to the rim of the Askja caldera. The track undulates gently past broken, jagged lava, and the only prominent vegetation is sparse lyme grass on black sand dunes. The river to the left eventually peters out on the broad, barren **Ódáðahraun**. ▶

The track runs through a broad hollow, rising sandy and gritty, and keeping left of a low, rounded hill. Cross a crest where jagged lava pokes through sand and descend gently to a sandy plain, where jagged lava lies left, with increasing lyme grass to the right. The track suddenly swings right, around 480m (1575ft), but walk straight ahead along a lesser track signposted 'Botni'.

The track becomes stonier, climbing onto broken lava, meandering and undulating. Creeping willow and small flowers find root-holds. Follow the margin between broken lava and ropy lava, while in the distance rise the humps of Sellandafjall and Bláfjall. The track is easier later, more sandy, gritty and convoluted as it avoids bouldery heaps of broken lava. At one point it splits and

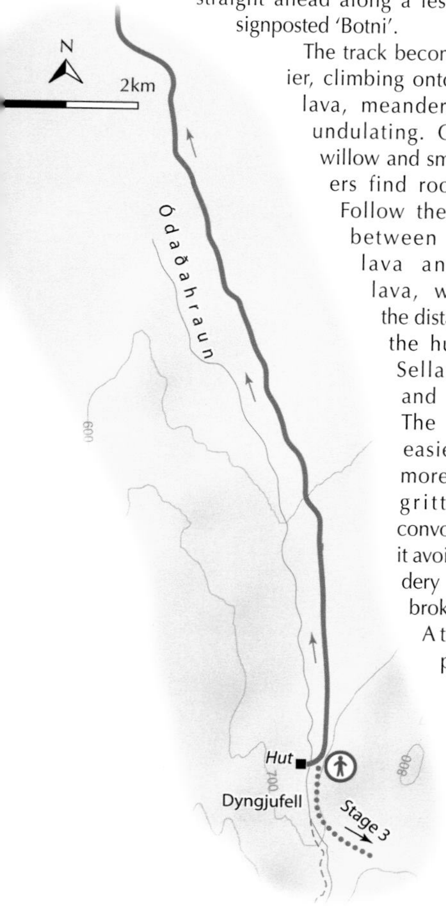

Herðubreið is visible far away to the right.

Map continues on page 238

237

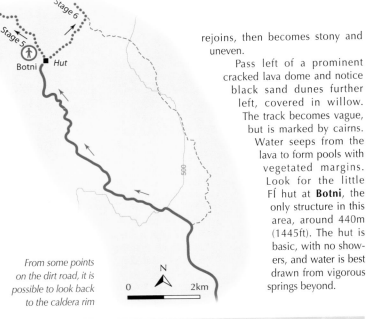

rejoins, then becomes stony and uneven.

Pass left of a prominent cracked lava dome and notice black sand dunes further left, covered in willow. The track becomes vague, but is marked by cairns. Water seeps from the lava to form pools with vegetated margins. Look for the little FÍ hut at **Botni**, the only structure in this area, around 440m (1445ft). The hut is basic, with no showers, and water is best drawn from vigorous springs beyond.

From some points on the dirt road, it is possible to look back to the caldera rim

Start	Botni
Finish	Svartárkot
Distance	15km (9½ miles)
Total ascent	20m (65ft)
Total descent	60m (195ft)
Time	4hrs 30mins
Terrain	An easy grassy track beside rivers and lakes, then a stony track
Map	1:100,000 'Mál og Menning – Atlaskort 21 Mývatnsöræfi'
Transport	None
Accommodation	Two huts at Stóraflesja

This is the shorter of two options for finishing the Askja Trail – the longer being Stage 6 of this trek. A grassy track wanders beside scenic rivers and lakes, then a stony track crosses a broad moorland to reach a large lake at Svartárkot.

Step out of the hut at **Botni**, head right and follow a meandering track through rugged lava and lush greenery, watching on the left to spot a vigorous spring. ▶ Follow the **Suðurá** downstream, where deep wheel-ruts cut the grass, with willow and birch alongside, as well as rushes, crowberry and flowers. The river is fascinating, powerful and convoluted as it splits and rejoins around islands and broadens to enter a lake populated by wildfowl.

This is the best water supply for the hut.

The track loops away from the river, passing another lake at **Mótunga** and continuing downstream. Watch for a ruined stone hut on the right. The track is sometimes on lava, meandering, rising and falling. The river features short rapids and lots of islands, while the track is flanked by birch scrub and grassy swathes. Two little huts at **Stóraflesja** are equipped with bunks. Continue along the track and detour briefly left to view rapids from rickety footbridges.

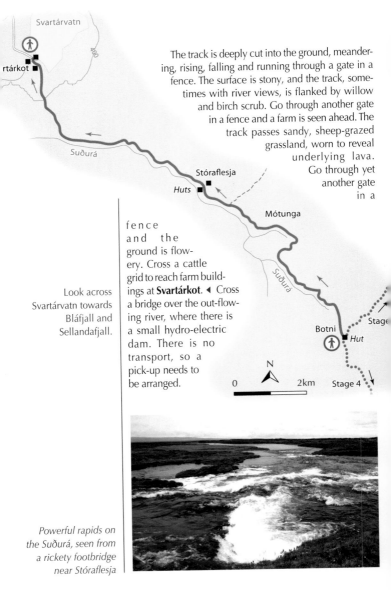

Svartárvatn

rtárkot ■

Suðurá

The track is deeply cut into the ground, meandering, rising, falling and running through a gate in a fence. The surface is stony, and the track, sometimes with river views, is flanked by willow and birch scrub. Go through another gate in a fence and a farm is seen ahead. The track passes sandy, sheep-grazed grassland, worn to reveal underlying lava. Go through yet another gate in a

Stóraflesja

Huts

Mótunga

Suðurá

fence and the ground is flowery. Cross a cattle grid to reach farm buildings at **Svartárkot**. ◀ Cross a bridge over the out-flowing river, where there is a small hydro-electric dam. There is no transport, so a pick-up needs to be arranged.

Look across Svartárvatn towards Bláfjall and Sellandafjall.

Botni ■ Hut

Stage

0   2km

Stage 4

N

Powerful rapids on the Suðurá, seen from a rickety footbridge near Stóraflesja

240

STAGE 6
Botni to Grænavatn

Start	Botni
Finish	Grænavatn
Distance	40km (25 miles)
Total ascent	40m (130ft)
Total descent	200m (655ft)
Time	11hrs
Terrain	Long; but easy walking along tracks, rising and falling gently
Map	1:100,000 'Mál og Menning – Atlaskort 21 Mývatnsöræfi'
Transport	None
Accommodation	None

This is the longer of two options for finishing the Askja Trail – the shorter being Stage 5 of this trek. Despite its length, it is simply a matter of following clear tracks, gradually heading north towards Mývatn.

Walk around the back of the hut at **Botni** to find a rugged track marked by red-tipped yellow posts, meandering over ropy lava to a junction. ▶ Turn left and the track rises and falls gently, but is uneven underfoot over a broad and stony rise. Cross ropy lava where the track winds through vegetated hollows. Later, the surroundings are grassy at **Botnaflesja**. Descend a little into a sandy, rocky hollow, then cross a gentle vegetated rise.

A small sign points back to Botni.

The track meanders through ropy lava, rising gently onto black ash. A cairn stands at a track junction, where a right turn is made. ▶ Crunch along an ash track at **Katlar**, undulating gently past short heath. Ford a river, **Hagalækur**, and rise over boulder-strewn ground and broken lava. Continue across ash and a boulder-studded plain at the foot of **Sellandafjall**. Go through a gate in a fence, passing grass and willow,

A small sign points back for Askja.

and the track runs briefly beside a river. The vegetation becomes increasingly dense, dominated by willow. Go through a gate in a fence, and the track crosses the river at a culvert overlooking a crumbling ravine.

The track climbs and vegetation

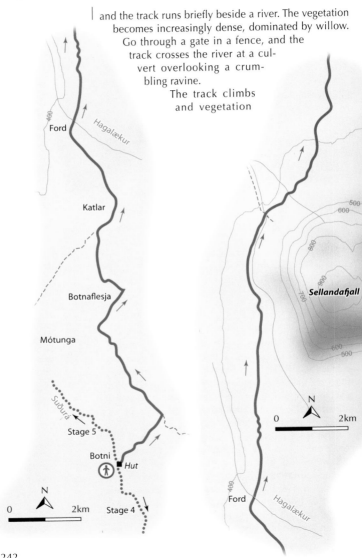

242

thins on stony hummocks. Stay on the clearest track, avoiding others, and eventually a view ahead reveals the complex lake of Mývatn. Descend gradually on stony slopes with clumps of bearberry. Cross a stony plain where fields have been created on the right. Cross a gravelly heath at **Randaskarð**, with lava to the right at **Sveigar**. Cross a cattle grid and

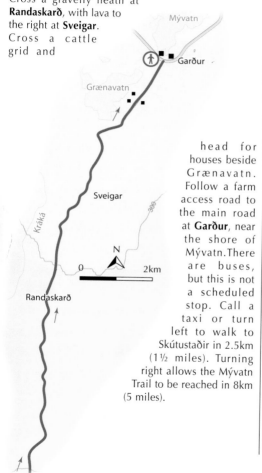

head for houses beside Grænavatn. Follow a farm access road to the main road at **Garður**, near the shore of Mývatn. There are buses, but this is not a scheduled stop. Call a taxi or turn left to walk to Skútustaðir in 2.5km (1½ miles). Turning right allows the Mývatn Trail to be reached in 8km (5 miles).

TREK 7
The Mývatn Trail

Start	Dimmuborgir
Finish	Reykjahlíð
Distance	55km (34 miles)
Time	3 days
Terrain	Generally easy, but with some steep and stony slopes, as well as rugged lava. It is possible to walk the route without a heavy pack, commuting to and from Reykjahlíð.
Facilities	Cafés at Dimmuborgir and the Nature Baths. Shop and restaurant at Reykjahlíð. Possible hot-dog stall at Leirhnjúkur.
Accommodation	Hotels, guesthouses and campsites at Reykjahlíð

Most walkers who base themselves at Reykjahlíð to explore around Mývatn walk a series of short and easy walks, generally driving cars from one to another. This is fine, but most of the best walks in the area can be linked together, and the 'Mývatn Trail' is of the author's own imagination, offering novice trekkers an opportunity to enjoy a long-distance trek without having to carry a heavy backpack.

Instead, with only a day-pack and a packed lunch, the trek can be walked by using paths leading to and from the village of Reykjahlíð, coupled with short, local bus services. The route naturally splits into three stages, and each stage explores notable geothermal hot-spot and abundant volcanic landforms. From several points there are views of Mývatn itself, a complex lake populated by a variety of birds and large numbers of annoying flies!

A short local taxi is needed to reach the start of the trail at Dimmuborgir, and after exploring a veritable maze-like area, the route climbs Hverfjall. Hot-spots lie beyond, and one area has been exploited to create the hot-water Nature Baths. The route leads to Reykjahlíð and all its facilities. On Stage 2, the following day, lava flows feature strongly, and more geothermal hot-spots are visited on the way to Víti and Krafla. Be sure to study the timetables for the SBA Norðurleið bus service, catching it in time to get from Víti back to Reykjahlíð. Trekkers will see how the geothermal area around Krafla has been tapped for steam to run power stations, and for hot water, piped to nearby properties. The next day, catch the bus back to Víti and follow Stage 3 to the remarkable geothermal area at Námaskarð, then walk back to Reykjahlíð.

Start	Borgarás, Dimmuborgir
Finish	Reykjahlið
Distance	15km (9½ miles)
Total ascent/descent	230m (755ft)
Time	5hrs
Terrain	Waymarked, convoluted paths and tracks across rugged lava and ash, as well as varied scrub
Maps	1:50,000 'Mál og Menning 8 – Akureyri Mývatn Dettifoss'; free 1:90,000 'Mývatn Lake', from the visitor centre
Transport	Taxi from Reykjahlið to Dimmuborgir
Accommodation	Accommodation and campsites at Reykjahlið

This stage links the popular maze-like Dimmuborgir with the shapely volcanic cone of Hverfjall, then wanders through a steaming geothermal hot-spot. There is an option to shortcut to Reykjahlið, while the main route allows a visit to the hot Nature Baths.

Start with a short ride in a local taxi to a café and souvenir shop at Borgarás. A viewpoint overlooks a natural maze of rocky ridges and pillars at **Dimmuborgir**. Go down through a gate, and by keeping right at path junctions a complete lap can be made around this amazing site. To explore further, make another lap using other paths. There are plenty of signposts and coloured markers – blue, red and yellow.

To leave this incredible place, watch for a mapboard and signpost for Grjótagjá and Reykjahlið. Climb through a cavernous hole in a cliff, descend and follow a yellow-pegged path, crossing a ladder-stile over a fence. A gentler path aims for stony slopes, where ropes push walkers right and left, zigzagging up steep, loose slopes of ash and stones to the crater rim of **Hverfjall**. ▶ Turn right to walk around the rim, rising to over 420m (1380ft).

Turn left for a short walk along the rim.

From the lowest point on the rim, a broad path marked by yellow pegs runs down black ash to a small car park and map-board. ◄ Cross a ladder-stile over a fence, marked 'Nature Baths'. Cross a level grassy area and follow pegs up onto ash and broken lava, passing steam vents. Follow a blue and orange river upstream, and cross a ladder-stile over a fence to reach the **Nature Baths** (café and bathing, tel 4644411).

Walk back across the ladder-stile, turn right and follow a peg-marked path beside the fence. Go down an ash track between fields and left along a vague track, following markers onto a clear track. Watch for another marked path and turn right to **Grjótagjá**. A cave here contains warm water – look inside, then climb onto fissured lava, later crossing a ladder-stile over a fence.

Follow an ash path, crossing yet another ladder-stile. Rise gently through forest to a junction and map-board. Keep straight ahead, rising and falling, to cross a pipe and a track. Follow a path across rugged moorland, watching for big holes. Just before reaching **Reykjahlíð**, turn left to go down metal steps into a deep fissure at Stóragjá. Reykjahlíð has accommodation, campsites, shop, post office and visitor centre (tel 4644460).

Signposts for Grjótagjá and Reykjahlíð offer a shortcut omitting the Nature Baths.

246

Walkers on the crater rim of Hverfjall, with Krafla rising in the distance

STAGE 2
Reykjahlíð to Víti

Start	Reykjahlíð
Finish	Víti, Krafla
Distance	20km (12½ miles)
Total ascent	400m (1310ft)
Total descent	100m (330ft)
Time	7hrs
Terrain	Waymarked paths over low hills and rugged lava flows, finishing with a steep climb
Maps	1:50,000 'Mál og Menning 8 – Akureyri Mývatn Dettifoss'; free 1:90,000 'Mývatn Lake' from the visitor centre
Transport	SBA Norðurleið link Reykjahlíð and Krafla
Accommodation	None – return to Reykjahlíð by bus

A gradual climb from Reykjahlíð reveals awesome 18th- and 20th-century lava flows. Leirhnjúkur features steaming vents and mud-pots, as does nearby Víti. Krafla can be climbed at the end in order to look back on the whole walk.

Walk to the swimming pool on the outskirts of **Reykjahlíð**, go around the back, cross a ladder-stile over a fence, and climb a slope of patchy bushes. The gradient eases and yellow pegs show the way to another ladder-stile over a fence. A grassy track crosses a rise, passing yet another ladder-stile. Cross a dip and note another yellow-pegged path joining from the left, and signposts. The pegs mark a path at variance with the track, but either can be used, rising and falling on the crest of **Langahlíð**.

Turn right later, as signposted 'Krafla', and go down to a lava flow, following its edge to the foot of **Hlíðarfjall** then turning right. ◄ Walk beside the lava, later climbing stony slopes above it, with wider views across the jagged flow. Climb past a couple of stony

There is a steep and stony path to the top of Hlíðarfjall.

Taking a break inside a big lava tube between Sáta and Leirhnjúkur

hollows, then the path drops back onto the lava. It is very rugged but surprisingly well trodden. Markers lead to an 'island' of green hills at **Sáta**. Pass these and continue across the lava. Watch on the left for the arches of a lava tube.

Cross a rise to go through a hollow where the lava crust sagged and cracked, then climb out of it. An easy path swings right below a big hole.

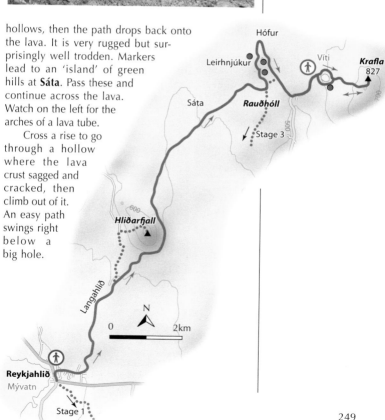

249

Follow the edge of the lava, passing a darker, more recent flow. Cross fissures and step up to signposts. Turn left to reach a junction with a broader path. ◄ Turn left to climb around the rugged slopes of **Leirhnjúkur**, either following a circular route or including spur paths to viewpoints and the rugged crater of **Hófur**. There are many steaming vents, but the highlight is a large mud-pot viewed from wooden decking. Go down steps to leave it, following duckboards and a broad path to a car park, toilets and hot-dog stall.

Shortcut right if time is pressing.

Turn left up to a road-end car park on a crater rim at **Víti**. This contains a tarn, and a path runs around the rim, dropping to mud-pots on the far side. Before dropping, consider climbing **Krafla** using a steep, rugged and obvious track. The 827m (2713ft) summit is spoiled by masts and a hut, but views back towards Mývatn are good. The end of the walk is back at the car park, timing your arrival to catch a bus back to Reykjahlíð.

STAGE 3
Víti to Reykjahlíð

Start	Víti, Krafla
Finish	Reykjahlíð
Distance	20km (12½ miles)
Total ascent	200m (655ft)
Total descent	500m (1640ft)
Time	7hrs
Terrain	Waymarked paths over low hills and rugged lava flows, with some steep ascents and descents
Maps	1:50,000 'Mál og Menning 8 – Akureyri Mývatn Dettifoss'; free 1:90,000 'Mývatn Lake' from the visitor centre
Transport	SBA Norðurleið link Reykjahlíð, Námaskarð and Krafla
Accommodation	Accommodation and campsites at Reykjahlíð

Buses run to Víti, at the foot of Krafla, and waymarked paths can be followed past Leirhnjúkur to Námaskarð. Explore an amazing geothermal site from top to bottom, then head back to Reykjahlið, maybe taking a hot bath on the way!

Have a look at the **Víti** crater, then walk down the road and turn right into a car park with toilets and a hot-dog stall. Follow a broad path towards Leirhnjúkur and turn left as signposted 'Námaskarð' and 'Reykjahlið'. ▶ Keep left whether signposted or not, following a path left of a fissure. Fells rise ahead and the path rises right of them. Cross a crumbling ash slope and a gap, then drop into a valley-like depression below **Rauðhóll**.

If the hot-spots weren't explored the previous day, visit them now.

Thick lava is piled on crumbling ash, and big boulders litter the area. Climb, then head down to walk alongside a lava flow. Turn a corner and yellow marker pegs run on and off the lava at **Hvithólaklif**. Go under power lines, cross the lava and a dirt track, and turn left beside the lava on the other side, reaching a junction and mapboard at **Arnarhóll**.

The extensive geothermal area of Námaskarð is a fascinating place to explore

Turn right up a vegetated hillside, rising and falling, watching for yellow pegs, and reach a stony crest with gnarled rock outcrops on **Dalfjall**. Drop steeply and continue on and off the crest. Cross a ladder-stile over a fence and follow wheel-marks through lyme grass in a sandy valley. Go up a narrow path and pass a rock wall, with rugged stumps and pinnacles to the left. Rise and fall as vegetation gives way to barren red and brown slopes, down to a road on the gap of **Námaskarð**. ◄

Cross the road and turn left downhill, then turn right up to a junction and climb a steep

Ahead, Námafjall gets dangerously muddy and slippery when wet, in which case turn right for Reykjahlíð.

path flanked by ropes. Walk from one rocky top to another along the crest of **Námafjall**, passing fumaroles. Cross

a broad dip before a final rocky top and keep right of the summit. Zigzag steeply down and wander from one fumarole to another at **Hverir**, passing large mud-pots and looking at information boards.

Climb back towards **Námaskarð**, cross the gap and follow the road down the other side. An ash path runs parallel to the road, levelling out past a blue pool near a power station. Turn left to reach the **Nature Baths** (café and bathing, tel 4644411). Keep right and cross a ladder-stile over a fence, then walk to **Reykjahlið** as described in Stage 1.

Walkers follow a signposted trail on the outskirts of Reykjahlið

9 SPRENGISANDUR AND KJÖLUR

Broad moorland near Gislaskáli, with Kjalfell seen in the distance (Trek 8 Stage 3)

Deep in the central highlands of Iceland, Sprengisandur and Kjölur are remote and uninhabited, covered in sand and gravel, with very little vegetation. They are Arctic deserts, between the glaciers of Vatnajökull, Hofsjökull and Langjökull. Despite being bleak and barren, cross-country routes evolved for summer travel and trade. The Sprengisandur Road was the least favoured, with barely enough vegetation to feed horses or livestock. The Kjölur Track, on the other hand, has had many incarnations, and while vehicles follow a clear dirt road today, the remains of older tracks and trails can still be traced with confidence.

In the middle of Sprengisandur, a couple of fine walks are available from the remote hut at Nýidalur (Walks 40 and 41). These explore a dale that was discovered only in 1845, as well as fells flanking the small ice-cap of Tungnafellsjökull. The Kjölur area is explored by linking a series of marked trails (Trek 8), taking advantage of opportunities to walk from hut to hut for a whole week.

Despite being remote, uninhabited and blocked by snow for most of the year, the Sprengisandur Road and Kjölur Track have good bus services in the summer. The Sprengisandur bus operates from Reykjavík and Landmannalaugar, through Nýidalur to Mývatn and Reykjahlið. The following day the journey is reversed, and so on through the week. The Kjölur Track has a daily bus service in both directions, including a spur to and from the mountain massif of Kerlingafjöll. Both bus services stop from time to time to allow passengers to walk to nearby waterfalls, including Goðafoss, near Mývatn, and Gulfoss, near Reykjavík.

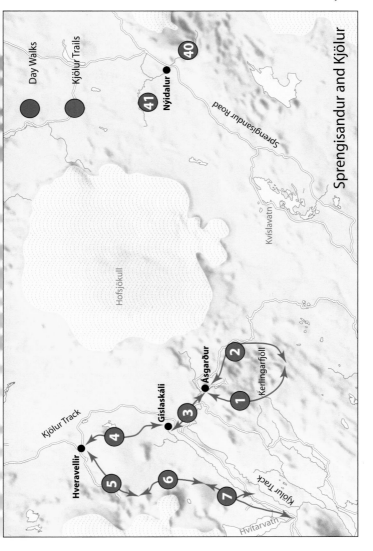

Sprengisandur and Kjölur

WALK 40
Nýidalur and Kaldagil

Start/Finish	Nýidalur
Distance	19km (12 miles)
Total ascent/descent	500m (1640ft)
Time	6hrs 30mins
Terrain	Glacial rivers need fording in a dale that is otherwise easy. A very steep climb is followed by a broad and stony crest.
Map	1:100,000 'Mál og Menning – Atlaskort 16 Hofsjökull'
Transport	Reykjavík Excursions serve Nýidalur from Reykjavík, Selfoss, Landmannalaugar and Reykjahlið

The verdant Nýidalur was discovered as late as 1845. It is notable for its range of flowers and offers easy walking, apart from fording glacial rivers. It is possible to climb steeply onto a stony crest and follow this back to the start.

Leave the FÍ huts at **Nýidalur**, around 800m (2625ft), and follow the dirt road in the direction of Mývatn, fording the glacial **Fjórðungakvísl**. Turn right upstream to cross minor streams. Keep away from the river, and it is necessary to climb above it on the slopes of **Þvermóður**. Cross a side-valley and continue up through the main dale,

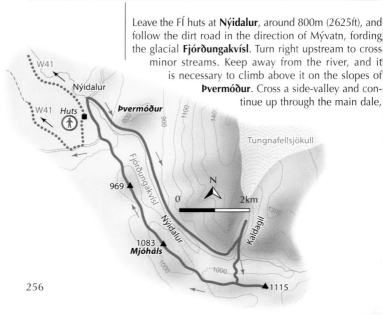

Nýidalur. Old wheel-marks can be traced, but they vanish on stony alluvial fans.

Eventually, the whole floor of the dale is stony. Swing left into a rugged, steep-sided valley at **Kaldagil**, around 900m (2950ft). Maybe catch sight of a glacier tongue coming from **Tungnafellsjökull**, then come back down. Ford the glacial river and go straight across the main valley to ford another river. ▸ Look very carefully at the very steep and stony southern slopes of the dale to spot a line of ascent that is mossier than any other part, with no rocky outcrops. Despite the steepness, the stones are stable and the gradient just about allows ordinary walkers to climb.

Reach a rounded crest and yellow marker posts. Turn left to sample good views from a rounded top at 1115m (3658ft), then double back. Cross a broad, stony, sparsely vegetated gap. Rise along the very broad, hummocky crest of **Mjóháls**, where marker posts lead through little gaps, passing a pool. The summit cairn stands at 1083m (3553ft). A long descent leads to a gap, and markers lead onto a stony hump with cairns at 969m (3179ft). Walk down as marked, join stony wheel-marks and turn left to follow them, soon forking right to join a dirt road. Turn right again to return to the huts.

A glimpse of Tungnafellsjökull, seen from the rugged Kaldagil

Alternatively, anyone unwilling to ford rivers should retrace their steps to Nýidalur.

WALK 41
Nýidalur and Sprengisandur

Start/Finish	Nýidalur
Distance	31km (19¼ miles)
Total ascent/descent	150m (490ft)
Time	8hrs 30mins
Terrain	Gently rolling stony tracks, then rugged stony slopes beside a river, vegetated in places
Map	1:100,000 'Mál og Menning – Atlaskort 16 Hofsjökull'
Transport	Reykjavík Excursions serve Nýidalur from Reykjavík, Selfoss, Landmannalaugar and Reykjahlíð

A little-used dirt road is followed a long way across the barren, stony desert of Sprengisandur. The glacial river of Fjórðungakvísl offers a clear, obvious and interesting route back to the huts at Nýidalur.

Leave the Fí huts at **Nýidalur**, around 800m (2625ft), either walking up the Sprengisandur road or following the river upstream. Either way, ford the shallow river and turn right as signposted 'Kvíslavatn' along a dirt road. This undulates gently across stony and sandy desert. It is difficult to gauge progress through this bleak and barren area, but it is a simple matter to follow the road, rising and falling repeatedly. At one point, orange posts block a lesser track on the right. ◄

This offers a way to shortcut the walk.

Keep to the main track, rising and falling, with increasingly barren views. Eventually, a shallow stream is easily crossed. Beyond this, a junction is reached where signposts are illegible, apart from one pointing back – 'Nýidalur 14km'. Turn right and a broad river comes into view, with banks streaked green. Cross a shallow stream – the same as crossed earlier – then follow the main river upstream. This is **Fjórðungakvísl** and it leads all the way back to the start, but the walk is only half-completed.

Cross lumpy moss, creeping willow, arctic river-beauty and stony, sandy areas. Later, drift right of the

river to avoid undercut banks, then cross rugged, bouldery humps rather than following the river. When a

The braided, glacial Fjórðungakvísl, seen near the huts at Nýidalur

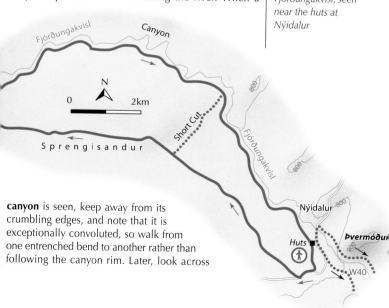

canyon is seen, keep away from its crumbling edges, and note that it is exceptionally convoluted, so walk from one entrenched bend to another rather than following the canyon rim. Later, look across

Broad, bleak, barren, stony Sprengisandur, with Tungnafellsjökull beyond

The shortcut joins here.

the river to spot a track marked by orange posts, but it is vague on this side of the river. ◄

Continue upstream, crossing stony and mossy slopes, and drop to a stony floodplain with more vegetation. The river becomes constricted, so climb over a ridge of moraine. Further upstream another constriction and another ridge of moraine are crossed. Keep away from the glacial river and ford a shallow, clear-water river to reach the **Nýidalur** huts on a grassy slope beyond.

TREK 8

The Kjölur Trails

Start	Ásgarður
Finish	Arbuðir or Hvítárnes
Distance	137 or 143km (85¼ or 88¾ miles)
Time	7 days
Terrain	Some rugged and pathless stretches at first, with river crossings, becoming easier in the middle, later finishing along dirt roads
Facilities	Restaurant at Ásgarður. Small shop at Gislaskáli. Restaurant at Hveravellir. Huts.
Accommodation	Huts and/or camping

There are three trails that can be conveniently linked end to end to explore Kjölur. The first of these (Stages 1–2) is a two-day circuit around the mountain massif of Kerlingarfjöll. The second (Stages 3–4) is a two-day link of the author's making, between Kerlingarfjöll and Hveravellir, taking in newly waymarked paths and an ancient cairned route. The third trail (Stages 5–7) is the Kjalvegur, which pre-dates the current Kjölur Track used by vehicles today. By all means amend and adapt the route, taking advantage of the fact that bus services are available at a number of points.

The **Kerlingarfjöll Circuit** is quite rugged and pathless in places, and involves fording a few rivers. Although a couple of huts are available on the trail, they are usually locked, and access needs to be arranged before leaving the start of the trail at Ásgarður. In poor weather, this trail is probably best avoided, as there are no waymarks or paths on some awkward stretches. After leaving **Kerlingarfjöll** a dirt road and a waymarked riverside path are followed most of the way to the Kjölur Track and a hut at Gislaskáli, suitable for an overnight break. From there, dirt roads are used to link with an ancient cairned route that leads most of the way to the busy geothermal hot-spot of **Hveravellir**. At this point the popular **Kjalvegur** is followed from hut to hut for three days, until it leads back to the Kjölur Track.

The same cross-country bus service serves all three trails, trundling slowly back and forth along the Kjölur Track in both directions every day, and also taking the spur road to Kerlingarfjöll. The bus runs between Reykjavík and Akureyri, the two largest settlements in Iceland.

STAGE 1
Kerlingarfjöll Circuit – Ásgarður to Klakkur

Start	Ásgarður
Finish	Klakkur
Distance	22km (13¾ miles)
Total ascent	650m (2130ft)
Total descent	500m (1640ft)
Time	8hrs
Terrain	Paths and waymarks at the start, then pathless and unmarked, with rivers and ravines to cross on stony fellsides
Maps	1:50,000 'Mál og Menning – 3 Kjölur Langjökull Kerlingarfjöll'; free 1:50,000 'Hiking Route around Kerlingarfjöll' from tourist information offices and Ásgarður
Transport	SBA Norðurleið serve Kerlingarfjöll from Reykjavík, Gulfoss, Akureyri and Hveravellir
Accommodation	Hut at Klakkur

Ásgarður is a huddle of huts with a small restaurant. The first half of this two-day circuit runs from Ásgarður to Klakkur, around the western flanks of Kerlingarfjöll. Careful route-finding is required on pathless and unmarked stretches.

Leave the huts at **Ásgarður**, cross a footbridge over a river, cross a small stream and climb. Grass gives way to a steep and stony slope, with a path marked '2' by wooden posts. Walk up the gentle crest of **Ásgarðshryggur** and head right as marked '9'. The ground is stony and gradients are gentle, with no path. Rise and fall across stony wash-outs, then descend to cross a trickle of water.

Climb to spot a trio of fells ahead, with the ice-caps of Langjökull and Hofsjökull in the distance. Marker posts are backed up with cairns and rocks painted '9', leading to a deep-cut valley where gullies converge. Ford the **Fremri-Ásgarðsá** and hug the edge of a plain before following

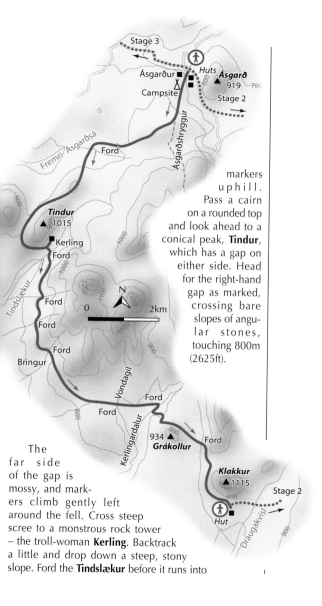

Stage 3

Ásgarður ■
Campsite
Huts
▲ Ásgarð
919
Stage 2

Fremri-Ásgarðsá

Ford

markers
uphill.
Pass a cairn
on a rounded top
and look ahead to a
conical peak, **Tindur**,
which has a gap on
either side. Head
for the right-hand
gap as marked,
crossing bare
slopes of angu-
lar stones,
touching 800m
(2625ft).

Tindur
▲ 1015
■ Kerling
Ford

Tindslækur

Ford

N

0   2km

Ford

Ford

Bringur

Vondagil

Ford

Ford

934 ▲
Grákollur

Ford

Klakkur
▲ 1115

Stage 2

Hut

Draugakvísl

The
far side
of the gap is
mossy, and mark-
ers climb gently left
around the fell. Cross steep
scree to a monstrous rock tower
– the troll-woman **Kerling**. Backtrack
a little and drop down a steep, stony
slope. Ford the **Tindslækur** before it runs into

a gorge, and climb the other side where a small side-valley joins. There is a sloping, stony shelf between the river and higher fells, without paths or markers, so look carefully to spot ways across a succession of steep-sided ravines. Generally, climb a little after crossing each one to find the easiest route. A gentle, stony gap is reached at **Bringur**, where two bigger ravines converge. Cross these and climb further, aiming for another gap, where dark stones give way to light stones.

Continue a gradual climbing traverse, then go gently down a stony plain. Find and cross the ravine of **Vondagil**, and cross a small stream beyond. Walk to a confluence of ravines at **Kerlingardalur**, and go down a crumbling slope of stones and grit, heading downstream to ford the river. When another stream comes in from the left, it is possible to climb from a wooden stake out of the ravine. Look ahead for widely spaced markers and walk towards the southern slopes of **Klakkur**, crossing a couple of streams flanked by moss. A track is reached, leading to a gleaming corrugated hut (administered from Ásgarður, tel 6647878 or 6647000, www.kerlingarfjoll.is).

Evening view of barren Kerlingarfjöll fellsides from the Klakkur hut

Streaks of moss flank a stream at the foot of the stony Klakkur

STAGE 2
Kerlingarfjöll Circuit – Klakkur to Ásgarður

Start	Klakkur
Finish	Ásgarður
Distance	28km (17½ miles)
Total ascent	350m (1150ft)
Total descent	500m (1640ft)
Time	11hrs
Terrain	Stony slopes, plains and ravines, with river crossings at the foot of fells
Maps	1:50,000 'Mál og Menning – 3 Kjölur Langjökull Kerlingarfjöll'; free 1:50,000 'Hiking Route around Kerlingarfjöll' from tourist information offices and Ásgarður
Transport	SBA Norðurleið serve Kerlingarfjöll from Reykjavík, Gulfoss, Akureyri and Hveravellir
Accommodation	Basic hut near Kisufell; huts at Ásgarður

The second half of this two-day circuit can be split early at a small hut below Kisufell. Beyond that, rivers are followed upstream and downstream, then a series of glacial rivers are crossed to return to Ásgarður.

A fairly clear track is followed across broad, stony areas between Klakkur and Kisufell

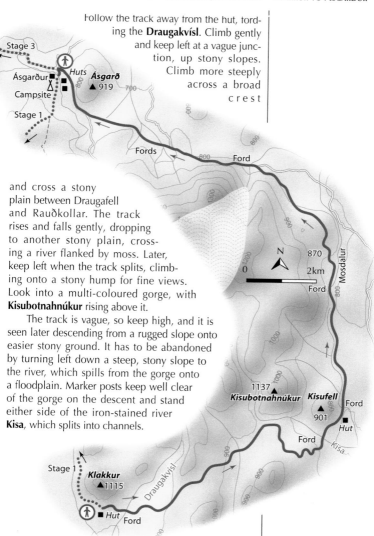

Follow the track away from the hut, fording the **Draugakvísl**. Climb gently
and keep left at a vague junction, up stony slopes.
Climb more steeply
across a broad
crest

and cross a stony
plain between Draugafell
and Rauðkollar. The track
rises and falls gently, dropping
to another stony plain, crossing a river flanked by moss. Later,
keep left when the track splits, climbing onto a stony hump for fine views.
Look into a multi-coloured gorge, with
Kisubotnahnúkur rising above it.

The track is vague, so keep high, and it is
seen later descending from a rugged slope onto
easier stony ground. It has to be abandoned
by turning left down a steep, stony slope to
the river, which spills from the gorge onto
a floodplain. Marker posts keep well clear
of the gorge on the descent and stand
either side of the iron-stained river
Kisa, which splits into channels.

A milky river is followed upstream from the hut below Kisufell

Ford it and continue across a stony plain to reach a small, basic hut near **Kisufell** (administered from Ásgarður, tel 6647878 or 6647000, www.kerlingarfjoll.is).

Walk across a level, grassy area, crossing small streams and a broader river, continuing upstream as marked. Traverse an awkward slope above the river, cut by stony gullies. The river is milky, but a couple of clear-water streams run into it, and a marker indicates that one of these is followed upstream. Cross and recross as the valley becomes narrow and rugged. There are little waterfalls, and a boulder-jam requires a scramble to pass. The stream becomes a mere trickle and a gentle, stony gap is crossed around 870m (2855ft).

Look down the fellside to see a stream in a rugged gorge. Walk parallel to the gorge on safe, stony slopes until the stream leaves it. Cross over it, and another stream, to hug the margin between mossy **Mosdalur** and stony slopes. When a waterfall is reached, the slope is too steep, so cross the river. When the slope eases, cross back and make a rising traverse through a broad gap. Drop down and rise while crossing small ravines, reaching a broad, gravelly plain. Rise gently, parallel to a track but well to the left of it, on sand and gravel.

The track fords a braided glacial river, rising and falling gently, and reaches another stony plain. The track climbs a hill, but veer left instead to find another glacial river carving a valley through stones. Ford it and climb, using a ravine to reach a stony, mossy shelf. The next stream is shallow, and the one after is a glacial river, with marker posts on both sides. Cross small ravines and climb over a hill, heading right to reach a dirt road. Follow this across the slopes of **Ásgarð**, going downhill and left to return to the huts at **Ásgarður**.

STAGE 3
Ásgarður to Gíslaskáli

Start	Ásgarður
Finish	Gíslaskáli
Distance	16km (10 miles)
Total ascent	150m (490ft)
Total descent	300m (985ft)
Time	6hrs
Terrain	Dirt roads and lightly trodden riverside paths, with some pathless stretches
Map	1:100,000 'Mál og Menning – 3 Kjölur Langjökull Kerlingarfjöll'
Transport	SBA Norðurleið serve Kerlingarfjöll and Gislaskáli from Reykjavík, Gulfoss, Akureyri and Hveravellir
Accommodation	Gíslaskáli hut

The walk away from Kerlingarfjöll is easy, and the dirt road need not be used much. The glacial river Jökulfall can be followed most of the way, passing a splendid waterfall. The little-known hut of Gíslaskáli is a fine place to stay.

Leave the huts at **Ásgarður**, following the dirt road away from Kerlingarfjöll. Pass a big boulder, follow the road down and cross a culvert on the Ásgarðsá. The road rises over a barren, stony area, descending gently to a broad, grassy dale. Cross a bridge over the powerful **Jökulfall** and admire it crashing into a gorge. Marker posts lead alongside the gorge, rising onto a stony plain. Follow a brow high above the river, looking down on a grotesque pinnacle, generally keeping clear of the edge. Go onto a high, boulder-strewn shelf, and later drop to a point above a waterfall. ◄

It is possible to go down to the river, then climb back.

Continue along the brow, dropping to the river later to pass a little hut, following the riverbank to rejoin the dirt road. Admire the waterfall of **Gýgjarfoss** and its convoluted gorge. Continue along a stony brow overlooking the river, rising and falling. Sometimes it is possible to see the river in the gorge, but at other times it is too deep and con-stricted. Eventually, the river surges from the gorge and is joined by the clear-water **Fossrófulækur**. Swing right to follow this upstream and cross it at a culvert, following the dirt road.

Walk up the road to a junction with the **Kjölur Track**, turning right along a broad crest and descending into a dip. A track heads left through a broad, grassy sheep-grazed area, leading to the hut of **Gíslaskáli**. There is usually space here when other huts are

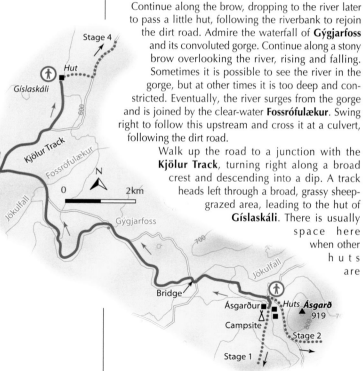

Stage 4

Hut

Gíslaskáli

Kjölur Track

Fossrófulækur

Jökulfall

N

0   2km

Gýgjarfoss

Bridge

Ásgarður

Campsite

Huts **Ásgarð**

919

Stage 2

Stage 1

full, and a small range of food is sold (tel 4868757, 8959500 or 8673571, www.gljasteinn.is).

The powerful Gýgjarfoss pours into a constricted rocky gorge

Stage 4
Gíslaskáli to Hveravellir

Start	Gíslaskáli
Finish	Hveravellir
Distance	26km (16 miles)
Total ascent	180m (590ft)
Total descent	120m (395ft)
Time	9hrs
Terrain	Mostly along dirt roads, with a pathless stretch across rugged moorland marked by cairns
Map	1:100,000 'Mál og Menning – 3 Kjölur Langjökull Kerlingarfjöll'
Transport	SBA Norðurleið serve Gislaskáli and Hveravellir from Reykjavík, Gulfoss, Kerlingarfjöll and Akureyri
Accommodation	Lodgings and campsite at Hveravellir

Quick walking along dirt roads and tracks leads to a monument at Beinahóll. Large cairns march across a rugged moor, passing a cave at Grettishellir. An extensive geothermal area can be explored at Hveravellir.

Follow the access track up from **Gíslaskáli** to a boulder-strewn crest. Turn left along the **Kjölur Track**, with views of Langjökull, Hofsjökull and Kerlingarfjöll. Cross a gentle dip, rise and note a prominent cairn on the left, and later cross a dip with a stream at **Eystri-Svártárbotnar**. Rise and fall gently, then turn left along a track signposted 'Beinahóll'. This crosses stony ground with little tufts of moss, flowers and willow, and later crosses ropy lava with great cracked 'blisters'. It is rugged underfoot as the track weaves and undulates, with Kjalfell

looming large. Reach the end of the track at the **Beinahóll** memorial. ◀

Five men died of exposure here in 1780. The scattered bones are the remains of their livestock.

Walk across pathless vegetated lava, heading for a line of prominent cairns. Turn right to follow them, and although the slope is gentle it is stony and bouldery. A rocky ridge at **Grettishellir** has a lava tube under it.

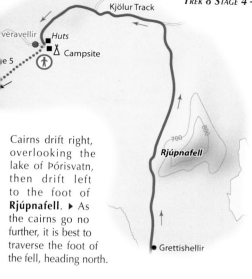

Cairns drift right, overlooking the lake of Þórisvatn, then drift left to the foot of **Rjúpnafell**. ▸ As the cairns go no further, it is best to traverse the foot of the fell, heading north.

Steam might be seen rising from distant Hveravellir, but there is rugged lava in that direction.

The monument at Beinahóll

273

This leads to the **Kjölur Track**, where vehicles are seen from time to time.

The next part of the trek, the Kjalvegur, starts here.

Turn left along the dirt road, going gently up and down to a signposted junction, turning left for **Hveravellir**. Walk up to another junction and turn left again, heading down to a car park and huts. ◄ There are lodgings, bar, campsite, hot pool and information about colour-coded trails exploring the hot springs, fumaroles, mud-pots and rugged lava (tel 8941293, www.hveravellir. is). Drinking water is sold in the bar, as surface water in this area is unsuitable for drinking.

Stage 5
Kjalvegur – Hveravellir to Þjófadalir

Start	Hveravellir
Finish	Þjófadalir
Distance	12km (7½ miles)
Total ascent	200m (655ft)
Total descent	140m (460ft)
Time	4hrs 30mins
Terrain	A rugged trail across lava, followed by an easy dirt road, ending with a short, steep descent
Map	1:100,000 'Mál og Menning – 3 Kjölur Langjökull Kerlingarfjöll'
Transport	SBA Norðurleið serve Hveravellir from Reykjavík, Gulfoss, Kerlingarfjöll and Akureyri
Accommodation	Basic hut at Þjófadalir

Many Kjalvegur trekkers follow a dirt road from Hveravellir, but this route follows a waymarked trail across rugged lava that links with the dirt road later. If Þjófadalir is reached early in the day, it is possible to continue easily to Þverbrekknamúli at the end of Stage 6.

Leave **Hveravellir**, around 620m (2035ft), following a board-walk up through the geothermal area and stepping off it where a little cone furiously vents pungent steam. A

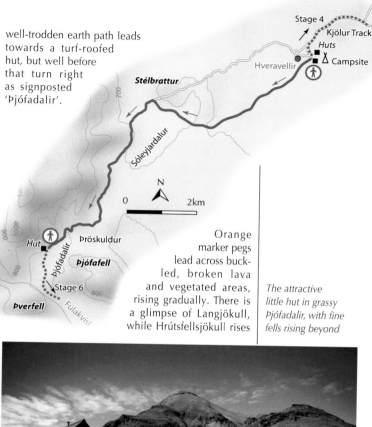

well-trodden earth path leads towards a turf-roofed hut, but well before that turn right as signposted 'Þjófadalir'.

Stélbrattur

Sóleyjardalur

Stage 4

Kjölur Track

Huts

Hveravellir

△ Campsite

N

0   2km

Hut

Þröskuldur

Þjófadalir

Þjófafell

Stage 6

Þverfell

Fúlakvísl

Orange marker pegs lead across buckled, broken lava and vegetated areas, rising gradually. There is a glimpse of Langjökull, while Hrútsfellsjökull rises

The attractive little hut in grassy Þjófadalir, with fine fells rising beyond

prominently ahead. Keep left of a rocky, rounded fell with boulder scree, where the lava ends.

Walk across stony slopes beyond, going gently down, then up and down to reach the edge of the lava, where there are impressive cracked 'blisters'. Drift slightly left beside a grassy sand and gravel plain, reaching a dirt road at **Sóleyjardalur**. A sign points back to Hveravellir and there are no more markers. Turn left to follow the sandy, dusty road through a gentle gap and across another grassy plain.

Climb the slopes of a subsidiary of **Þjófafell**, continuing steeply up to a gap and a car park. Look into the fine grassy **Þjófadalir**, flanked by fells, with Langjökull above and Hrútfellsjökull beyond. Drop steeply down, looking for the path, and walk through the dale to the FÍ hut. It is basic, with no showers, and water is drawn from a nearby spring.

STAGE 6
Kjalvegur – Þjófadalir to Þverbrekknamúli

Start	Þjófadalir
Finish	Þverbrekknamúli
Distance	14km (8¾ miles)
Total ascent	120m (395ft)
Total descent	300m (985ft)
Time	5hrs 30mins
Terrain	Level moorland and a short hill-walk at the end, with some steep slopes
Map	1:100,000 'Mál og Menning – 3 Kjölur Langjökull Kerlingarfjöll'
Transport	None
Accommodation	Hut at Þverbrekknamúli

The Kjalvegur is popular with horse-riders, and most of this stage follows parallel ruts trodden by horses across broad moorland. A glacial river is spanned by a footbridge over a narrow gorge. Small, steep-sided hills are crossed at the end.

Walk gently down through **Þjófadalir** on an easy, grassy path. Cross a river with a view of distant Kerlingarfjöll. Follow the river downstream, although there may be no water in it. Hrútfellsjökull appears in view ahead as the path crosses lumpy grassland, sand and stones, reaching a fenced horse **corral**. There are faded signposts, so keep right of the enclosure and walk straight ahead. Although there are cairns, the rutted path is obvious, pulling away from the river. Pass water-holes in a bouldery dip and later walk beside the powerful, murky, glacial **Fúlakvísl**.

The river runs into a gorge and shouldn't be approached closely. It leaves the gorge and splits on shoals of shingle, gravel, sand and mud. The path runs from cairn to cairn on broken lava, and there is later low, dense willow near the river. Follow the river as it turns around the foot of rounded hills, before it squeezes through an incredibly narrow gorge. Look for a tiny **footbridge** and cross it. The gorge is narrow enough to jump, but the penalty for slipping is death!

A path climbs diagonally up a steep, stony slope on **Múlar**. Follow marker posts over a gentle, stony rise and down to a gap. Climb a more vegetated slope, rising and falling, then go down a steep, stony slope that levels out on a grassy shelf. Ahead is a low fell, **Þverbrekknamúli**, with a huge floodplain beyond. Walk down ropy lava to

Stage 5
Hut
Þröskuldur
Þjófafell
Þjófadalir
Þverfell
Corral
N
0   2km
Fremra-Sandfell
Fúlakvísl
Footbridge
Múlar
Þverbrekkur
Þverbrekknamúli
Hut
Footbridge
Fúlakvísl
Stage 7

Looking across rolling moorland from the Kjalvegur to the fells of Kerlingarfjöll

Some walkers spend an extra day here to climb the ice-capped Hrútfellsjökull.

the FÍ hut at the foot of the fell. This is rather basic when its water supply fails, with the nearest alternative source 1km (½ mile) away. ◄

STAGE 7
Kjalvegur – Þverbrekknamúli to Arbuðir or Hvítárnes

Start	Þverbrekknamúli
Finish	Arbuðir or beyond Hvítárnes
Distance	19 or 25km (12 or 15½ miles)
Total ascent	30m (100ft)
Total descent	150m (490ft)
Time	7hrs 30mins or 9hrs
Terrain	Easy riverside paths, then care is needed later where paths and tracks lead in several directions
Map	1:100,000 'Mál og Menning – 3 Kjölur Langjökull Kerlingarfjöll'
Transport	SBA Norðurleið serve Arbuðir from Reykjavík, Gulfoss, Kerlingarfjöll, Hveravellir and Akureyri
Accommodation	Huts at Arbuðir and Hvítárnes

This stage of the Kjalvegur is easy, with gentle gradients, but keep an eye on paths and tracks in places. There is a choice of two huts towards the end, and two ways to reach the Kjölur Track and its buses.

Leave the hut at **Þverbrekknamúli** and follow tall posts past a cairn on a rise, descending through willow and birch to the glacial **Fúlakvísl**. Cross a high footbridge, turn right and rejoin the rutted horse trail at a cairn bearing a warning triangle. There are extensive views. A vehicle track is followed that becomes sandy where it runs through willow. Cross another vehicle track and follow rutted paths through low, mixed vegetation. Areas of lava lie near the river around **Þverbrekknaver**.

When slopes of Baldheiði allow, views stretch to Hvítárvatn and Langjökull. The river surges through a rocky gorge and a deep, steepsided, stony cutting. The path pulls away from the river, weaving about, becoming a sandy groove through low scrub. Cairns lead to a ford on a small river, with a choice of routes.

For Arbuðir

Ford the river and follow a path gently uphill, heading southwards over a stony slope. There are other paths, but the idea is to keep straight ahead, eventually crossing a stony crest and a dirt road. Walk down to ford the **Svartá** and reach the hut at **Arbuðir** (tel 4868757, 8959500 or 8673571, www.gljasteinn.is). Buses run on the adjacent Kjölur Track.

Map continues on page 280

279

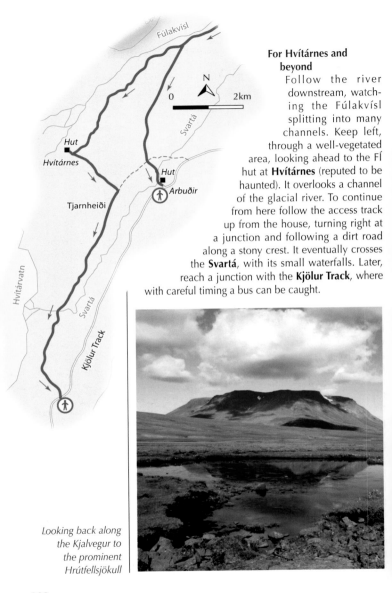

For Hvítárnes and beyond

Follow the river downstream, watching the Fúlakvísl splitting into many channels. Keep left, through a well-vegetated area, looking ahead to the FÍ hut at **Hvítárnes** (reputed to be haunted). It overlooks a channel of the glacial river. To continue from here follow the access track up from the house, turning right at a junction and following a dirt road along a stony crest. It eventually crosses the **Svartá**, with its small waterfalls. Later, reach a junction with the **Kjölur Track**, where with careful timing a bus can be caught.

Looking back along the Kjalvegur to the prominent Hrútfellsjökull

10 HORNSTRANDIR PENINSULA

Little streams are crossed by small footbridges on the way out of Hesteyri (Trek 9 Stage 1)

Hornstrandir is the most remote north-western peninsula in Iceland. It is an important nature reserve, noted for its range of birds and population of Arctic foxes. No roads serve this area, and snow lingers a long time. As a result, there is only a brief period in the summer when people visit Hornstrandir. Many families from Ísafjörður occupy summer houses and cabins, mostly clustered beside a handful of inlets. A ferry operates from Ísafjörður to various points around the peninsula, and a number of interesting and scenic trails are partly marked and sometimes well trodden. With careful planning, trekkers can explore Hornstrandir in some detail, but it is essential to take all food supplies and

camping equipment there. Tidal rivers may need to be forded, so be aware of the tide times.

Despite the apparent remoteness of Hornstrandir, ferries operate from the little town of Ísafjörður, and this can be reached in a number of ways. The bus journey from Reykjavík or Akureyri to Ísafjörður can be completed in a very long day, but connections don't work every day, so careful study of timetables is required. Flying from Reykjavík to Ísafjörður speeds up the journey, and if there is time to transfer to the ferry, then Hornstrandir can be reached the same day. Sjóferðir ferry timetables should be checked in advance (tel 4563879, www.sjoferdir.is).

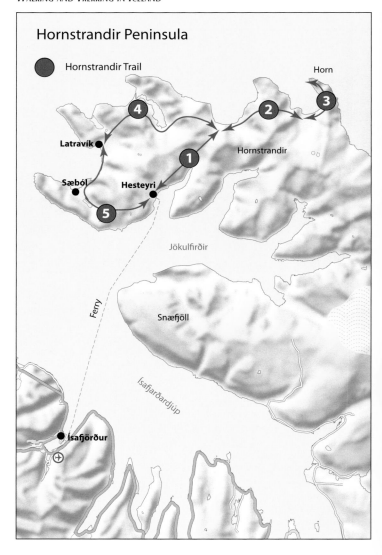

Hornstrandir Peninsula

Hornstrandir Trail

Horn

Latravík

Hornstrandir

Sæból   Hesteyri

Jökulfirðir

Ferry

Snæfjöll

Ísafjarðardjúp

Ísafjörður

TREK 9

The Hornstrandir Trail

Start/Finish	Hesteyri
Distance	First three-day trek – 42km (26 miles); Second three-day trek – 61km (38 miles); six-day option – 100km (62 miles)
Time	3–6 days
Terrain	Although some paths are marked by posts or cairns, most are not, and some routes aren't well-trodden on the ground. There are some steep and rugged slopes, some tidal rivers that need fording, and the possibility of snow on the ground.
Facilities	Doctor's House at Hesteyri offers basic lodgings, food and drink
Accommodation	Apart from basic lodgings at Hesteyri, camping

Three options for interesting treks are offered here (two three-day treks and one six-day trek), depending how walkers arrange their ferries and how much food they are carrying. **First three-day trek** – catch a ferry to Hesteyri, and complete Stages 1, 2 and 3 to Hornvík. **Second three-day trek** – catch the ferry to Hesteyri and complete Stages 1, 4 and 5 in a circuit leading back to Hesteyri. The **six-day option** combines all these stages, starting from Hesteyri – complete Stages 1, 2 and 3, then double back along Stage 2 to link Stages 4 and 5, returning to Hesteyri. The only place offering basic lodgings and food on Hornstrandir is the Doctor's House at Hesteyri (tel 8535034, www.hesteyri.net).

STAGE 1
Hesteyri to Hlöðuvík

Start	Hesteyri
Finish	Hlöðuvík
Distance	15km (9½ miles)
Total ascent/descent	500m (1640ft)
Time	6hrs
Terrain	Steep, stony slopes and gentle vegetated slopes, sometimes wet, with some streams to ford
Maps	1:55,000 'Mál og Menning – 9 Hornstrandir'; 1:100,000 'Ferðakort – Hornstrandir'; 1:100,000 'Vestfirðir & Dalur 1'
Transport	Sjóferðir ferry links Ísafjörður and Hesteyri
Accommodation	Camping and hut at Hesteyri; camping at Hlöðuvík

This popular cairned trail crosses the Hornstrandir peninsula at a narrow point, over the gap of Kjaransvíkurskarð. Turning right at Kjaransvík leads towards Horn (Stages 2 and 3), and turning left allows a circuit to be completed back to Hesteyri (Stages 4 and 5).

Step ashore at **Hesteyri** and turn right along a path flanked by angelica, reaching the Doctor's House (café and hut accommodation). Cross footbridges over river channels and walk beside **Hesteyrarfjörður**. A ruined whaling station can be seen ahead and a path heads there. However, after crossing a stream, turn left up a slope of bare earth and stones, aiming for a cairn on a brow.

Map continues on page 286

Cross a stream and rise gently on flowery

284

slopes, then climb steeply to another cairn on another brow, enjoying views back to Ísafjörður. Rise gently past a cairn beside a stream, then cairns cross rough, stony ground to a vegetated area where the path vanishes. Look for more cairns heading gently down a rugged slope, later rising and falling, and crossing several streams around **Innri-Hesteyrarbrúnir**. Keep an eye on an obvious gap in the fells ahead. Climb the steep and stony slope of Andbrekkur, passing cairns on the gap of **Kjaransvíkurskarð**, around 430m (1410ft). ▶ Wind down the other side on a steep, bouldery slope onto a gentler slope. All the way down through the dale, there are short, steep, rugged 'steps', separated by gentler, vegetated slopes. At first the cairned path is well to the left of the river, **Kjaransvíkursá**, then moves closer to its waterfalls and cascades. Ford the inflowing **Þverá**, walk down a flowery moorland to the sea at **Kjaransvík**, and turn right. ▶

Looking back down to Hesteyri, and along Hesteyrarfjörður, to distant Ísafjörður

Snow often lingers into summer here.

Turn left for Stage 4.

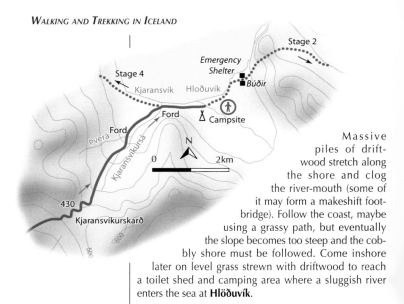

Massive piles of drift-wood stretch along the shore and clog the river-mouth (some of it may form a makeshift foot-bridge). Follow the coast, maybe using a grassy path, but eventually the slope becomes too steep and the cob-bly shore must be followed. Come inshore later on level grass strewn with driftwood to reach a toilet shed and camping area where a sluggish river enters the sea at **Hlöðuvík**.

STAGE 2
Hlöðuvik to Hornvík

Start	Hlöðuvik
Finish	Hornvík
Distance	12km (7½ miles)
Total ascent/descent	380m (1245ft)
Time	5hrs
Terrain	Steep ascents and descents, crossing gaps in the fells. Some scrambling on a rugged coastal path.
Maps	1:55,000 'Mál og Menning – 9 Hornstrandir'; 1:100,000 'Ferðakort – Hornstrandir'; 1:100,000 'Útivera Vestfirðir & Dalur 1'
Transport	Sjóferðir ferry links Ísafjörður and Hornvík
Accommodation	Campsite at Hornvík

Steep, rugged and attractive fells lie between Hlöðuvík and Hornvík, and gaps between them bear a good path. There is also a very rugged coastal path between Rekavík and Hornvík, equipped with a rope at one point.

Leave the camping area at **Hlöðuvík** and cross a foot-bridge over the river. Continue along the coast

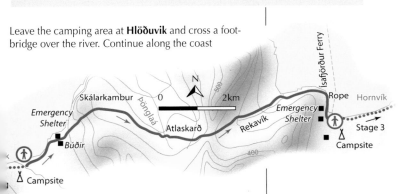

to a huddle of huts at **Búðir**. ▶ Cross a little footbridge, and as the path splits keep left to avoid most of the boggy ground ahead, although both paths reach the foot of a waterfall. Climb into a corrie which has a small tarn. Zigzag steeply to find

One hut is an emergency shelter.

Looking down to Buðir and Hlöðuvík from the rugged gap of Skálarkambur

287

a way up the rocky headwall, crossing a gap between rocky summits at **Skálarkambur**, over 300m (985ft).

The descent is at a gentle gradient, but on a bouldery, stony slope. Follow cairns and a good path across little streams, then cross the broader **Þönglaá**. Climb a steep and stony slope, dropping down the other side to cross little streams. Then climb a steep and worn route above the gap of **Atlaskarð** before dropping onto it, at 327m (1073ft). ◄ Follow the path down into the broad, green, often flowery dale of **Rekavík**, which levels out in a wet and boggy area. Pass wooden decking (the owner dislikes people stopping here) and drop to a river-mouth, crossing a driftwood logjam.

> From here there is a view of Hornvík looking like a lake, with Hornbjarg rising beyond.

Climb and follow a path across a grassy slope above the sea, taking care as it gets steep and crumbly. Drop to a boulder beach and walk to a rock tower. Pass behind it, up and down a crumbling slope protected by a rope. Follow the boulder beach past an emergency hut, ferry landing and overgrown ruins, reaching a campsite at **Hornvík**, where there are a couple of huts and toilets.

STAGE 3
Hornvík and Horn

Start/Finish	Hornvík
Distance	15km (9½ miles)
Total ascent/descent	560m (1840ft)
Time	5hrs
Terrain	Tidal river crossing and coastal walking, reaching sheer cliffs and some very steep slopes
Maps	1:55,000 'Mál og Menning – 9 Hornstrandir'; 1:100,000 'Ferðakort – Hornstrandir'; 1:100,000 'Útivera Vestfirðir & Dalur 1'
Transport	Sjóferðir ferry links Ísafjörður and Hornvík
Accommodation	Campsite at Hornvík

The 'Horn' of Hornstrandir is quite popular, despite its remoteness. The cliffs are populated by birds, and the steep slopes are remarkably well vegetated with grass and flowers. Tidal river crossings require careful timing.

Leave most of your things at the campsite and walk along the beach at the head of **Hornvík**. There are two tidal river-mouths to ford, or a lengthy walk inland to avoid them. Pass rocky outcrops and a waterfall at Steinþors-standur, and walk along an awkward storm-beach at the foot of a cliff at **Skipaklettur**. A narrow, awkward path crosses tiny streams and boggy patches on a well-vegetated slope. Cross a bigger stream and pass a toilet shed at a camping area. Drift back towards the shore to pass a shed below a couple of houses at **Horn**.

Rise across a grassy, flowery slope, and the path steepens on a stony slope, running close to an edge. Gentler grassy slopes lead to an abrupt cliff edge at **Horn**. Turn right to follow a narrow path near the cliffs of **Hornbjarg**, dropping to a gap, with views of a pinnacle ahead. Climb straight past masses of flowers and drift right across a very steep slope, reaching a narrow crest on **Miðfell**. ▶

Cross the crest where it was reached, swinging left across and down a very steep, grassy, flowery slope. Take great care stepping down to a gap near an overhanging

Left here leads to a summit over 360m (1180ft), while right leads along a grassy crest for views.

289

Tidal rivers have to be forded to reach the rugged and attractive peninsula of Horn

cliff. Use a knotted rope for the descent, gradually level out and head for a prominent gap. Look ahead to a pinnacle of rock and the conical summit of Kálfatindar, with a tarn down to the right. Leave the gap and cross hummocky ground to the tarn, **Miðdalsvatn**, keeping right to cross its outflow.

Follow a path up across a stony, grassy slope onto a ridge. Turn left up a rocky scramble onto a higher part of the ridge, around 300m (985ft). Keep right along a shelf to reach a gap, passing the hump of Eílifstindur to reach the gap of **Almenningaskarð**. Turn right down a path through **Innstidalur**, which leads to the houses at **Horn**, so turn left to aim for the camping ground passed earlier, although the ground is boggy in places. All that remains is to retrace steps along the shore, crossing the two tidal rivermouths, to finish.

Fljóta

Glúms

STAGE 4
Kjaransvík to Látravík

Start	Kjaransvík
Finish	Látravík
Distance	24km (15 miles)
Total ascent/descent	950m (3115ft)
Time	9hrs
Terrain	Rugged fells with steep ascents and steeper, stony descents. The lower parts are pathless in places.
Maps	1:55,000 'Mál og Menning – 9 Hornstrandir'; 1:100,000 'Ferðakort – Hornstrandir'; 1:100,000 'Útivera Vestfirðir & Dalur 1'
Transport	Sjóferðir ferry links Ísafjörður and Látravík
Accommodation	Camping at Hlöðuvík and Látravík

This is a tough day's walk, with two distinct ascents and descents over rugged fells. The shallow tidal lake of Fljótavatn is located in between, and if necessary this long day could be split by camping in its broad dale.

Leave **Kjaransvík** (or the nearby camping ground at Hlöðuvík) and walk around the western side of the bay. A grassy path rises across little streams, reaching a bigger stream with waterfalls. Walk upstream to find wooden posts and a path, crossing the stream at a higher level. Climb a slope that becomes steep and stone-strewn, where marker posts split as they

Map continues on page 292

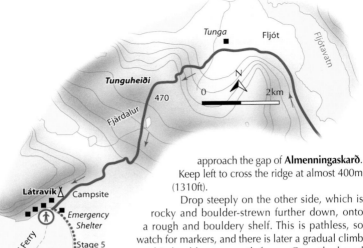

approach the gap of **Almenningaskarð**. Keep left to cross the ridge at almost 400m (1310ft).

Drop steeply on the other side, which is rocky and boulder-strewn further down, onto a rough and bouldery shelf. This is pathless, so watch for markers, and there is later a gradual climb past big boulders as a path forms. Cross the broad gap of **Þórleifsskarð**, over 400m (1310ft). Posts run down the other side, but end on a steep and stony path on a bouldery slope. There is a rock-step halfway down to four little tarns. Pass between the two leftmost tarns and spot a couple of posts over a bouldery rise.

Widely spaced posts and cairns lead down through **Þórleifsdalur**, from boulders to vegetated slopes, crossing a stream. The slope steepens and the path peters out, with fine views of flat, grassy, boggy ground near **Fljótavatn**. There is no path, so pick a way around to the other side of

Boggy pool beside the slightly tidal lake of Fljótavatn, below Glúmsstaðafoss

292

the lake, crossing inflowing streams below the waterfall of **Glúmsstaðafoss**. The ground near the tidal lake can be wet and muddy, so stay near the foot of the fell while heading down-dale, reaching a broad area of grass and pools at **Fljót**.

Keep well left of a solitary hut at **Tunga** and cross a few streams. Look around the fellsides and pick out all the streams in view. Spot the one furthest right and climb to the right of it. Pick up and follow a cairned path which later zigzags up a steep, bouldery slope, followed by chunky scree, onto the broad crest of **Tunguheiði**, around 470m (1540ft). Cairns march across, then the descent is a series of steep, rugged 'steps' and gentler shelves, with cairns all the way.

Keep right of a tarn in **Fjárdalur**, cross its outflow and walk down a broad, gentle, stony slope. Drop down more big 'steps', the last one being almost a cliff, so keep right to drop to a rugged moorland and reach a track. Turn left, then right, to a camping ground and a few huts at **Látravík** (one is an emergency shelter).

Stage 5
Látravík to Hesteyri

Start	Látravík
Finish	Hesteyri
Distance	22km (13¾ miles)
Total ascent/descent	350m (1150ft)
Time	9hrs
Terrain	Sandy beach and rocky coast, then a track and path cross rugged uplands
Maps	1:55,000 'Mál og Menning – 9 Hornstrandir'; 1:100,000 'Ferðakort – Hornstrandir'; 1:100,000 'Útivera Vestfirðir & Dalur 1'
Transport	Sjóferðir ferry links Ísafjörður, Hesteyri, Sæból and Látravík
Accommodation	Camping and hut at Hesteyri; camping at Sæból

Sandy beach walks with river crossings are followed by a rocky headland, where the tide must be out. Huts are passed at Sæból, and a track heads inland past a church. Rugged uplands are crossed on the way back to Hesteyri.

Leave **Látravík** along the sandy beach, crossing river-mouths either side of **Mannfjall**, which has wind-blown sand against it. The rivers must be forded at low tide, and beware of soft sand. Continue along the beach, which becomes more rugged at the foot of **Hvarfnúpur**. Again, the tide must be out. Scramble over boulders and bare rock, then a stout chain helps while stepping down to slippery seaweed-covered boulders. Scramble up and down more rock, then a cobbly beach leads to a sandy beach where a small river is crossed.

Follow a track through grass, passing a campsite just before a white cabin. After passing a couple more huts at **Sæból**, a track heads left, straight across a boggy dale. There is a gentle ascent, followed by a stony rise and a footbridge over a stream. The track is stony and undulating as it rises through the dale, keeping left of a house and a church at **Staður**, above the lake of **Staðarvatn**.

Walkers wait beside Hesteyrarfjörður for the ferry back to Ísafjörður

Look carefully for a path, drifting down towards old telegraph poles, but keeping well left of them. Climb across a rugged slope with boggy patches, then a steep zigzag path reaches cairns on a stony gap at almost 280m (920ft) on **Fannalægðafjall**. Lines of cairns lead right and left, but follow a well-trodden path between them, which becomes a rugged track. There is a steeper descent on **Sléttuheiði**,

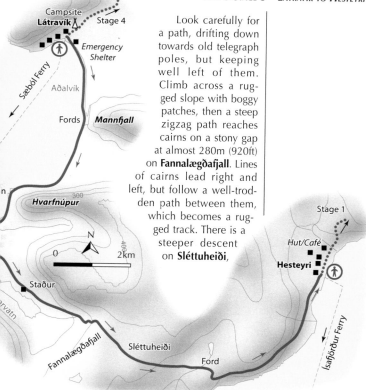

and the track later becomes a path. Ford a river with a tarn upstream and a waterfall downstream. Rise gently past a small pool, picking up a line of cairns. The path rises and falls across a fellside above **Hesteyrarfjörður**.

Follow the path down towards the coast and it becomes stony and boggy. Follow old telegraph poles through rough vegetation or walk on vegetated sand (or follow the sandy beach at low water). Pass a campsite and continue to the ferry landing or to the café in **Hesteyri**.

The little harbour town of Ísafjörður crouches at the foot of Eyrarfjall (Walk 42)

11 THE WESTFJORDS

Looking back down through Sunndalur towards the inlet near Suðureyri (Walk 43)

Many visitors to Iceland omit the north-western part of Iceland, the Westfjords, and that is their great loss. The Westfjords is almost a separate island, and legend has it that three trolls spent a night digging through a narrow isthmus to create an island, but were turned to stone at sunrise. Tarmac only stretches so far, leaving motorists to follow convoluted dirt roads around a succession of fjords and across several mountain passes. There are only a handful of villages, and while most of them have bus services, these don't operate every day. If trying to reach the Westfjords from Reykjavík or Akureyri, check bus timetables in advance and travel on those days when connections work best. Alternatively, fly with Air Iceland from Reykjavík to Ísafjörður or Eagle Air to Bildadalur.

A selection of day-walks are described throughout the Westfjords, starting at Ísafjörður (Walk 42) and making the most of opportunities to start and finish at villages such as Suðureyri, Flateyri (Walk 43) and Þingeyri, which are all linked by buses. Most of the mountains in this area are flat-topped, but the highest mountain, Kaldbakur (Walk 44), is more shapely. The ascent of Lómfell (Walk 45) can be attempted by taking a short break while travelling through the Westfjords, while the walk from Foss to Krossholt (Walk 46) requires more thought to reach the start and finish. Many walkers head for sheer cliffs at Látrabjarg, but only for a short walk, so Walk 47 offers a longer walk. By prior arrangement, Látrabjarg can be reached by bus from Patreksfjörður.

The most interesting way to and from the Westfjords is to use the ferry from Stykkishólmur to Brjánslækur. An interesting short walk is available from Brjánslækur (Walk 48) for those who arrive too early for a ferry. It is also possible to 'jump ship' halfway across Breiðafjörður and spend time on the delightful little island of Flatey (Walk 49).

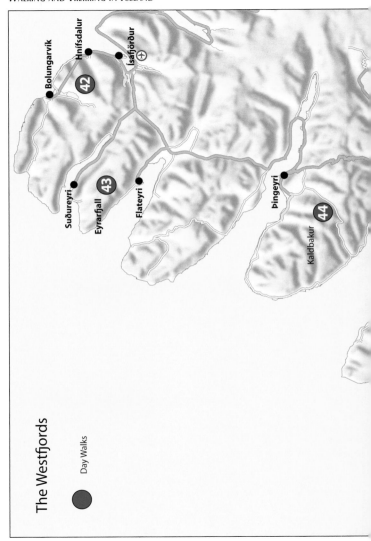

The Westfjords

Day Walks

Lómfell

45

Ferry

49

Flatey

48

46

Krossholt

Foss

Breiðafjörður

Bíldudalur

Patreksfjörður

47

Látrabjarg

299

WALK 42

Hnífsdalur, Bolungarvík and Ísafjörður

Start	Hnífsdalur or Bolungarvík
Finish	Ísafjörður
Distance	15 or 18km (9½ or 11 miles)
Total ascent/descent	650m (2130ft)
Time	5hrs or 6hrs
Terrain	Easy roads and tracks in rugged valleys, with scrambling required over a ridge. Some bouldery, boggy, pathless slopes.
Maps	1:100,000 'Mál og Menning – 9 Hornstrandir'; 1:100,000 'Ferðakort – Hornstrandir'; 1:100,000 'Útivera Vestfirðir & Dalur 2'
Transport	The airport Fly-Bus links Ísafjörður, Hnífsdalur and Bolungarvík (tel 8921417)

Take a bus from Ísafjörður to neighbouring Hnífsdalur or Bolungarvík – this route starts from either village to climb through scenic dales across rugged passes. Both options combine for a rugged scramble and a descent to Ísafjörður.

From Hnífsdalur

In **Hnífsdalur**, look at a street plan near a bus shelter, as you need to follow Heiðarbraut, which doesn't have its name displayed. The road is flanked by houses, then becomes a track rising gently through a dale, passing a sign for Seljalandsdalur and Bolungarvík. Cross a cattle grid and the track falls, rises, and falls again while approaching a **farm**.

Fork left well before the farm, climbing a grassy track that becomes stony. Cross a stream, descend, then climb gradually towards the river, **Hnífsdalsá**, and its waterfalls. Head upstream to find a place to cross, and continue up a moorland slope following a power line. Cross little streams flanked by vivid moss. Drift left of the power line before reaching the gap of **Heiðarskarð**.

From Bolungarvík

Follow the road towards Ísafjörður, turning right as sign-posted for Syðridalur. The road becomes stony, passing a golf course and the lake of **Syðradalsvatn**. Cross a cattle grid and pass a turning for the farm of Miðdalur, with the farm of **Hanhóll** ahead. Turn right up a track with a 'walking' sign, which rises and falls, crossing a bridge over a stream. Go up a bit, then down to a bridge over a river at a hydro-electric **power station**. The track ahead is signposted 'Hnífsdalur'.

Climb the track and watch the bends – first a prominent left, later a gradual right – then go under a power line and climb towards a stream with waterfalls. Turn left, later right, then left at a junction. Climb and keep straight ahead at another junction, lev-elling out. The track runs gently downhill

Little streams and lots of boulders are passed before scrambling near Þjófar on bare rock to a small dam. Keep right, behind the dam, climbing a rough, stony track under a power line. The track vanishes on steep, rugged, wet slopes streaked with moss, but keep left of the power line to the gap of **Heiðarskarð**, around 500m (1640ft). Turn right to traverse a rugged slope and link with the route from Hnífsdalur.

Both routes combine to aim for a broad gap flanked by rock towers. Getting there involves crossing stony, bouldery slopes with mossy patches and pools. A steep, stony, bouldery climb bears a couple of marker posts, and care is needed on crumbling earth to reach a knife-edge gap, around 600m (1970ft), west of the rocky top of **Þjófar**. Follow posts steeply down stones and broken rock, swinging left to cross awkward, bouldery slopes. More vegetation flanks **Seljalandsdalur** later, as well as wet and boggy ground.

The aim is to walk towards the head of the fjord whenever it is in view, until a solitary **ski station** is seen. Aim well left of this to avoid fences and land on its access road. Simply follow the bendy road downhill, through a tunnel in an avalanche embankment, continuing straight towards **Ísafjörður** along Seljalandsvegur.

WALK 43
Suðureyri to Flateyri

Start	Suðureyri
Finish	Flateyri
Distance	15km (9½ miles)
Total ascent/descent	650m (2135ft)
Time	5hrs
Terrain	Easy roads and tracks at the start and finish. Steep, bouldery slopes and a stony plateau in the middle.
Map	1:100,000 'Útivera Vestfirðir & Dalur 2'
Transport	Local buses link Ísafjörður, Suðureyri and Flateyri

This walk is almost a simple dale-to-dale walk, linking two coastal villages. However, it climbs onto a broad, bleak, stony plateau where stout cairns mark the route, and there is an optional detour onto Eyrarfjall for a bird's-eye view of Flateyri.

Suðureyri offers accommodation, food and drink, and is easily explored. Walk through the village by road, and a dirt road continues around the rocky headland of **Brimnes**. Climb to a junction and keep straight ahead across an embankment to the farm of **Staður** and its little church. Pass between buildings and watch for a little sign in a field for Klofningsheiði and Flateyri.

Go down the field and through a gateway in a fence, where a stony track climbs beyond. Follow this until it expires and cross the **Þverá**. Look carefully for faded red posts among stony hummocks, vegetated hollows, boulders and small pools fringed by bog cotton. If posts aren't seen quickly, they should be spotted later by keeping well to the left of

304

Sunndalur, near steep scree. A narrow path rises gently through the dale. Follow it carefully when boulders are reached, especially when making a steep climb, then traverse a bouldery slope to the head of the dale. Pass a cairn, and the path swings right to cross a stream on mossy stones.

Climb to a big cairn crowned with a cross, and follow more cairns over the broad, stony crest of **Klofningsheiði**, over 620m (2035ft). ▶ Follow cairns gently downhill, reaching a cairn overlooking steep-sided **Klofningsdalur**. Follow an old track downhill, swinging left into the dale. Rockfall debris includes big boulders from cliffs and screes that almost obscure the track further down.

Turn left down an easier vegetated track, leaving the dale and swinging left across a slope. Drift right down to a lower track, turning left to go through a gateway in a fence and cross a stream. Turn right down another track to the shore of Önundarfjörður and turn left along a dirt road into **Flateyri**, where there is accommodation, food and drink. A memorial near the church recalls an avalanche in October 1995, which killed 20 people. Massive embankments have been built to safeguard against a repeat of the tragedy.

The village of Flateyri sits on flat land at the foot of the steep-sided Eyrarfjall

Smaller cairns and tall posts head left for a stony, pathless route to Eyrarfjall and a view of Flateyri. This is 3km (2 miles) there and back, with minimal ascent and descent.

305

WALK 44
Þingeyri and Kaldbakur

Start/Finish	Þingeyri or Alftamýrarheiði
Distance	5 or 35km (3 or 21¾ miles)
Total ascent/descent	1100m (3610ft)
Time	2hrs or 10hrs
Terrain	Easy valley tracks, followed by steep, stony, rocky fellside
Map	1:100,000 'Útivera Vestfirðir & Dalur 2'
Transport	Sterna serve Þingeyri from Ísafjörður and Patreksfjörður

Kaldbakur is the highest peak in the Westfjords, flanked by similarly rugged peaks that give the impression of an Alpine enclave. Using a 4WD to Alftamýrarheiði leaves only a short walk to Kaldbakur, but from Þingeyri it is a long way.

Leave **Þingeyri** along the coast road, passing fish-drying sheds, and continue around the airport, where the road becomes stony. Turn left as signposted 'Kirkjubólsdalur' and reach a junction. If walking, turn right to follow the dirt road to the farm of **Kirkjuból**. ◄ Pass between the farmhouse and outbuildings and go through gates in fences. It is mostly a gentle, grassy descent through fields, later joining the vehicle route.

If driving, keep left, cross a bridge and take the second track on the right, later fording two rivers to join the walking route.

Turn right to cross a stream and follow the **Kirkjubólsá** upstream. The track is stony as it climbs from the river, rising and falling through **Kirkjubólsdalur**, with splendid views of fells. Climb higher through Tröllárdalir and the track becomes convoluted before the gap of **Alftamýrarheiði**, around 550m (1805ft). ◄ Go down the other side into **Fossdalur**, around a bend and down the track, with an eye on Kaldbakur and the broad gap to the right of it.

Beware a path climbing from the gap, which is very steep, crumbling and dangerous, so cannot be recommended.

◄ Leave the track and use grassy slopes to avoid steep and stony slopes as much as possible, and climb to a broad, stony gap around 620m (2035ft). Turn left and

4WDs should be parked off the track here.

climb increasingly steeply on a stony and vegetated slope, looking for traces of a path. Pass a chunky rock outcrop, then more rock rears impressively above it. Keep to the trodden path, scrambling where necessary. The top of **Kaldbakur** is level, but bouldery, with a cairn at 998m (3274ft) and a guestbook. Views of nearby peaks are splendid, while distant slopes support broad plateaux. Snæfellsnes and its ice-cap are in view. Simply retrace steps back to the track, if driving away, or to **Þingeyri** if walking.

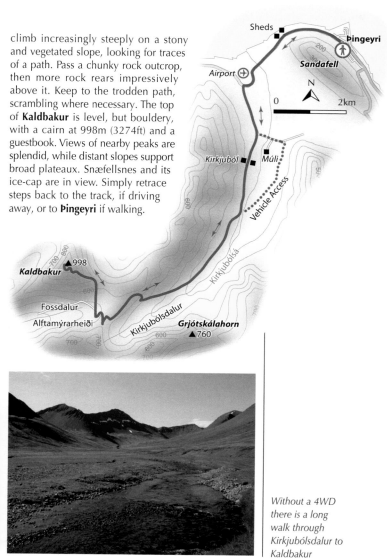

Without a 4WD there is a long walk through Kirkjubólsdalur to Kaldbakur

307

WALK 45

Helluskarð and Lómfell

Start/Finish	Helluskarð
Distance	7km (4½ miles)
Total ascent/descent	320m (1050ft)
Time	2hrs 30mins
Terrain	Rough, rocky, boulder-strewn slopes with waymark posts
Map	1:100,000 'Útivera Vestfirðir & Dalur 4'
Transport	Sterna cross Helluskarð between Patreksfjörður and Ísafjörður

When Hrafna-Flóki settled in Vatnsdalur in the ninth century, the winter was harsh and all his cattle died. In spring he climbed a fell, possibly Lómfell, and saw ice in the fjords. He coined the name 'Ísland' (Iceland) for the whole country and left, never to return.

There is a junction of dirt roads near the gap of **Helluskarð**. Descend towards Brjánslækur, passing small pools either side of the road, with the tarn of **Þverdalsvatn** ahead. Before reaching it, on the left of the road, is a signpost for Lómfell. Follow red-tipped marker pegs and infrequent small cairns up a rugged slope, staying left of a stream. The ground is bouldery, with little rugs of vegetation. Cross a stream as marked.

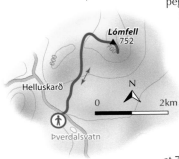

Later, there is a steep climb onto a bouldery shoulder, then drift right for an even steeper, rockier climb. Watch for markers to follow a vague, gritty path onto the rocky crest of **Lómfell**. The summit cairn stands at 752m (2467ft), but continue to a lower

cairn, where there is a guestbook, for a better view. The broad, bleak plateau of Gláma and an abundance of tarns contrasts with the island-studded Breiðafjörður, with Snæfellsnes beyond. There are other rough and rocky hills nearby, and a glimpse of Suðurfirðir. Retrace steps back to the road.

The slopes of Lómfell are rough and bouldery almost all the way

WALK 46

Foss to Krossholt

Start	Foss
Finish	Krossholt
Distance	15km (9½ miles)
Total ascent/descent	500m (1640ft)
Time	6hrs
Terrain	The start and finish feature dense woodland, with moors and rocky uplands between
Map	1:100,000 'Útivera Vestfirðir & Dalur 4'
Transport	Airport bus from Patreksfjörður, Talknafjörður and Bildudalur to Bildudalur airport, 6km (3¾ miles) from Foss. Sterna serve Krossholt from Patreksfjörður, Brjánslækur and Ísafjörður.

This old route is an obvious shortcut from coast to coast over a low, rugged gap, and it is often referred to as the 'Postman's Path'. The route, which splits halfway along to provide a choice of routes to Krossholt, is cairned over high ground, but is almost lost in dense birch bushes at either end.

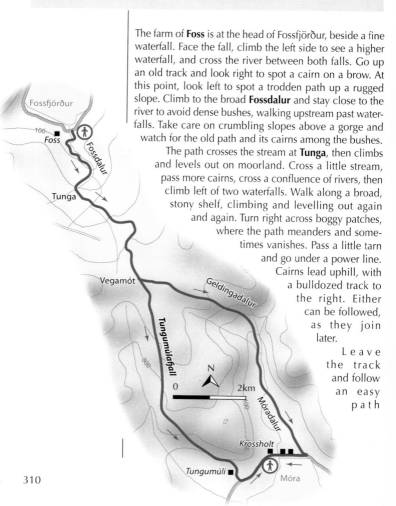

The farm of **Foss** is at the head of Fossfjörður, beside a fine waterfall. Face the fall, climb the left side to see a higher waterfall, and cross the river between both falls. Go up an old track and look right to spot a cairn on a brow. At this point, look left to spot a trodden path up a rugged slope. Climb to the broad **Fossdalur** and stay close to the river to avoid dense bushes, walking upstream past water-falls. Take care on crumbling slopes above a gorge and watch for the old path and its cairns among the bushes.

The path crosses the stream at **Tunga**, then climbs and levels out on moorland. Cross a little stream, pass more cairns, cross a confluence of rivers, then climb left of two waterfalls. Walk along a broad, stony shelf, climbing and levelling out again and again. Turn right across boggy patches, where the path meanders and some-times vanishes. Pass a little tarn and go under a power line. Cairns lead uphill, with a bulldozed track to the right. Either can be followed, as they join later.

Leave the track and follow an easy path

310

Two waterfalls are passed as the 'Postman's Path' climbs from Tunga to Vegamót

through a rocky, boulder-strewn area, with a little tarn to the right. Watch for cairns when the path is vague, climbing through wild and rocky terrain. Gradients are gentle, and after a pool on the right, pass the tangled remains of an old fence. Cairns stand on outcrops to right and left of a gap at **Vegamót**, around 260m (855ft), and walkers can go either way.

Via Tungumúli

Turning right, keep right of another little pool, descending and rising gently. Cairns run along a rocky outcrop to the left, but a trodden path runs along the foot, later vanishing among rock, boulders, stones and grit. Keep an eye on cairns, which rise and fall as the slopes of **Tungumúlafjall** become a little more vegetated. Cross a little stream and a crest, then cross a streambed. Eventually, cairns lead down a slope where creeping bushes appear. Cross another streambed, climb a little, then pick up a zigzag path downhill. This drifts onto a ledge with cliffs above and below, while dense bushes hamper progress. Aim for a couple of little houses at **Tungumúli**. Follow the access track to a road and turn left to reach **Krossholt**, where chalets offer lodgings.

Via Mórudalur

Turning left, go up a rugged slope and follow cairns across a broad, gentle slope of rock, stones and grit, with

311

a little pool to the right. Go gently down, with a larger pool to the right. Climb onto a brow to see more cairns, keeping right of them on a falling traverse on a rugged slope. Cross a little valley and turn round a sheer rock outcrop to see **Geldingadalur**. Drop from a rocky brow on uneven scree, picking up stretches of old paths. Drift closer to a stream, avoiding bushes, to see waterfalls. Pass a confluence of streams and follow the streambed of the **Móra** past another confluence, always on the right. The riverbed becomes broad and bouldery and should be crossed. Later, pick up and follow a track across a tributary. Continue past taller bushes and ford a stream, following the track through **Mórudalur** to a road, then turn right to reach **Krossholt** and its chalets.

WALK 47
Brunnaverstöð and Látrabjarg

Start/Finish	Brunnaverstöð
Distance	20km (12½ miles)
Total ascent/descent	500m (1640ft)
Time	7hrs
Terrain	Sheer coastal cliffs and stony slopes, with dirt roads back to the start
Map	1:100,000 'Útivera Vestfirðir & Dalur 4'
Transport	Sterna serve Látrabjarg only by prior request, from Patreksfjörður, Brjánslækur, Þingeyri and Ísafjörður (tel 4565518)

Most people drive all the way along a dirt road to Látrabjarg just to look over the cliff edge, then drive away. It is worth spending time bird-watching, of course, but there are opportunities to explore longer and to camp overnight.

Enjoy this walk to the fullest extent by camping at **Brunnaverstöð** (the site of an old fishing station). Follow

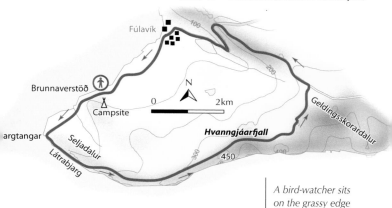

the dirt road up across boulder scree and onwards to white buildings and a road-end car park at **Bjargtangar**.

A bird-watcher sits on the grassy edge of sheer cliffs at Látrabjarg

A stone-paved path with steps climbs to an abrupt cliff edge at **Látrabjarg**, one of the best sites in Iceland for bird-watchers. Puffins, razorbills, guillemots and gulls nest on sheer cliffs.

Turn left to follow the cliff path carefully. A grassy slope, sometimes tussocky, rises from **Seljadalur** to the cliffs, and there are sometimes shortcuts from gap to gap to avoid some of the climbing. However, the path keeps climbing as the cliffs get higher. By the time **Hvanngjáarfjall** is reached, the cliffs rise almost 450m (1475ft), although the summit of the fell is flat. Views stretch from the Westfjords across Breiðafjörður to Snæfellsnes.

Two parallel paths lead down to a broad gap on

313

mossy, stony slopes, with a view down to the dirt road used later in the day. Rise onto the next broad top, and the path becomes vague on the descent as the deep **Geldingsskorardalur** opens ahead. Look left, inland, spotting a path leading to a turning space at the end of a track. Walk in that direction to a monument and notice. ◄

Follow the track as it rises, falls and bends across stony slopes to a junction with another track. Turn left to continue along a stony crest, with views down to an enormous beach at Breiðavík. Descend to a junction with the dirt road and zigzag down past a tarn to a huddle of houses at **Fúlavík**. Continue along the dirt road to return to **Brunnaverstöð**.

The Dhoon, a British trawler, was wrecked in December 1947, and local farmers mounted a rescue.

WALK 48
Brjánslækur and Surtarbrandsgil

Start/Finish	Brjánslækur
Distance	6km (3¾ miles)
Total ascent/descent	200m (655ft)
Time	2hrs
Terrain	A simple valley walk on a track and moorland paths
Map	1:100,000 'Útivera Vestfirðir & Dalur 4'
Transport	Sterna serve Brjánslækur from Patreksfjörður, Þingeyri and Ísafjörður. Baldur ferry serves Brjánslækur from Stykkishólmur (tel 4332254, www.seatours.is).

Instead of waiting a couple of hours for a ferry at Brjánslækur, use the time to go on this short walk to the 'protected natural monument' of Surtarbrandsgil, where beds of crumbling lignite (brown coal) are full of wafer-thin fossilised plants.

The start of this walk lies between the ferry office/**café** and the blue farm of **Brjánslækur**. First, go to one of these places and ask permission to explore Surtarbrandsgil, or join a guided walk if a ranger is present. With permission

Surtarbrandsgil   Café ⊞   Flatey and Stykkishólmur

Lækjará   Brjánslækur   Ferry →

granted, read the notices at a gate and follow a track up through a large field. Go through a gate at the top and head left along a path on a slope of bilberry, crowberry and birch. Stay well above the **Lækjará** and follow it upstream. When the valley bends right, a little ravine features small waterfalls. Walk past a twin waterfall and join a path with red-tipped markers, which are used on the return.

Stay on the marked path into the rugged canyon of **Surtarbrandsgil**, walking beside the stream. Note the hard and soft beds of rock and tottering pinnacles. A fenced-off area must not be entered, as this is where the bulk of fossils are found – in rocks that split almost as thinly as the pages of a book. However, some specimens have been left for display purposes. ▶ Trees and plants grew here beside a lake when the climate was warmer. They were later buried and compressed into lignite.

There is no way past a waterfall in the canyon, so retrace steps, but follow the path marked by red-tipped pegs. This leads back to the large field. Go down to the road and turn left for the ferry office/**café**.

Enjoy looking at the fossil specimens, but do not break or remove them.

A crumbling cliff at Surtarbrandsgil is packed with lignite beds and fossilised plants

315

WALK 49

Flatey and Breiðafjörður

Start/Finish	Ferry pier, Flatey
Distance	4km (2½ miles)
Total ascent/descent	30m (100ft)
Time	1hr 30mins
Terrain	Easy tracks and paths, mostly coastal
Map	Free leaflet map from ferry ticket offices
Transport	Baldur ferry serves Flatey from Stykkishólmur and Brjánslækur (tel 4332254, www.seatours.is)

When you take the ferry across Breiðafjörður, you can 'jump ship' and explore the island of Flatey for no extra charge, but mention this when you buy tickets. Half of the bird species that breed in Iceland have been noted on the island.

Most visitors to Flatey walk straight from the pier to the village of Þorpið along a gravel track, but there is a quiet route around the grassy, western point of **Tröllendi**. A grassy path above a rocky shore passes marshy pools. Pass a notice about Flatey and a tall, painted stone landmark, then join and follow the track to the village of **Þorpið** and its tiny harbour. ◄

Follow the track past some lovely restored 19th- and 20th-century houses, and continue along a grassy path on low cliffs. Reach a notice at **Lundaberg**, the highest point on the island at only 16m (52½ft), and look for

The hotel/café offers food, drink and accommodation.

puffins. Further along there may be a big 'STOP' notice, from mid-May to mid-July, when eider ducks are nesting. Further along, past a narrow neck of land, the entire eastern end of the island at **Eyjarendi** may be closed for the same period, and is savagely defended by terns. This end of the island is rugged underfoot, and views of mainland Iceland seem to completely embrace Flatey. Eventually, pass a board listing bird species, followed by a couple of wrecked wooden boats, to leave the restricted area.

It is possible to pick a way along the coast and return to the pier, but it is better to head inland to the church and adjacent 'library' to study a view indicator. ▶ Walk back towards the village and keep left to follow the gravel track back to the pier in time for the ferry.

The little village of Þorpið and its tiny harbour on the interesting island of Flatey

A monastery was founded on Flatey in the 11th century, but no trace remains.

12 SNÆFELLSJÖKULL AND SNÆFELLSNES

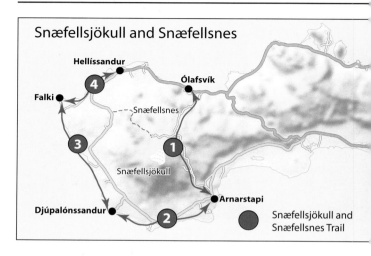

The long western peninsula of Snæfellsnes has a very rugged coastline, and the ice-capped peak of Snæfellsjökull dominates. According to legend, this is where Arne Saknussemm gained access to the underworld, which later inspired Jules Verne to write *A Journey to the Centre of the Earth.*

The whole area was designated as a national park in 2001. The peninsula is quite easy to reach from Reykjavík, being served daily by bus. Furthermore, a circular bus service operates daily around the western end of the peninsula from Hellissandur and Ólafsvík. This bus stops from time

to time to allow passengers to enjoy short walks, notably along a splendid coast path linking the villages of Arnarstapi and Hellnar.

A long-distance trek is offered in this area, but visitors who want short walks will find plenty of them. It is worth going to the national park visitor centre at Hellnar, and obtaining a free map of hiking trails. Cautious walkers may also climb Snæfellsjökull on glacier tours operated from Arnarstapi by Snjófell www.snjofell.is, tel 4356783. This company can also offer transport up and/or down the dirt road between Arnarstapi and Snæfellsjökull, but this must be arranged in advance.

TREK 10
The Snæfellsjökull and Snæfellsnes Trail

Start	Ólafsvík
Finish	Hellissandur
Distance	72km (46 miles)
Time	4 days
Terrain	A high-level dirt road at the start, with an optional glacier climb requiring care. Mostly low level and coastal afterwards, but with some very rugged lava.
Facilities	Hotel, shops and restaurants at Ólafsvík. Guest house and restaurants at Arnarstapi. Hotel and café at Hellnar. Hotel and restaurants at Hellissandur.
Accommodation	Hotel at Ólafsvík; guest house at Arnarstapi; hotel at Hellnar; hotel at Hellissandur. Wild camping is discouraged in the national park.

Although there are plenty of opportunities for short walks in the area, it is well worth linking these into a longer trek. The 'Snæfellsjökull and Snæfellsnes Trail' is of the author's imagining, connecting an obvious high-level dirt road, close to Snæfellsjökull, with a series of coastal paths, many of which are waymarked. The resulting four-day trek takes in the best parts of the national park, and if it proves too rugged in places, then walkers can bail out by bus at certain points.

The first stage is along a dirt road from Ólafsvík to Arnarstapi, with the option of climbing Snæfellsjökull. If you want to take this option, check the glacier conditions in advance with Snjófell, tel 4356783. The next three stages explore the rugged coast between Arnarstapi and Hellissandur. Bear in mind that there is no accommodation, and water is exceptionally sparse around the coast. Wild camping is discouraged by the national park authorities, although it happens discreetly. Should trekkers not wish to camp, then pick-ups and drop-offs need to be arranged, or careful study of bus timetables is needed to join and leave the route.

STAGE 1

Snæfellsjökull – Ólafsvík to Arnarstapi

Start	Ólafsvík
Finish	Arnarstapi
Distance	22km (13½ miles); extension onto Snæfellsjökull adds 10km (6¼ miles)
Total ascent/descent	800m (2625ft); extension onto Snæfellsjökull adds 800m (2625ft)
Time	8hrs; extension onto Snæfellsjökull adds 4hrs
Terrain	Entirely along a dirt road through high fells, with an option to climb Snæfellsjökull, which involves glacier walking
Maps	1:55,000 'Mál og Menning – 10 Snæfellsnes'; free 1:85,000 'Trails in Snæfellsjökull National Park' from the national park visitor centre
Transport	Sterna serve Ólafsvík from Reykjavík, Borgarnes and Stykkishólmur. A circular service runs from Ólafsvík to Arnarstapi, Hellnar and Hellissandur.
Accommodation	Guesthouse and campsite at Arnarstapi

A scenic dirt road runs from Ólafsvík to Arnarstapi, reaching 700m (2295ft) on the slopes of Snæfellsjökull. It is possible to climb onto the glacier, if conditions allow, and strong walkers may still be able to complete the distance down to Arnarstapi, if they are prepared to finish late.

Follow the coast road from **Ólafsvík**, past the campsite and viewpoints, turning right as signposted 'Snæfellsjökull'. Climb a dirt road through **Fossardalur**, spotting a waterfall in the river. Keep ahead where another track heads right, and the gradient is gentler, with more waterfalls in view. The road pulls away from the river with a view of Snæfellsjökull. Climb across the slopes of **Hrói** and swing right behind it, passing a track junction, then swing left downhill, crossing a stream in a dip at **Tághálsar**.

Climb steeply, easing to cross a couple of streambeds, then the way steepens again. There is a slight

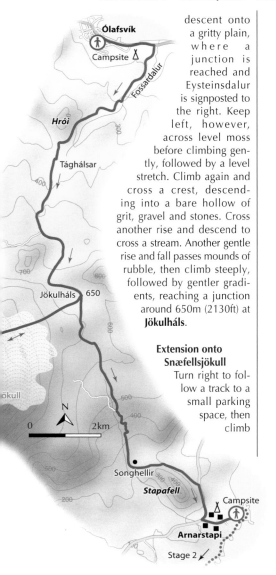

descent onto a gritty plain, where a junction is reached and Eysteinsdalur is signposted to the right. Keep left, however, across level moss before climbing gently, followed by a level stretch. Climb again and cross a crest, descending into a bare hollow of grit, gravel and stones. Cross another rise and descend to cross a stream. Another gentle rise and fall passes mounds of rubble, then climb steeply, followed by gentler gradients, reaching a junction around 650m (2130ft) at **Jökulháls**.

Extension onto Snæfellsjökull

Turn right to follow a track to a small parking space, then climb

The long and winding dirt road leading towards Snæfellsjökull is easy to walk

Sometimes the glacier is riddled with cracks and should be avoided altogether.

a steep, bouldery slope. There may be snowmobiles parked, operated by Snjófell (www.snjofell.is, tel 4356783), and if the glacier is in good condition it is a simple matter to follow snowmobile tracks. ◄ Many people do this without ice axes, crampons or ropes. Keep right on the ice to start, later swinging left past dark, rounded humps. Make a rising traverse towards three rocky peaks, reaching the foot of a striking rock tower. This is the highest point on Snæfellsjökull, at 1446m (4745ft), but as it involves rock-climbing walkers should avoid it. Enjoy extensive views from Reykjanes to the Westfjords, then retrace steps.

Continue along the main dirt road, climbing a slope of lightweight, light-coloured pumice, levelling out over 700m (2295ft), with fine views. Cross more of the pumice, rising and falling, and eventually darker rock and gravel appear, with a little more vegetation. Follow the track downhill towards the steep-sided **Stapafell**, and suddenly swing left to cross a rocky ridge. The cave of **Sönghellir**, once used as a habitation, is down to the left and worth a quick visit. Walk down the lower slopes of Stapafell, enjoying coastal views and eventually reaching a road junction. Turn right, and later left as signposted for **Arnarstapi**, where there is food, drink and accommodation.

STAGE 2
Snæfellsnes – Arnarstapi to Djúpalónssandur

Start	Arnarstapi
Finish	Djúpalónssandur
Distance	19km (12½ miles)
Total ascent/descent	100m (330ft)
Time	7hrs 30mins
Terrain	Easy cliff coast path at the start, drifting inland later and more rugged towards the end
Maps	1:55,000 'Mál og Menning – 10 Snæfellsnes'; free 1:85,000 'Trails in Snæfellsjökull National Park' from the national park visitor centre
Transport	Sterna operate a circular route from Ólafsvík to Arnarstapi, Hellnar and Hellissandur
Accommodation	Hotel at Hellnar. Wild camping is discouraged, but it happens anyway.

A short, scenic, interesting, popular cliff path links Arnarstapi and Hellnar, and this is also accessible to day-walkers by using the circular bus service. The continuation to Djúpalónssandur is quieter and rugged in places, and not always marked.

Towers of rock flank the attractive little harbour at Arnarstapi

Arnarstapi has a scattering of summer-houses, a couple of restaurants, guesthouse and campsite. Follow the road towards the wonderfully scenic little harbour, with views of Snæfellsjökull. A path signposted 'Hellnar' runs around a grassy headland, meandering, rising and falling, with red-tipped marker pegs. Signs indicate points of interest, including a couple of blow-

A path runs past the 'Baldur' sculpture to return to Arnarstapi.

holes in the cliffs and headlands, and there is a cliff-edge viewpoint at **Gatklettur**. ◀ Cross a

Spend time exploring the rugged cliff coast around Reykjanesviti at the end of the Reykjavegur

lava and sandy hollows. Keep right at two junctions, approaching a **power station**. Blue markers head left of the track, crossing a concrete hot-water conduit. ▶ Cross two tracks close together, join and follow another track as marked, and reach a staggered junction. Keep left, rising and winding on sand and pumice, and cross a rugged little gap.

'Power Plant Earth' is open Saturday and Sunday afternoon at the power station (tel 4361000, **www. powerplantearth.is**).

Ahead is a **lighthouse**, and the blue markers make a bee-line towards it across stones and sand, joining a track at the foot of a grassy hill. Turn right to reach a rugged cliff-line at **Reykjanesviti**, at the end of the Reykjavegur.

Reykjanesviti

This rugged peninsula should be explored in detail. Climb the grassy hill to the lighthouse, follow cliff paths, especially a circuit marked by green posts, read notices about birds and note the distant rock stack of Eldey and its huge gannet colony. Before leaving, visit the huge, vigorous mud-pot of Gunnuhver, which belches sulphurous steam and recently devoured its own access road and viewpoint, although new viewpoints have been installed.

2 FJALLABAK AND ÞÓRSMÖRK

Sunshine and storm creates a rainbow over the fells near Landmannalaugar (Walk 14)

Situated in South Iceland, the nature reserves of Fjallabak and Þórsmörk are very popular with walkers, and indeed some might claim that they are over-crowded. The main base for exploring Fjallabak is Landmannalaugar, but there are several huts available, and all of them allow camping alongside. The fells around Landmannalaugar are streaked with an amazing variety of pastel shades, with permanent snow and ice on the higher fells.

Day walks from Landmannalaugar include Suðurnámur and Bláhnúkur (Walks 14 and 15). Another fell walk is available from the huts at Hvanngil (Walk 16), which also includes fine waterfalls. On the doorstep of Fljótsdalur Youth Hostel, Þórólfsfell can be climbed (Walk 18). At Þórsmörk, Valahnúkur rises above woodlands to offer splendid views (Walk 17). Nearby huts offer accommodation, but this is a popular area that can get crowded.

There are daily buses, operated by Reykjavík Excursions and Trex, to Landmannalaugar and Þórsmörk from Reykjavík. A bus service runs on alternate days from Reykjavík to Hvanngil and Fljótsdalur, and it allows good access to some of the walks. Landmannalaugar can also be reached from Skaftafell (Section 3) using a Reykjavík Excursions bus that stops to allow passengers to enjoy a short walk to a fine waterfall at Eldgjá.

This section also includes a visit to the Vestmannaeyjar (Westman Islands). The walk on the largest island, Heimaey (Walk 19), can be reached by buses linking with ferries at Landeyjahöfn or Þorlákshöfn. There are also flights from Reykjavík airport to Heimaey.

Iceland's classic long-distance trail, the Laugavegur, which is flanked by the quiet Hellismannaleið and busy Skógar Trail, is also described in this section. Together, these three trails offer a splendid nine-day trek (Trek 2) through amazing and varied terrain.

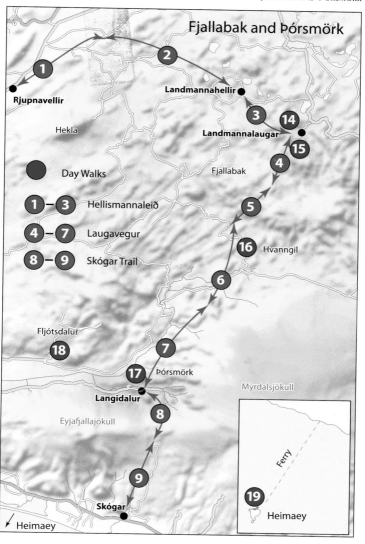

Fjallabak and Þórsmörk

Rjupnavellir

Hekla

Landmannahellir

Landmannalaugar

Fjallabak

Hvanngil

Day Walks

1 – 3   Hellismannaleið

4 – 7   Laugavegur

8 – 9   Skógar Trail

Fljótsdalur

Þórsmörk

Langidalur

Mýrdalsjökull

Eyjafjallajökull

Skógar

Heimaey

Ferry

Heimaey

95

WALK 14

Landmannalaugar and Suðurnámur

Start/Finish	Landmannalaugar
Distance	9km (5½ miles)
Total ascent/descent	400m (1310ft)
Time	3hrs
Terrain	Steep and stony fells with small river crossings on the descent
Map	1:25,000 'FÍ – Landmannalaugar Map of Hiking Trails', but get it corrected at the hut as many trails are shown incorrectly
Transport	Reykjavík Excursions serve Landmannalaugar from Reykjavík, Hveragerði, Selfoss, Skaftafell and Kirkjubærklauster. Trex (tel 5876000, www.trex.is) serves Landmannalaugar from Reykjavík, Hveragerði and Selfoss.

This popular half-day walk wanders along the crest of the fells above Landmannalaugar, returning across a stony floodplain and crossing a lava flow. It can be combined with Walk 15 onto Bláhnúkur.

Leave **Landmannalaugar**, at 590m (1935ft), by walking along the dirt road, crossing a clear hot river and a murky cold river using footbridges. Continue along the dirt road with a steep

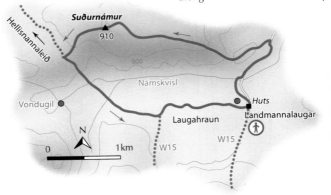

footbridge over a flower-fringed stream, leave Arnarstapi and go through a gate in a fence. Rugged lava lies ahead and the path is quite contorted. After going through a gateway in a drystone wall, the path is easier to a café. Follow a road up into **Hellnar** to reach the national park visitor centre, which also has a café. ▸

There is a hotel nearby.

Walk up the road, passing a left turn for a house at Laugarbrekka, then head left to follow a track gently downhill beside a fence. Follow the fence across a heath, go under a power line and eventually reach low cliffs near **Merarvík**. Turn right along the cliffs, which may be undercut in places. Pass two old fences and pick up a narrow, grassy path. Pass another old fence later, and cross a stream near a waterfall called **Foss**. Easy grassy paths run to a drystone wall, and there is rugged lava beyond. The path heads inland across heath, returning to the cliffs – very close to the edge.

Look ahead to see a distinct rise at **Svalþúfa**, where kittiwakes nest on cliffs. Look for red-tipped markers down the far side, and cross low-lying lava to reach amazing twin rock towers at **Lóndrangar**. Continue past storm beaches and driftwood towards buildings. Markers keep right of all except the building furthest inland. Head for a lighthouse and hug the rugged coast, or use tracks inland to go faster, reaching a mass of boulders at **Þrælavík**.

A grassy, marked path continues, rising and falling, rugged in places. Low-lying parts are strewn with coloured buoys, while quoits are often thrown over markers. Look back to the lighthouse, but no landmarks are seen ahead. Step over a low drystone wall

and cross grassy, flowery hills, passing a crumbling turf-roofed hut. Cross another drystone wall and join a clear path. Inland is a car park and toilets, where a pick-up could be arranged, while another path drops to a grey, stony, sandy beach at **Djúpalónssandur**.

STAGE 3
Snæfellsnes – Djúpalónssandur to Öndverðarnes

Start	Djúpalónssandur
Finish	Öndverðarnes
Distance	19km (12½ miles)
Total ascent/descent	100m (330ft)
Time	7hrs 30mins
Terrain	Mostly rugged coastal walking on broken lava, with some easy stretches, but also some very rugged parts
Maps	1:55,000 'Mál og Menning – 10 Snæfellsnes'; free 1:85,000 'Trails in Snæfellsjökull National Park' from the national park visitor centre
Transport	Sterna operate a circular route from Ólafsvík to Arnarstapi, Hellnar and Hellissandur
Accommodation	Wild camping is discouraged, but it happens anyway

This is the most rugged day along the Snæfellsnes coast. There are markers at first, but they need to be spotted carefully in some places. After an easy stretch there is a very rugged stretch without markers, ending with a good track.

Note Poor quality for drinking. A thin layer of fresh water 'floats' on salt water.

The beach at **Djúpalónssandur** is flanked by jagged rocks, while inland lie two small pools. ◀ Twisted iron on the beach is all that remains of the British trawler Epine, wrecked in March 1948 with few survivors. Watch for a signpost, follow a rugged path uphill, cross a gentle heath and descend to the cove of **Dritvík**, where there is an emergency shelter. Watch carefully above the hut to find a path in a groove between stony mounds. There is a lot

of meandering, rising and falling, and once the cliff coast is regained there are red-tipped markers.

Some stretches are rough and stony, and there is a distinct short drop with a small cave to the left. Keep looking for markers, twisting and turning past humps and hummocks, with areas of grass and crowberry. Pass a storm beach, then a bouldery storm beach with lots of coloured buoys. A track heads inland at **Hólahólar** and the markers split, so keep left between rugged lava and a vegetated slope of pumice. ▶

Continue across broad plains of grass and crowberry, often with a bouldery storm beach, coloured buoys and driftwood to the left. Walk back onto lava and cross a low drystone wall, later passing left of old farm ruins. A larger grassy plain leads to a drystone sheepfold and pic-nic table at the end of a track at **Klofningur**. Watch for markers through blocky moss-covered lava, passing old enclosures, pools and a ruined farm at **Beruvík**. ▶

The coast ahead is unmarked, with lots of rock, little ascents and descents, and muddy pools which are best avoided. Shortcut little headlands and find red-tipped markers on the low, grassy point of **Eyrar**. ▶ Follow

The rugged bay at Dritvík, with its orange-painted emergency shelter

Right offers a short walk around a volcanic crater.

A marked path runs inland to the road.

These markers lead inland to the road.

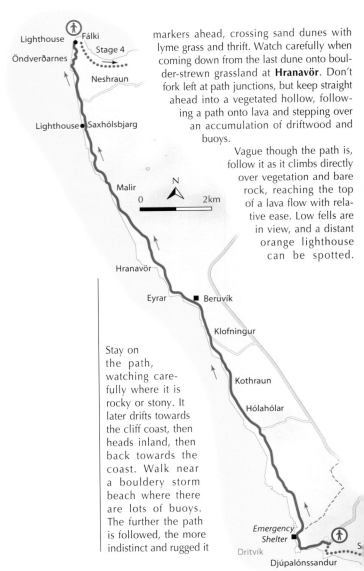

markers ahead, crossing sand dunes with lyme grass and thrift. Watch carefully when coming down from the last dune onto boulder-strewn grassland at **Hranavör**. Don't fork left at path junctions, but keep straight ahead into a vegetated hollow, following a path onto lava and stepping over an accumulation of driftwood and buoys.

Vague though the path is, follow it as it climbs directly over vegetation and bare rock, reaching the top of a lava flow with relative ease. Low fells are in view, and a distant orange lighthouse can be spotted.

Stay on the path, watching carefully where it is rocky or stony. It later drifts towards the cliff coast, then heads inland, then back towards the coast. Walk near a bouldery storm beach where there are lots of buoys. The further the path is followed, the more indistinct and rugged it

The little lighthouse at Saxhólsbjarg, where the cliffs are colonised by birds

becomes, until any route can be followed as long as it reaches the lighthouse at **Saxhólsbjarg**. ▶

Simply follow a track, keeping straight ahead at a signposted junction. Reach another orange lighthouse at **Öndverðarnes**. There is rolling grassland here, the ruins of a farm, and an interesting well at **Fálki**, dug into a sand dune. Although poor quality for drinking, this water is sufficient as a source if treated or boiled.

Notices explain about the bird life and former egg-gathering.

STAGE 4

Snæfellsnes – Öndverðarnes to Hellissandur

Start	Öndverðarnes
Finish	Hellissandur
Distance	12km (7½ miles)
Total ascent/descent	50m (165ft)
Time	4hrs
Terrain	Some rugged coastal walking, with and without paths, and some easier stretches, ending with a track and road
Maps	1:55,000 'Mál og Menning – 10 Snæfellsnes'; free 1:85,000 'Trails in Snæfellsjökull National Park' from the national park visitor centre
Transport	Sterna operate a circular route from Ólafsvík to Arnarstapi, Hellnar and Hellissandur
Accommodation	Hotel at Hellissandur

This stretch of the Snæfellsnes coast isn't too difficult, and if it needs to be made easier, there is a track and road a little further inland. Hellissandur has some interesting features, including a maritime museum.

Leave **Öndverðarnes**, heading inland to a prominent cairn on a fissured hump. Walk down towards the coast to pick up and

follow a path, sometimes two or three paths, through grassy and stony areas. Pass an old fence and look ahead for cairns through rugged, fractured lava, partly vegetated with grass, crowberry and bilberry. There is a vague path, but avoid being drawn off-route by a large cairn to the right. The path is often vague where it crosses sand, but join a dirt road and follow it to a tarmac road at **Skarðsvík**, where there is a sandy beach.

Follow the road a little, leaving it to trace old wheel-marks over sandy grassland, speckled with thrift, on low cliffs. Stay on vegetated areas when it gets rugged. Follow the road across the broad, sandy river channels of **Gufuskálamóður** to a road junction. Turn left along the road, but quickly head back towards the coast. The ground is stony, gritty and sandy, with rocks and lyme grass. Reach a road-end car park at **Írskrabrunnur**, where a dry well is surmounted by a whale bone.

Continue as signposted along a marked path, reaching a memorial stone at Gufuskálavör. Walk along the low, bouldery coast alongside a fence enclosing a tall mast and Iceland's main **ICE-SAR** rescue training base. As

One of the cairns that are followed across rugged lava on the way to Skarðsvík

A pleasant sandy beach at Skarðsvík, on the way towards Hellissandur

the fence drifts inland there is more room between it and the coast. Turn the point of **Brimnes** and pass a painted day-mark, following a track between a building and an old harbour at Krossavík. Walk to the road and turn left up into **Hellissandur**. There is a museum on the right and a hotel on the left, as well as shops and a café.

APPENDIX A
Route summary tables

Section 1 – Reykjavík, Reykjanes and Hengill

Walk	Start	Finish	Distance	Total ascent/descent	Time	Page
1	Ráðhús, Reykjavík	Ráðhús, Reykjavík	20km (12½ miles)	100m (330ft)	5hrs	42
2	Esjustofa	Esjustofa	9km (5½ miles)	800m (2625ft)	3hrs	45
3	Fitjar, near Keflavík	Grindavík	18km (11 miles)	150m (490ft)	6hrs	47
4	Grindavík	Vogar	18km (11 miles)	150m (490ft)	6hrs	49
5	Grindavík	Hafnir	21km (13 miles)	150m (490ft)	7hrs	53
6	Krýsuvík or Vestarurlækur	Krýsuvík or Vestarurlækur	12 or 16km (7½ or 10 miles)	150m (490ft)	3hrs or 4hrs	56
7	Seltún	Seltún	8km (5 miles)	150m (490ft)	3hrs	58
8	Seltún	Seltún	13km (8 miles)	350m (1150ft)	4hrs 30mins	60
9	Þingvellir	Þingvellir	10km (6¼ miles)	80m (260ft)	3hrs 30mins	62
10	Hveragerði or Rjúpnabrekkur	Hveragerði or Rjúpnabrekkur	10 or 17km (6¼ or 10½ miles)	500m (1640ft)	3hrs 30mins or 5hrs 30mins	65
11	Ölfusvatn	Ölfusvatn	21km (13 miles)	500m (1640ft)	7hrs	67
12	Hellisheiði	Hveragerði	19km (12 miles)	ascent: 420m (1375ft); descent: 620m (2035ft)	6hrs 30mins	69
13	Nesjavellir	Nesjavellir	18km (11 miles)	875m (2870ft)	6hrs	72

Trek 1 – The Reykjavegur

Stage	Start	Finish	Distance	Total ascent	Total descent	Time	Page
1	Nesjavellir	Múlasel	11km (7 miles)	500m (1005ft)	350m (1150ft)	4hrs	76
2	Múlasel	Bláfjallaskáli	31km (19¼ miles)	450m (1475ft)	250m (820ft)	11hrs	78
3	Bláfjallaskáli	Kaldársel	16km (10 miles)	100m (320ft)	500m (1640ft)	5hrs	81
4	Kaldársel	Djúpavatn	19km (12 miles)	300m (985ft)	175m (575ft)	7hrs 30mins	83
5	Djúpavatn	Bratthals	14km (8¾ miles)	125m (410ft)	250m (820ft)	5hrs	86
6	Bratthals	Þorbjörn	13km (8 miles)	100m (330ft)	150m (490ft)	4hrs 30mins	88
7	Þorbjörn	Reykjanesviti	23km (14¼ miles)	125m (410ft)	150m (490ft)	8hrs	91

Section 2 – Fjallabak and Þórsmörk

Walk	Start	Finish	Distance	Total ascent/descent	Time	Page
14	Landmannalaugar	Landmannalaugar	9km (5½ miles)	400m (1310ft)	3hrs	96
15	Landmannalaugar	Landmannalaugar	7km (4½ miles)	450m (1475ft)	2hrs 30mins	98
16	Hvanngil	Hvanngil	10km (6¼ miles)	270m (885ft)	3hrs	100
17	Langidalur or Húsadalur	Langidalur or Húsadalur	6km (3¾ miles)	330m (1080ft)	2hrs	103
18	Fljótsdalur Youth Hostel	Fljótsdalur Youth Hostel	17km (10½ miles)	500m (1640ft)	5hrs 30mins	105
19	Heimaey (harbour or airport)	Heimaey (harbour or airport)	9km (5½ miles)	270m (885ft)	9hrs	107

Trek 2 – Hellismannaleið, Laugavegur and Skógar Trail

Stage	Start	Finish	Distance	Total ascent	Total descent	Time	Page
1	Rjúpnavellir	Áfangagil	19km (12 miles)	320m (1050ft)	200m (655ft)	6hrs	111
2	Áfangagil	Landmannahellir	22km (13½ miles)	550m (1805ft)	250m (820ft)	8hrs	113
3	Landmannahellir	Landmannalaugar	17km (10½ miles)	550m (1805ft)	540m (1770ft)	6hrs	116
4	Landmannalaugar	Hrafntinnusker	12km (7½ miles)	530m (1740ft)	80m (260ft)	4hrs 30mins	119
5	Hrafntinnusker	Álftavatn	12km (7½ miles)	130m (425ft)	600m (1970ft)	4hrs 30mins	121
6	Álftavatn	Botnar/Emstrur	16km (10 miles)	200m (655ft)	270m (885ft)	6hrs	123
7	Botnar/Emstrur	Langidalur or Húsadalur	15km (9½ miles)	350m (1150ft)	600m (1970ft)	6hrs	126
8	Langidalur or Básar	Fimmvörðuháls	13km (8 miles)	900m (2950ft)	70m (230ft)	5hrs	129
9	Fimmvörðuháls	Skógar	16km (10 miles)	50m (165ft)	1050m (3445ft)	5hrs 30mins	132

Section 3 – Skaftafell and Vatnajökull

Walk	Start	Finish	Distance	Total ascent/descent	Time	Page
20	Sandfell	Sandfell	23km (14¼ miles)	2000m (6560ft)	12hrs	136
21	Svinafellsjökull	Svinafellsjökull	20km (13 miles)	2000m (6560ft)	11hrs	138
22	Skaftafell	Skaftafell	20km (12½ miles)	1075m (3525ft)	7hrs	140
23	Skaftafell	Skaftafell	8km (5 miles)	300m (985ft)	2hrs 30mins	144
24	Skaftafell	Skaftafell	28km (17½ miles)	300m (985ft)	8hrs	146
25	Café at Jökulsárlón	Café at Jökulsárlón	16km (10 miles)	100m (330ft)	4hrs	148

Section 4 – Snæfell and Lónsöræfi

Walk	Start	Finish	Distance	Total ascent/descent	Time	Page
26	Snæfellsskáli	Snæfellsskáli	16km (10 miles)	1050m (3445ft)	6hrs	153

Trek 3 – The Lónsöræfi Trail

Stage	Start	Finish	Distance	Total ascent	Total descent	Time	Page
1	Bjálafell	Geldingafellsskáli	25km (15½ miles)	400m (1310ft)	480m (1575ft)	10hrs	157
2	Geldingafellsskáli	Egilssel	20km (12½ miles)	530m (1740ft)	680m (2230ft)	8hrs	160
3	Egilssel	Múlaskáli	10km (6¼ miles)	150m (490ft)	580m (1900ft)	4hrs	162
4	Múlaskáli	Stafafell	30km (18½ miles)	400m (1310ft)	580m (1900ft)	10hrs	164

Section 5 – Egilsstaðir and the Eastfjords

Walk	Start	Finish	Distance	Total ascent/descent	Time	Page
27	Egilsstaðir	Egilsstaðir	16km (10 miles)	400m (1310ft)	5hrs	170
28	Neðri-Stafur	Seyðisfjörður	8km (5 miles)	ascent: 100m (330ft); descent: 520m (1705ft)	2hrs 30mins	172
29	Lagarfljót (southern end)	Lagarfljót (southern end)	6km (3¾ miles)	250m (820ft)	2hrs	174
30	Hallormsstaður	Hallormsstaður	8km (5 miles)	250m (820ft)	2hrs 30mins	176
31	Vatnsskarð	Vatnsskarð	20km (12½ miles)	480m (1575ft)	7hrs	178

Stage	Start	Finish	Distance	Total ascent	Total descent	Time	Page
1	Seyðisfjörður	Loðmundarfjörður	23km (14¼ miles)	650m (2130ft)	650m (2130ft)	9hrs	182
2	Loðmundarfjörður	Húsavík	15km (9½ miles)	500m (1640ft)	400m (1310ft)	5hrs	185
3	Húsavík	Breiðavík	15km (9½ miles)	400m (1310ft)	500m (1640ft)	5hrs 30mins	187
4	Breiðavík	Bakkagerði, Borgarfjörður	21km (13 miles)	800m (2625ft)	800m (2625ft)	8hrs	189

Section 6 – Jökulsárgljúfur

Walk	Start	Finish	Distance	Total ascent/descent	Time	Page
32	Ásbyrgi	Vesturdalur	8km (5 miles)	100m (330ft)	2hrs 30mins	194
33	Vesturdalur	Vesturdalur	13km (8 miles)	200m (655ft)	4hrs	196
34	Dettifoss	Dettifoss	6km (3¾ miles)	80m (260ft)	2hrs	198

Trek 5 – The Jökulsárhlaup

Stage	Start	Finish	Distance	Total ascent	Total descent	Time	Page
1	Dettifoss	Vesturdalur	20km (12½ miles)	150m (490ft)	350m (1150ft)	6hrs 30mins	203
2	Vesturdalur	Ásbyrgi	14km (8½ miles)	100m (330ft)	150m (490ft)	5hrs	206

Section 7 – Akureyri and Eyjafjörður

Walk	Start	Finish	Distance	Total ascent/descent	Time	Page
35	Akureyri	Akureyri	20km (12½ miles)	1200m (3940ft)	7hrs	212
36	Harbour, Hrísey	Harbour, Hrísey	7km (4½ miles)	100m (330ft)	2hrs 30mins	214
37	Sandvík or the airport, Grímsey	Sandvík or the airport, Grímsey	12km (7½ miles)	200m (655ft)	3hrs 30min	217

Section 8 – Kverkfjöll and Askja

Stage	Start	Finish	Distance	Total ascent/descent	Time	Page
38	Car park beyond Sigurðasáli	Car park beyond Sigurðasáli	20km (12½ miles)	1000m (590ft)	8hrs	223
39	Herðubreiðarlindir	Herðubreiðarlindir	10km (6¼ miles)	50m (165ft)	7hrs	225

Trek 6 – The Askja Trail

Stage	Start	Finish	Distance	Total ascent	Total descent	Time	Page
1	Herðubreiðarlindir	Bræðrafell	18km (11 miles)	180m (590ft)	40m (130ft)	7hrs	228
2	Bræðrafell	Drekagil	20km (12½ miles)	280m (920ft)	100m (330ft)	7hrs	230
3	Drekagil	Dyngjufell	23km (14¼ miles)	750m (2460ft)	900m (2950ft)	9hrs	233
4	Dyngjufell	Botni	20km (12½ miles)	50m (165ft)	250m (820ft)	6hrs 30mins	236
5	Botni	Svartárkot	15km (9½ miles)	20m (65ft)	60m (195ft)	4hrs 30mins	239
6	Botni	Grænavatn	40km (25 miles)	40m (130ft)	200m (655ft)	11hrs	241

Trek 7 – The Mývatn Trail

Stage	Start	Finish	Distance	Total ascent	Total descent	Time	Page
1	Dimmuborgir	Reykjahlíð	15km (9½ miles)	230m (755ft)	230m (755ft)	5hrs	245
2	Reykjahlíð	Víti, Krafla	20km (12½ miles)	400m (1310ft)	100m (330ft)	7hrs	248
3	Víti, Krafla	Reykjahlíð	20km (12½ miles)	200m (655ft)	500m (1640ft)	7hrs	250

Section 9 – Sprengisandur and Kjölur

Walk	Start	Finish	Distance	Total ascent/descent	Time	Page
40	Nýidalur	Nýidalur	19km (12 miles)	500m (1640ft)	6hrs 30mins	256
41	Nýidalur	Nýidalur	31km (19¼ miles)	150m (490ft)	8hrs 30mins	258

Trek 8 – The Kjölur Trails

Stage	Start	Finish	Distance	Total ascent	Total descent	Time	Page
1	Ásgarður	Klakkur	22km (13¾ miles)	650m (2130ft)	500m (1640ft)	8hrs	262
2	Klakkur	Ásgarður	28km (17½ miles)	350m (1150ft)	500m (1640ft)	11hrs	266
3	Ásgarður	Gíslaskáli	16km (10 miles)	150m (490ft)	300m (985ft)	6hrs	269
4	Gíslaskáli	Hveravellir	26km (16 miles)	180m (590ft)	120m (395ft)	9hrs	271
5	Hveravellir	Þjófadalir	12km (7½ miles)	200m (655ft)	140m (460ft)	4hrs 30mins	274
6	Þjófadalir	Þverbrekknamúli	14km (8¾ miles)	120m (395ft)	300m (985ft)	5hrs 30mins	276
7	Þverbrekknamúli	Arbuðir or Hvítárnes	19 or 25km (12 or 15½ miles)	30m (100ft)	150m (490ft)	7hrs 30mins or 9hrs	278

Section 10 – Hornstrandir Peninsula
Trek 9 – The Hornstrandir Trail

Stage	Start	Finish	Distance	Total ascent	Total descent	Time	Page
1	Hesteyri	Hlöðuvík	15km (9½ miles)	500m (1640ft)	500m (1640ft)	6hrs	284
2	Hlöðuvík	Hornvík	12km (7½ miles)	380m (1245ft)	380m (1245ft)	5hrs	286
3	Hornvík	Hornvík	15km (9½ miles)	560m (1840ft)	560m (1840ft)	5hrs	288
4	Kjaransvík	Látravík	24km (15 miles)	950m (3115ft)	950m (3115ft)	9hrs	291
5	Látravík	Hesteyri	22km (13¾ miles)	350m (1150ft)	350m (1150ft)	9hrs	293

Section 11 – The Westfjords

Walk	Start	Finish	Distance	Total ascent/descent	Time	Page
42	Hnifsdalur or Bolungarvik	Ísafjörður	15 or 18km (9½ or 11 miles)	650m (2130ft)	5hrs or 6hrs	300
43	Suðureyri	Flateyri	15km (9½ miles)	650m (2135ft)	5hrs	303
44	Þingeyri or Alftamýrarheiði	Þingeyri or Alftamýrarheiði	5 or 35km (3 or 21¾ miles)	1100m (3610ft)	2hrs or 10hrs	306
45	Helluskarð	Helluskarð	7km (4½ miles)	320m (1050ft)	2hrs 30mins	308
46	Foss	Krossholt	15km (9½ miles)	500m (1640ft)	6hrs	309
47	Brunnaverstöð	Brunnaverstöð	20km (12½ miles)	500m (1640ft)	7hrs	312
48	Brjánslækur	Brjánslækur	6km (3¾ miles)	200m (655ft)	2hrs	314
49	Ferry pier, Flatey	Ferry pier, Flatey	4km (2½ miles)	30m (100ft)	1hr 30mins	316

Section 12 – Snæfellsjökull and Snaefellsnes
Trek 10 – The Snæfellsjökull and Snaefellsnes Trail

Stage	Start	Finish	Distance	Total ascent	Total descent	Time	Page
1	Ólafsvík	Arnarstapi	22km (13½ miles)	800m (2625ft)	800m (2625ft)	8hrs	320
2	Arnarstapi	Djúpalónssandur	19km (12½ miles)	100m (330ft)	100m (330ft)	7hrs 30mins	323
3	Djúpalónssandur	Öndverðarnes1	9km (12½ miles)	100m (330ft)	100m (330ft)	7hrs 30mins	326
4	Öndverðarnes	Hellissandur	12km (7½ miles)	50m (165ft)	50m (165ft)	4hrs	330

APPENDIX B

Glossary of place-name elements

It is useful for walkers to know the meaning of at least a few place-name elements, especially those that appear regularly on maps, as these generally refer to very specific landscape features and so might help with navigation. Some of the most common are given below.

Icelandic	English
...á	river (suffix; eg in jökulsá)
austur	east
berg	rock
bjarg	cliff
borg	rocky hill
brekka	slope
brú	bridge
bær	farm/district
dalur	dale/valley
eldborg	lava cone
eldgjá	lava fissure
ey	island
fell/fjall	fell/mountain
fljót	big river
foss	waterfall
garður	garden/enclosure
gil	gill/ravine
gígur	crater
gljúfur	canyon
græn	green
hagi	pasture
háls	ridge
heiði	heath
hellir	cave
hnúkur	peak
hóll	rounded hill
höfn	harbour
hraun	lava

Icelandic	English
hryggur	ridge
hús	house
hver	hot spring
ís	ice
jarð	ground/earth
jökul	glacier
jökulhlaup	glacier flood
jökulsá	glacier river
kambur	crest
kirkja	church
klettur	cliff/steep rock
kvísl	river/tributary
land	land
leir	clay
leira	muddy
lind	spring
lón	inlet
lækur	stream
múli	rounded mountain/headland
mýri	mire/bog
nes	ness/headland
norður	north
reykur	reek/smoke/steam
sand	sand
skáli	hut
skarð	gap/pass
skógur	wood/forest

Icelandic	English	Icelandic	English
slétta	plain/level	*vatn*	water/lake
snjó/snæ	snow	*veður*	weather
staður	place	*vegur*	path/way
steinn	stone/rock	*vest*	west
strönd	strand/beach	*vikur*	pumice
suður	south	*vík*	bay/cove
svæði	area/region	*ytri*	outer
sæluhús	emergency hut	*þing*	parliament/meeting
tjörn	tarn/small lake		
tunga	tongue of land	*þorp*	village

Thank goodness for pictograms!

APPENDIX C
Further information

General
Iceland Government – www.government.is

Iceland Tourism – www.visiticeland.com

Around Iceland – www.heimur.is/heimur/world – Highly recommended free book containing incredibly detailed practical information for visitors. Consider a copy of this book as an essential accompaniment while travelling in Iceland.

Getting to Iceland
Icelandair – www.icelandair.com – Flights from London, Manchester, Glasgow, Europe and North America to Keflavík

Iceland Express – www.icelandexpress.com – Flights from London, Europe and New York to Keflavík

Norröna – www.smyrilline.com – Ferry from Denmark and the Faroe Islands to Seyðisfjörður

Getting around Iceland
Air Iceland – www.airiceland.is – Flights from Reykjavík to Akureyri, Ísafjörður, Grímsey, Egilsstaðir and Vopnafjörður

Eagle Air – www.eagleair.is – Flights from Reykjavík to Vestmannaeyjar, Höfn, Húsavík, Sauðárkrókur, Gjögur and Bildudalur

Stræto – tel 5402700, www.straeto.is – Buses around greater Reykjavík

Sterna – tel 5511166, www.sterna.is – Scheduled bus services and tours

Reykjavík Excursions – tel 5805400, www.re.is – Scheduled bus services and tours

SBA Norðurleið – tel 5500720, www.sba.is – Scheduled bus services and tours

Bus 'passports' – www.icelandonyourown.is – For cheaper bus travel

Salty Tours – tel 8205750, www.saltytours.is – Minibus tour around Reykjanes

Trex – tel 5876000, www.trex.is – Buses to Landmannalaugar and Þorsmörk

Stafafell Travel – tel 6996684, www.eldhorn.is/stafafell – Minibus to Lónsöræfi

Jeeptours – tel 8982798, www.jeeptours.is – Jeep to Snæfell and Lónsöræfi

Egilsstaðir buses – Seyðisfjörður tel 4721515; Hengifoss-Hallormsstaður tel 4761399; Borgarfjörður – tel 8948305

National parks
Þingvellir – www.thingvellir.is/english/national-park

Vatnajökull – www.vatnajokulsthjodgardur.is/English

Snæfellsjökull – www.ust.is/snaefellsjokull-national-park

Maps of Iceland
Online map of Iceland – atlas.lmi.is/kortasja_en – Very versatile and well worth going through its various styles of mapping and using the 'measure' function

Landmælingar Íslands, National Land Survey of Iceland – www.lmi.is – Producers of maps in a variety of styles, and holders of an extensive map archive

Ferðakort – www.ferdakort.is – Sellers of Landmælingar Íslands mapping

Mál og Menning – www.forlagid.is – Useful 'Atlaskort' and 'Hiking Maps'

There are plenty of other useful maps quoted throughout this guidebook.

Huts and hostels
Ferðafélag Íslands (FÍ, or Iceland Touring Association) – tel 5682533, www.fi.is – FÍ also arrange a walking and trekking programme

Útivist – tel 5621000, www.utivist.is – Útivist also arrange a walking and trekking programme

HI-Iceland (youth hostels) – tel 5756700, www.hostel.is

Guiding and glacier skills
Icelandic Mountain Guides – tel 5879999, www.mountainguides.is

Glacier Guides – tel 5712100, www.glacierguides.is

Icelandic Travel – Dick Phillips
Dick Phillips, Whitehall House, Nenthead, Alston, Cumbria CA9 3PS, tel 01434-381440, www.icelandic-travel.com – Dick has provided practical help and advice for thousands of British visitors to Iceland for over 50 years. Dick's Icelandic base is Fljótsdalur Youth Hostel, which houses an impressive library on all things Icelandic.

Safety and emergencies
Emergencies – police, ambulance, fire service – tel 112

ICE-SAR (Search and Rescue) – tel 112, www.landsbjorg.is

Weather forecast – tel 9020600 (recorded message), www.vedur.is

Road conditions – tel 1777, www.vegaverdin.is

Safetravel.is – Magazine-style publication full of safety advice – www.safetravel.is

Before you leave...
The Blue Lagoon – tel 4208801, www.bluelagoon.com – Bathe outdoors in hot salt water on the way to the airport, with bus transport and luggage transfer arranged.

GUESTBOOK/GESTABÓK

Visitors to Iceland encounter 'guestbooks' everywhere – in hotels and huts, at museums and visitor centres, even at picnic sites, waterfalls and the summits of lofty mountains. Here is a 'guestbook' of your very own.

GUESTBOOK/GESTABÓK

GUESTBOOK/GESTABÓK

LISTING OF CICERONE GUIDES

For full information on all
our guides, and to order
books and eBooks, visit our
website:
www.cicerone.co.uk.

Walking – Trekking – Mountaineering – Climbing – Cycling

Over 40 years, Cicerone have built up an outstanding collection of 300 guides, inspiring all sorts of amazing adventures.

 Every guide comes from extensive exploration and research by our expert authors, all with a passion for their subjects. They are frequently praised, endorsed and used by clubs, instructors and outdoor organisations.

All our titles can now be bought as **e-books** and many as iPad and Kindle files and we will continue to make all our guides available for these and many other devices.

Our website shows any **new information** we've received since a book was published. Please do let us know if you find anything has changed, so that we can pass on the latest details. On our **website** you'll also find some great ideas and lots of information, including sample chapters, contents lists, reviews, articles and a photo gallery.

It's easy to keep in touch with what's going on at Cicerone, by getting our monthly **free e-newsletter**, which is full of offers, competitions, up-to-date information and topical articles. You can subscribe on our home page and also follow us on **Facebook** and **Twitter**, as well as our **blog**.

Cicerone – the very best guides for exploring the world.

CICERONE

2 Police Square Milnthorpe Cumbria LA7 7PY
Tel: 015395 62069 info@cicerone.co.uk
www.cicerone.co.uk